RAILWAYS OF THE WORLD 6

Railways of the USA

RAILWAYS OF THE WORLD

The Southern Pacific classification yard at West Colton, California, on a
cold moonlit night. Situated 50 miles east of Los Angeles it lies at the
intersection of the main line to the Pacific Northwest, and the
transcontinental route through Arizona and Texas to the Mississippi River
gateways to the east.

RAILWAYS OF THE WORLD 6

Railways of the USA

O. S. NOCK

B.SC., C.ENG., F.I.C.E., F.I.MECH.E.
HONORARY FELLOW AND PAST PRESIDENT,
INSTITUTION OF RAILWAY SIGNAL ENGINEERS

WITH 81 PHOTOGRAPHS
AND 42 MAPS AND DIAGRAMS

ADAM AND CHARLES BLACK · LONDON

FIRST PUBLISHED 1979
A. & C. BLACK (PUBLISHERS) LIMITED
35 BEDFORD ROW, LONDON WC1R 4JH

© 1979 O. S. NOCK

ISBN 0 7136 2006 4

British Library Cataloguing in Publication Data

Nock, Oswald Stevens
    Railways of the world.
    6: Railways of the USA
    1. Railroads
    I. Title
    385   HE1021

    ISBN 0-7136-2006-4

Set, printed and bound in Great Britain by
Fakenham Press Limited, Fakenham, Norfolk

Contents

Illustrations

Southern Pacific classification yard, West Colton, California *Frontispiece*

BLACK AND WHITE PLATES

MAPS AND DIAGRAMS

Acknowledgements

The author and publishers thank the following for permission to use photographs:

Atchison Topeka and Santa Fe Railway for 4(1); 26(1); 26(2).

Burlington Northern for 13(2); 14(1); 14(2); 15(1); 15(2); 21(1); 30(1).

California State Museum for 29(1); 29(2).

Chessie System for 1(2); 2(2); 2(3).

Conrail for 4(2); 9(3); 31(2); 32.

Family Lines System for 12(1); 12(2); 12(3); 13(1).

R. H. Kindig for 2(1); 17; 20(1); 20(2); 20(3); 22(1); 22(2); 22(3); 23(2); 23(3); 25(1); 25(2); 25(3); 27(1); 27(2); 27(3); 31(1).

O. S. Nock for 1(1); 1(3); 3(3); 7(1); 7(2); 9(1); 9(2); 10(1); 10(2); 10(3); 11(1); 11(2); 16(1); 16(2); 16(3); 19(1); 19(2); 23(1); 24(1); 24(2); 24(3).

Norfolk and Western Railway for 5(1); 5(2); 6(1); 8(1); 8(2); 11(3).

Dr P. Ransome-Wallis for 31(3).

Southern Pacific for 6(2); 21(2); 28(1); 28(2); 30(2).

Photos 3(1); 3(2); 18(1); 18(2); 18(3); 18(4) are from the author's collection.

The coloured frontispiece is reproduced by courtesy of Southern Pacific.

The maps were drawn by Mrs C. Boyer of Corsham from data in the author's collection.

Preface

Throughout my life as a professional engineer concerned with railway signalling and brake equipment it was part of my duties to make a constant study of American practice, and with my inborn enthusiasm for railways in all their multifarious activities this opened up a far wider field. Consequently, when this series of books was planned I looked forward to writing the American volume with particular pleasure. By way of preliminary homework I read once again the many books on American locomotive practice and history in my own library, those on signalling and marshalling yard techniques, and everything I could find upon past history. The literature is certainly prodigious; but when the time came for me to start in earnest, and to go to see for myself, I gained the impression that some of my American railroad friends were somewhat aghast at the mileage I proposed to cover, and the note-taking on which I was bent, all within the span of six weeks. I would certainly have liked to make it longer, but long-standing engagements in the United Kingdom set parameters at each end. Aghast some of them may have been, but one and all they responded with a warmth of welcome and friendship that made the trip one of the most memorable in my life.

To mention all of them by name would add many pages to the book, but those who accompanied me on numerous specific excursions are mentioned in the text, with my grateful thanks. Apart from that I must express my special gratitude to Richard E. Briggs, Vice-President of the Association of American Railroads, who acted as general coordinator with the various companies for the establishment of my itinerary; to John Ragsdale, of Amtrak, who arranged numerous travelling facilities on passenger trains; to Stanley E. G. Hillman, Chairman of Illinois Central Gulf; Howard Skidmore, Vice-President of the Chessie System; L. E. Hoyt, Vice-President Southern Pacific Corporation, and Howard Gilbert, Director Press

xii

Relations of Conrail, all of whom received me most cordially, and saw to it that my 'dash round America', as one of them expressed it, was as pleasant as it was profitable.

Two others must be specially mentioned. I have been fortunate, now over a period of nearly forty years, of the pen-friendship of Dick Kindig, of Denver, Colorado, one of the foremost of American railway photographers, and for the privilege of including many of his magnificent action pictures in this book. The other is the late E. C. Poultney, for many years a close friend and fellow member of the Institution of Locomotive Engineers. After his death, some years ago, his son very kindly bequeathed to me his father's technical library and papers, which included a great amount of material on American railroads, particularly the Pennsylvania, the New York Central, and the Chesapeake and Ohio. I have quoted freely from some of these papers in my own book.

I was welcomed in many American homes, and the talk frequently centred upon links with the United Kingdom, and what life was like over here today. I brought back greetings to my own family, and especially to Olivia my wife, who I found was well known to many American railroad folks through her participation in so many of my earlier books, and my mention of her in the prefaces. Now, because of increasing physical disability she is no longer able to do the typing; but her interest and encouragement is undiminished, even though she has to play the less glamorous role of holding the fort at home while the 'old man' is flitting round the world. My thanks to her, and my indebtedness to her are just as deep as when she was able to come with me.

Silver Cedars,   O. S. NOCK,
High Bannerdown,
Batheaston,
Bath.   October 1978

Introduction

The railroads of the United States today have a character unlike those in any other part of the world, in their relation to the social and business life of the country and in the seemingly anomalous position they now hold. Elsewhere, as earlier books in this same series have shown, there is strong continuity of tradition in style, in quality and frequency of service; but a traveller who knew the railroads of the USA in the 1930s, or even during the war years, could well rub his eyes in almost disbelieving astonishment at the virtual disappearance of most of the great passenger trains of yester-year. And yet Americans in all walks of life and occupations are travelling their country as never before. When I made an extensive tour in the early summer of 1977 I covered a considerable mileage by road and air, as well as by trains of all kinds, and I saw in the magnificent network of major highways one reason why travel by train has gone out of fashion, even though the speed limit on roads everywhere is 55 m.p.h. But the network of internal airlines is no less comprehensive, and in several stages of my itinerary where there were no passenger trains at all to provide links in the chain, I was able very conveniently to get from point to point by air.

For all that, however, I must, at the very outset, correct an impression popularly held in Europe that the railroads of America are staggering sadly towards their end. It is true that one very large group in the north-east of the country was lifted from outright bankruptcy and complete closure only by Government action; but elsewhere the railroads are prospering as freight carriers in the grand manner, and they provide a fascinating study. In riding the trains today, visiting the great centres of traffic control, and talking to railroad men of every grade, right across the country, I was delighted to find also the sense of pride in past achievements held by so many of them. There is a common misconception that Americans have little time for historical sentiment, and the oft-quoted remark of Henry Ford, which I can now believe to be apochryphal — 'History is bunk' — would seem to support this. But from my own travels I found that nothing is further from the truth. The way in which busy men took of their time to show me, with infectious enthusiasm, magnificent museum pieces was enlightening. What some of my friends were not so enthusiastic in reminding me, however, was the way in which certain organs of the press, the radio, and television on the eastern side of the Atlantic have, for reasons best known to themselves, indulged in programmes that can at best be described as 'hatchet jobs': seeking out only the worst, and grossly over-emphasising it, while making not the slightest attempt to present the other side of the picture.

To persons who recall those major misrepresentations it will prob- ably come as a surprise to learn that over an overwhelming proportion of America's vast railway mileage a magnificent service of transporta- tion is being performed by privately owned companies, with profit to the shareholders, satisfaction to the traders and contentment of the staff. There are, as everywhere else on railways the world over, dark areas, and I have made no attempt to slur hurriedly over them — in fact, when the itinerary for my visit was being planned, one railroad manager was only too anxious to show me his 'lousy railroad', and to explain the steps they were taking to get it right.

I returned home with a multitude of impressions, six well-filled notebooks, many rolls of exposed film, and a mass of printed documentation of all kinds from pioneer history to the most modern operating practice. How was such a library to be coalesced into a single book? Deep as is my own interest in the steam locomotive and its history, the overriding impression of my 13,000 miles of travel in the USA is of the railroads as mighty freight carriers, and it is this impression that forms the backbone of the book. It is, however, a treatment that has given plenty of opportunity for excursions into past history, particularly as many examples of splendid steam locomotives are preserved, not only in museums, but on pedestals beside the scenes of their former labours. It is, of course, very much a personal book, and I am conscious that many extensive areas are absent. I did not travel at all over the tracks of the Missouri Pacific, the former New York Central, the Seaboard Coast Line, or of the Union Pacific, though at various points I saw much of the latter railroad in action. But I hope that lack of direct personal contact has not left their stature diminished in any way.

My arrival in Boston, in May 1977, was actually not my earliest contact with American railroads. My first was with the Southern Pacific, in San Francisco many years earlier; later, in Pittsburgh and its environs, I became very conscious of the close association of the Westinghouse organisation with the former Pennsylvania. But the birth of American railroading took place on the eastern seaboard; and so I am going to skip over the intervening coastline, to start in earnest on this book at Baltimore.

CHAPTER ONE

Baltimore, the birthplace

> The enterprise undertaken by the people of Baltimore in establishing railroad communication between tidewater and the Ohio River, with its far reaching water connections, was the greatest undertaking the world had then contemplated in land transportation.
>
> *Angus Sinclair*

I had been in America for no more than a few days when I came to Baltimore. There had been business to attend to in New York and Philadelphia, but that was quickly disposed of, and I hastened on, because no one with a love of railways and a sense of history could wait to reach this gracious city, the very cradle of American railroads. Franklyn Carr of the Chessie System met me and in a very short time we were driving to the Baltimore and Ohio Railroad Museum, at Mount Clare. As a railway enthusiast I had first become fully conscious of this great American railroad just fifty years earlier from the publicity worked up in England over the visit of the Great Western 4−6−0 locomotive *King George V*, to take part in the centenary celebrations of the B. & O., in 1927. But at the time I am sure that very few British enthusiasts appreciated the tremendous significance of this centenary.

Angus Sinclair's words, which I quote at the head of this chapter, in no way exaggerate the position. Cast the mind back to the railway situation in Europe in the early spring of 1827: the Stockton and Darlington had been open for less than two years, and Timothy Hackworth was struggling to keep the early locomotives at work; so troublesome was the position that George Stephenson was having to fight hard to ward off those who advocated cable haulage for the Liverpool and Manchester Railway, while in France, on the mineral lines working around St Etienne there was no question of locomotive haulage. Yet here in Baltimore, a group of public-spirited men, in February 1827 determined upon the construction of a double-tracked railroad from Baltimore to the Ohio River: 380 miles — *three hundred and eighty miles!* Why such a tremendous project? The Ohio River flowed in a generally south-westerly direction to debouch into the Mississippi at Cairo. It was rich agricultural land, but between it and the eastern seaboard lay the ranges of the Appalachian, and Allegheny Mountains. They were not starkly rugged like the Rockies, but completely clad — as today — in dense forest land, and the merchants of Baltimore saw clearly that if a trade route could be pioneered through those ranges it would be of great advantage to the city, and all the district around it. British railway promoters faced with opposition on every hand, and wearied by long and acrimonious struggles in Parliamentary committees, might well have rubbed their eyes in wonder when following the first meeting of the projectors on 19 February, an Act of Incorporation by the State of Maryland was granted on 28 February, and confirmed by the State of Virginia on 8 March — *seventeen days* from the very first meeting to the final 'go-ahead'.

It is fairly obvious, however, that all concerned did not fully appreciate what they had let themselves in for; but with unanimity of purpose and immense goodwill, the planning of the Baltimore and Ohio Railroad speedily got under way. Today it is the oldest railway in the world to retain its original name. Unlike the contemporary situation in England, none of the promoters of the B. & O. were engineers, and because the famous military academy at West Point had the only engineering school in the whole American nation, the Army was called upon to establish the route. The first surveys were made under the direction of two United States Topographical Engineers, Lieut. Col. Stephen H. Long, and Capt. William G. McNeill, and a United States Civil Engineer, William Howard. To minimise the cost of construction they took a very winding course beside the west branch of the Patapsco River to the minor watershed of Parr Spring Ridge, and then dropped down towards the Monocacy River, itself a

1. Original concept of the Baltimore and Ohio Railroad in competition with early canal routes

tributary of the Potomac. It then headed across fairly level country to a dramatic location, where the Potomac cuts through the Caboctin Mountains in a ravine reminiscent of some parts of the Rhine, and the railway had to be engineered along a narrow ledge between great beetling crags and the water's edge, at two successive points known as the Lower and Upper Point of Rocks.

It was at Point of Rocks that I made my first personal acquaintance with the original B. & O. main line, which there makes a triangular junction with the direct line from Washington. Branches were at first known as 'lateral rail roads', and from the outset one such was projected from where the main line first came alongside the Patapsco River, near Elkridge Landing, nine miles from Baltimore. This 'lateral' road ran direct to Washington, to make a total distance of 37½ miles from Baltimore. It will be at once appreciated in passing that the B. & O. had almost from the outset a subsidiary route that was longer than the Liverpool and Manchester; and at the beginning of the branch

3

there stands today a structure of outstanding historical interest. After the War of Independence, and the establishment of Washington as the capital city of the emergent nation, much of the basic planning of the city layout and its finest buildings were the work of the great architect Benjamin H. Latrobe. He had two sons, John H. B., and Benjamin H., who were trained to be an engineer and a lawyer respectively. Both gave almost lifelong service to the B. & O., but oddly enough in exactly opposite spheres to those in which they had been trained. John H. B. became a lawyer and was B. & O. counsel for sixty-four years; Benjamin H. eventually became Chief Engineer, and planned the route through the wild mountain country leading to the Ohio River. One of his earliest works, however, was the viaduct over the Patapsco River, 700 ft long, with eight elliptical arches in massive stone, carrying the Washington branch shortly after its divergence from the old main line. Like many of the pioneer railway structures in Great Britain, although this viaduct was built so long ago it is still capable of carrying the vastly heavier locomotives and trains of today. The Thomas Viaduct, as it is known, was brought into service in 1835.

The main line from Baltimore had been opened through to Harper's Ferry in 1834, a picturesque spot at the confluence of the Shenandoah and the Potomac Rivers, and scene of one of many sharp engagements in the Civil War. Abraham Lincoln had travelled to Washington by the B. & O. in 1861 for his inauguration as President, and the railroad and its employees who remained loyal to the Union cause was constantly harried by raids from the Confederate forces. Locomotives were sabotaged and bridges blown up, as ample evidence of the vital west-east lifeline that this still-new railroad represented. In one raid on Martinsburg, upstream from Harper's Ferry, Stonewall Jackson's men destroyed no fewer than forty-four locomotives! But the bridges at Harper's Ferry have a history as chequered by the vicissitudes of floods as by civil war. The bridge on which the tail end of the Chessie Steam Special stood briefly, and from which I took the photograph (Plate 7:1), dates only from 1931. The Baltimore and Ohio Railroad had reached a temporary terminus on the Maryland shore opposite to Harper's Ferry in 1834. A wooden bridge to carry a roadway had been built five years earlier, and the first railroad bridge was opened in 1836 to be combined with this. Then, when the line along the Shenandoah valley was completed to Harper's Ferry in 1836, connection was made with the B. & O. by a 'Y' junction in the *middle of the timber bridge*. This most curious construction provided connection with the B. & O. in the direction of Baltimore, and a separate span from the Shenandoah valley line was needed to link up. It must have been a fascinating structure; but it did not last long. After it had been washed away three times by floods, and subsequently rebuilt, it was replaced in 1852 by a single suspension truss bridge of wrought iron.

Then came the Civil War. Even before hostilities had begun generally, John Brown in his famous attack on the town in 1859, tore down the bridge. It was rebuilt, only to be burnt by Stonewall Jackson two years later. Again and again it was damaged, and the line breached in the course of the fighting. The Shenandoah valley was constantly harassed by the Confederate troops, and the B. & O. main line was a vital link between the north and Federal headquarters at Washington. In less troubled times, and from 1931 until 1936 there had been three bridges over the Potomac River, but the one furthest downstream which had been built in 1870 and used after 1893 for road traffic, had been destroyed by floods in 1936. The bridge to the right of the picture (Plate 7:1) was the main railway crossing from 1893; but after the destruction of the third bridge it was adapted, by planking the surface, to carry both road and rail traffic. The junction of the Shenandoah valley line, as can be seen in the picture, is now just inside the short tunnel, instead of in mid-stream.

Reverting now to earlier days, by the time war broke out the line had actually reached the Ohio River, at Wheeling, and there was some interesting engineering work on the more westerly sections. Instead of massive masonry arches there were examples of Albert Fink's patent inverted suspension truss, in wrought iron — alas, more easily damaged by saboteurs. In 1863 Confederate raiders destroyed a fine example across the Monongehela River at Fairmount. This early history was brought more vividly home to me when, several days after my first arrival in Baltimore, I was able to travel over part of the line by the Chessie Steam Special; but I must not at this stage 'jump the gun' as it were, and it is now time to enter the sanctuary of Mount Clare, Baltimore.

Inside the roundhouse, and taking in also the larger exhibits that are

5

necessarily outside, there is displayed virtually the entire history of steam traction on the railroads of the USA. One can relive the excitement of the race on the B. & O. in August 1830 between Peter Cooper's *Tom Thumb* and a horse, on parallel tracks; see one of the famous 'Grasshopper' locomotives of Davis and Gartner, dating back to 1832, and walk round the stalls surrounding the central turntable to see the gradual evolution in passenger cars, freight train cabooses and yard switchers right down to the first generation diesel-electric locomotives. And standing on the turntable, the appropriate centrepiece of it all, is the 4–4–0 *James Mason*, an example from 1856 of *the* American type of locomotive. In the USA of the nineteenth century this type was so much a maid-of-all-work, so universal throughout the land, that there was a great deal more than patriotic conceit in bestowing upon it so all-embracing a name. The 4–4–0 type was certainly developed in North America, and in the first place derived its type name in the same way as 'Atlantics', 'Pacifics', 'Prairies' and 'Hudsons' in later years; but the 4–4–0 of North America — the true 'American' — was in many ways different from the neat, inside-cylindered 4–4–0s that became so popular on the railways of Britain in later years. The 'American' locomotive was synonymous with the development and expansion of railroads themselves throughout the length and breadth of the Continent.

It needs no more than a glance at a map of the first section of the Baltimore and Ohio Railroad to appreciate how the 'American' type of locomotive came to be developed. In following the course of the Patapsco River the line twists and turns like a corkscrew, and the rigid wheelbase designs of locomotive that were being developed in Europe, and which were being imported in limited numbers into North America, were speedily found unsuitable. The 'American' type stood as firm as a three-legged stool on any rough ground, because its form of suspension was precisely that of a three-legged stool. Its frame was supported only at three points. One was at the pivot point of the leading four-wheeled bogie. The four-coupled wheels had compensated suspension, in that their axle boxes on each side of the engine were carried on a scale beam connected to the frame only at its centre point. These points of attachment, on each side, formed the second and third 'legs' of the stool. Locomotives of this type rode very

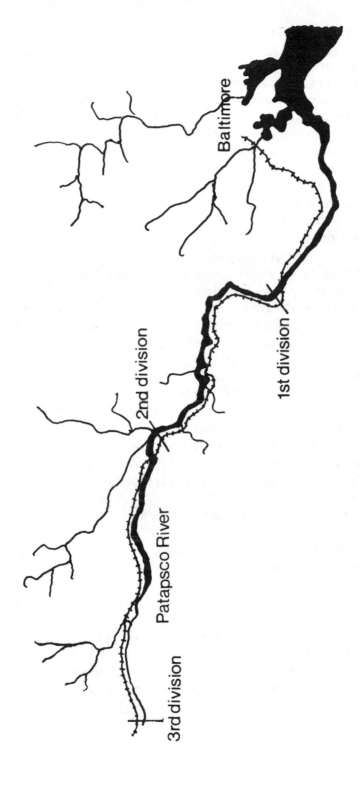

2. First section of the Baltimore and Ohio Railroad showing the winding route following the Patapsco River

smoothly and safely, on the sharply curved and lightly laid tracks of America. The *William Mason* was a typical early example so far as the actual machinery was concerned. Its finish is perhaps less decorative than some of its contemporaries elsewhere in the USA, but it carries a tremendous example of a spark-arresting smoke stack, and an enormous headlamp. In North America the railroads are not fenced, and the locomotive crews always had to keep a sharp look-out for animals and other obstructions, and the headlamp threw a piercing beam of light ahead in the night time.

It was at Mount Clare also that Samuel F. B. Morse placed the test wires for the sending of his first messages by the code that carries his name. Here indeed one is not only at the birthplace of American railroads in the constructional and mechanical sense, but also, in the telegraph, at the very foundation of their working. Because of the great distances involved and the lack of appreciable habitation along the routes, there was no early development of traffic control systems as in Europe, with the accompaniment of many signals along the lines. The telegraphic 'train order' was the only means of giving train crews the authority to proceed. Messages were sent from one depot to another by telegraph, and the operators had to decode the messages, write them out on slips of paper, and hand them to the engine crew. There were times when orders were misunderstood, or wrongly transcribed, and then disaster could strike in the form of a head-on collision on single track. In view of the vast number of train movements that by the end of the nineteenth century were so regulated, the mishaps were notably few. On the B. & O. the hazards of head-on collision did not arise, because the main line was double track from the outset.

The Ohio River was the original objective of the B. & O. Railroad, but once attained it proved an obstacle to further expansion, and connection to large and developing interests in the states of Ohio and Indiana had to be made by a slow and cumbersome ferry service across the river at Wheeling. This obstacle was surmounted in 1871 when a bridge crossing between Benwood, West Virginia, and Bellaire, Ohio, was completed. It had two large spans across the navigable part of the river, and a number of approach spans, and with its opening the B. & O. had a direct line from Baltimore to Chicago. From that same

8

bridge head at Bellaire another line of the B. & O. penetrated west-wards to Columbus, Ohio, and thence to Cincinnati, where it forked again, with the northern arm going to Indianapolis and Springfield, Illinois, and the southern arm to St Louis. So while the original concept of the B. & O. was to bring the products of Ohio and West Virginia to tidewater at Baltimore, the railroad gained three great tentacles stretching west to Chicago and to the banks of the Missis-sippi River. Over the years an enormous freight traffic developed, and from this brief sketch of the beginnings we can leap the years to look now at twentieth-century business.

The tremendous upsurge in the sheer tonnage of freight conveyed is vividly reflected in the almost sensational increase in the size and tractive power of locomotives within a very short space of time. To look for a moment at what was happening on some other American railroads; on the Western Maryland, for example, freight power had shot up from small 2−8−0s at the turn of the century to 2−8−8−2 compound Mallets of 105,600 lbs tractive effort by 1915. On the St Louis-San Francisco, the tractive effort of freight locomotives — non-articulated at that — had increased from 28,300 to 71,480 lbs in fourteen years, and an even greater increase was to be noted on the Burlington, from 2−6−2s of 21,900 lbs in 1900 to 2−10−2s of 71,500 lbs in 1912. The Denver and Rio Grande Western had reached 93,400 lbs tractive effort as early as 1913. It was equally significant that as recently as 1909 an entirely new railway, the Virginian, run-ning for much of its way parallel to the Norfolk and Western, was built for the express purpose of carrying coal from the West Virginia fields for export from Sewells Point, near Norfolk, at the entrance to Chesapeake Bay. One important factor that was making the operation of much heavier mineral trains practicable and safe was the improved techniques in braking developed by the Westinghouse company, and it was on the still-new Virginian Railway that some remarkable demonstration runs were made in 1921, as described in Chapter Four.

To meet traffic developments in the years between the two world wars the articulated locomotive on the B. & O. as on many other American railroads became a fast mixed traffic unit, with four high-pressure cylinders instead of the true Mallet arrangement of com-pound working. The older articulateds, being slow freighters, or bank engines, had little attention paid to their riding qualities at any speed more than about 25 m.p.h. Above that they could become unpleasantly rough and unstable at the front end. But in the later 1930s the need to run the long-distance freights in heavier formations and at higher speed led to careful studies of the riding qualities of the articulateds, because there was a limit to the size in which fixed wheelbase locomotives could be built.

The B. & O. had perhaps more experience with articulated locomotives than any other railroad in the USA, because they had been the very first to introduce the type in North America. In 1904 they had purchased some locomotives of the 0−6−6−0 type from the American Locomotive Co., and one of them, shown at the St Louis Exposition of that year, created immense interest. But even at the slow speeds involved in banking duties, on the heavy gradients through the Alleghenies they proved unstable. This type was followed in 1911 by some huge 0−8−8−0s, having a nominal tractive effort of 105,000 lbs and weighing 206 tons, without their tenders. But without any guiding influence at the front end, they also proved unsuitable for main line running, and were restricted to banking, or helper duties, and yard work.

Normally the B. & O. built most of its locomotives at the Mount Clare shops, but all the articulateds were purchased from one or another of the great firms. The turning point from the older conception of the articulated as a Mallet compound for the heaviest of slow speed duties to that of a giant main line hauler of fast tonnage trains began in 1924 on the neighbouring and allied road to the B. & O., the Chesapeake and Ohio, in a class of forty-five locomotives of the 2−8−8−2 type with four high-pressure cylinders. They were very large engines, with an all-up weight, engine only, of 252 tons, and a tractive effort of 103,500 lbs. Furthermore, although they were nominally limited to a maximum speed of 35 m.p.h., their crews found that they ran freely and steadily up to 55 m.p.h. This was because of a better distribution of the weight between the set of driving wheels carried on the forward articulated unit, and those on the fixed frame, and to the use of a two-wheeled leading truck ahead of the cylinders. The fact that these locomotives could be used at fast freight train speed on river-level gradients, as well as in hard slogging over the mountains, was of great assistance in regulating freight movement. It was found that these engines could haul trains of 50 per cent greater gross tonnage than the previous 2−6−6−2 compound Mallets.

The ultimate in articulateds for the B. & O. came in 1944 when Baldwins built a class of twenty of the 2−8−8−4 type. In size they aptly represent the culmination of the historic locomotive saga of Mount Clare, although these giants were not actually built there; their stupendous proportions make a breathtaking comparison with Peter Cooper's *Tom Thumb* of 1830! The '7600' class of 1944 were essentially fast running freight engines, with 5 ft 4 in. coupled wheels, and a total engine weight of 280 tons. The tender, with two-thirds full-capacity of coal and water added another 135 tons — altogether a nice little engine! The nominal tractive effort was 115,000 lbs, but perhaps of all the various statistics the most arresting is that the diameter of the boiler was something approaching twice the gauge of the rails, 8 ft 4 in. against 4ft 8½in. One could hardly imagine the B. & O. using any fuel other than bituminous coal, and in the huge firebox there were five thermic siphons to assist in the rapid circulation of water, and free steaming. The equipment also included two Westinghouse cross-compound air compressors for the locomotive and train brake system. Unlike the practice of the Chesapeake and Ohio, which I saw and was able to photograph, in having the air compressors on the smokebox front, the B. & O. '7600' class carried them on the right-hand side of the boiler.

I was naturally interested in the means of disposal of the vast tonnages of coal brought down to Baltimore by the B. & O., amounting to about 40 million tons annually. To some extent, Baltimore is handicapped as a port for exporting coal by its geographical situation near the head of Chesapeake Bay, but it will be greatly improved on the completion of the Chesapeake and Delaware Canal, which will provide a short cut saving more than 100 miles over the present need to circumvent the Virginia Capes. The development of Curtis Bay near Baltimore, however, extends back to over fifty years, when the needs of wartime Europe called for much help from the USA. Great though the development then was, however, it is much surpassed by the installations that Willis Cook took me to see in 1977. By the 1950s the changes in methods of transportation were made primarily for economic reasons, and the more refined uses of coal demanded facilities that were not available at Curtis Bay. The challenges from other basic sources of energy, notably oil, made it essential to keep at high efficiency every link in the chain from receipt of coal at the pits, during its conveyance, and to its handling at the point of export. Only by such efforts could the economic advantages of coal be sustained.

The new facilities, which I had the pleasure of seeing in operation, were brought into service in 1968. Arriving loaded coal trains pull into outer receiving yards, and are initially divided as to whether the loads are for export, or for harbour and coastwise delivery. Export coal is further classified to meet blending demands, and cars are then spotted in an eight-track load yard, each track of which has a capacity of 300 cars. All of these tracks are served by 40-ton electric side-arm locomotives that operate on narrow gauge tracks between the ordinary rail tracks. When loading export coal the cars are 'spotted' by the electric side-arm locomotive within reach of an electrically operated car positioner, capable of handling twelve loaded cars. This positioner is controlled by the car dumper operator, and it feeds them automatically into a rotary dumper. This can handle up to two 120-ton cars in tandem, and it can deal with a maximum capacity of 6000 tons of coal per hour. It is a fine modern example of fully mechanised bulk mineral handling.

Back at Mount Clare, one of the preserved locomotives standing among the outside exhibits is a green-painted 'Pacific', the *President Washington*, and it recalls a very interesting phase of B. & O. history. For many years Baltimore remained the eastern terminus of the line, but with a constantly increasing traffic the need for direct rail communication with Philadelphia and New York became apparent. A new line was built from Baltimore to Philadelphia, and passenger service was inaugurated in 1886. At that time there was no through service to New York and onward passengers were ticketed by the so-called Bound Brook route, which was operated jointly by the Philadelphia and Reading, and the Central of New Jersey. Furthermore there was then no direct rail connection east and west of the Patapsco River in Baltimore itself, and trains were transferred by ferry. To obviate the delay and inconvenience involved a joint project of the B. & O. and the then-Maryland Central was launched to construct a Belt Line, tunnelling for more than 1½ miles under the very heart of Baltimore City, and making a connection between Camden station, the original B. & O. terminus, and the more recently constructed Philadelphia Division. The completion of this line was in 1895, and the celebrated 'Royal Blue' trains thereafter ran through between Washington and New York without the need of any ferry connection.

From the inception of this through service locomotives of the B. & O. worked the trains only as far as Philadelphia. There they were taken over by the Reading as far as Bound Brook, and thence by those of the C.R.R. of N.J. This arrangement lasted until April 1918, when of course the railroads were under Government control. Then, by an order issued by the Director General of Railroads, the B. & O. trains were transferred from Jersey City terminal to the Pennsylvania station in New York, and the route-ing east of Bound Brook was over the Lehigh Valley Railroad to West Newark Junction and thence over the Pennsylvania. Under this arrangement the B. & O. trains were hauled throughout from Philadelphia to Manhattan Transfer by locomotives of the Reading company, and electrically over the last 8·8 miles into the terminus. This arrangement lasted for not more than eight years, and in September 1926 the original route was taken up again, with the difference that the B. & O. locomotives worked through from Washington to Jersey City, 226 miles. The B. & O. had been using 'Pacific' locomotives on its heavily graded routes since 1906, but to meet the requirements of this eminently prestige run the new 'President', or 'P 7' class was introduced in 1927. In the centenary year of the B. & O. particular attention was paid to neatness of outline and handsome finish. They were painted olive green with gold and maroon striping and gold lettering, while on their smokebox doors they carried the insignia of the company, consisting of the initials B. & O. surmounted by the dome of the Capitol, of Washington. The machinery was designed for a running speed of 80 m.p.h. and these engines gave excellent service.

The third partner in the present Chessie System is the Western Maryland, which arose as a direct competitor of the B. & O., running closely parallel to it for much of the way between Cumberland, Virginia, and Baltimore. It was to Cumberland that I travelled with

13

Tom Johnson in the Chessie Steam Special in May 1977, and having arrived there on a Saturday evening there was much discussion as to whether the rejuvenated Reading 4−8−4 No. 2101 hauling the steam special would be able to take the heavy 18-car train of about 1250 gross trailing tons up the heavy grade to the summit of the Alleghenies on the run to Pittsburgh scheduled for the following day. This was Western Maryland territory for the first 94 miles, after which the train would enter upon metals of the former New York Central for the last 58 miles, on easy descending gradients to Pittsburgh. But from Cumberland for 23 miles the ascent averages 1 in 57, and this was a tremendous proposition, even for a 4−8−4 locomotive having a tractive effort of 68,000 lbs; because even though she has a booster providing an additional 11,000 lbs when cut in, one would not normally expect to use this tractive power continuously for 23 miles of toiling uphill grade. With a 400-ton locomotive and tender, and 1250 tons of train, a gravitational force of 29 tons had to be overcome, apart from any frictional resistances. The tractive effort of main engine *plus* booster amounts to 35 tons, so it was going to make an all-out effort essential.

Locomotive No. 2101 of the Reading has an unusual pedigree. The company had a class of heavy freight 2−8−0s, known as 'I 10'. They were essentially slow speed units, and by the 1940s were becoming outdated. But the boilers, 7 ft 4 in. diameter, with an enormous firebox having a grate area of 94·5 sq. ft were still good, and by no means life-expired, and so thirty of these were taken and formed the basis of a new 4−8−4 fast mixed-traffic design. The boilers were not large enough as they were, so an additional ring was added at the smokebox end, increasing the length of the tubes from 13 ft 6 in. to 20 ft, and a longer smokebox was fitted. Fortunately, the excellent design of the boiler permitted an increase in the steam pressure from 220 to 240 lbs per sq. in. and the internals of the boiler were rearranged to provide a combustion chamber ahead of the firebox. Four thermic siphons were fitted, one in this chamber, and three in the firebox proper. Apart from the rear end of the boiler everything else about the 4−8−4s that emerged was new: a one-piece cast steel bed frame, with cylinders cast integrally; 5 ft 10 in. coupled wheels, and roller bearings to all carrying wheels. The new engines were numbered 2100 to 2109, but they went into traffic in the closing years of the great steam era and were used no more than sporadically, and in 1955, as the saying goes, No. 2101 was 'put into mothballs'. How she was rescued from retirement and brought back into full working order would fill a book in itself.

Before relating how No. 2101 fared on the run to Pittsburgh, it is worth recalling what the Western Maryland used to do with their freight hauls in steam days. At one time the Class '12' 2−10−0s were the standard power, having a tractive effort of 90,300 lbs. Westbound from Cumberland their load rating was one of 1900 tons, but this was not taken without assistance. In the case of very heavy trains no fewer than three helpers were sometimes needed, one coupled on ahead of the train engine and two more pushing in rear. On the comparatively easy gradients from Baltimore No. 2101 had given an impressive performance, and on the Sunday morning as I watched her being prepared they hoped to climb the great bank without help. But while I was watching a westbound freight drew into Cumberland station headed by *five* diesels. I wondered. Unfortunately from the viewpoint of No. 2101 I had to go south that day, but my hosts telephoned later, and we learned that she had climbed the bank unassisted — just! The summit of the Alleghenies on this route is 2373 ft above sea level, with an ascent of 1747 ft in the 23 miles from Cumberland.

CHAPTER TWO

The Chessie System

The Chesapeake and Ohio of today, of which the official name, by the way, is 'railway' and not 'railroad', is a mighty freight hauler, and as such I saw some of its manifold activities; but until the great slump in passenger business it ran a series of splendid sleeping car trains in which, as the publicity folks assured us, one slept like a kitten. In that happy phrase there was born a legend, the legend of 'Chessie'. The adorable kitten, fast asleep on a pillow, became the mascot, the insignia of the Chesapeake and Ohio. In due course she grew up and married and with 'Peake', her 'old man', had many more little 'chessies', who were also pictured fast asleep on the luxurious night expresses from Washington. Today 'Chessie' is more than a legend; she is an institution, the name officially adopted by the association of three great railroads. Her portrait, still fast asleep (!), graces official notepaper; her profile is carried on locomotives, box-cars, cabooses and elsewhere — strangely enough in one respect, since there is only one remaining passenger train over the line.

The Chesapeake and Ohio, like its partner the Baltimore and Ohio, is a great carrier of coal. This traffic originates in the great coalfields of eastern Kentucky and West Virginia, and coal is conveyed north-westwards to Cincinnati and Chicago, to Toledo and Detroit, all for internal and heavy industrial use. The other flow is eastwards for export, or for coastwise distribution, through the great port of Newport News, at the mouth of the James River, at the entrance to Chesapeake Bay. These traffics are concentrated at Russell Yard, Kentucky, for the first named, and at Hinton, West Virginia, for the second. The strategic location of these two yards in relation to the

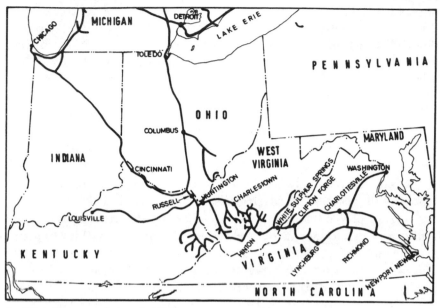

3. The Chesapeake and Ohio system

originating traffic will be clearly apparent from the accompanying sketch map. Centrally for the whole system, a veritable 'Crewe' of the Chesapeake and Ohio, is Huntington, the site of the large mechanical engineering works and its headquarters. Unlike its partners in the present Chessie System, the C. & O. makes its way through the hill ranges of West Virginia without any very severe gradients on the sections of maximum loading. Northward from Russell Yard to Columbus, en route for Toledo and Detroit, the principal ascent extends for 17¼ miles, of which only 1¼ miles are as steep as 1 in 143, and the remainder varies between level, and 1 in 500. Eastbound from Hinton, over the Allegheny Division, the going is harder, with 12½ miles at 1 in 143. For westbound empties over this same section the gradient is 1 in 88 for 10 miles from Clifton Forge.

The hardest going is on the westbound run over the Mountain Division, from Charlottesville to Clifton Forge. Here there is a stretch of 13 miles continuously climbing at 1 in 70-75, and another stiff bank from Staunton at 1 in 66. It was for this section that the very first American locomotives of the 4−8−2 type were introduced, as long

17

ago as 1911. They had cylinders 29 in. diameter by 28 in. stroke, 5 ft 2 in. diameter coupled wheels, but at that time the techniques of boiler design limited the steam pressure to 180 lbs per sq. in. Nevertheless the tractive effort was big enough for that period — 58,000 lbs. They were primarily intended for passenger trains over this 95¾ mile sub-division, a run of a little over three hours.

The line runs through beautiful country in this area, amid the richly wooded slopes of the Appalachian Mountains; but by the Amtrak passenger train of today, the *James Whitcomb Riley* between Washington and Chicago, it is traversed in the middle of the night. (In unexpected circumstances, however, I saw it to the best possible advantage from a light aeroplane.) My friends of the 'Chessie' had very kindly laid on a splendid business car attached to the rear of the *James Whitcomb Riley* to take us by night from Washington to Huntington, leaving at 9.35 p.m. and arriving 7.21 a.m. next morning. The Chesapeake and Ohio reaches Washington by trackage rights over eighty-five miles of the Southern Railway, from Orange, and from the observation platform at the rear end of the car the departure from Washington is dramatically beautiful, with the Capitol building, brilliantly floodlit, seen precisely in line with the track for some distance. When we reached Charlottesville however, just before midnight, we learned that because of a derailment farther west the train would not be able to take its normal route. It was at first thought that a big detour to the south via the Norfolk and Western would be necessary, and the arrangements were still uncertain when I turned in for the night. There was little rest for my friends of the Chessie however. Consultation with the Norfolk and Western made it clear that we should not have arrived back on Chessie metals, at Huntington, until late in the following afternoon, with no time to follow out the programme they had laid on for me. So at Waynesboro, where the train itself passed on to the N. & W. our business car was taken off the *James Whitcomb Riley* and attached to the rear of the first eastbound freight, and worked back to Charlottesville. There my friends had the light aeroplane ready to take us over the mountains, some 200 miles, to Huntington.

The nature of the routes followed by the heaviest coal hauls have dictated the development of a different type of freight locomotive on the C. & O. from that found on other American railroads. With easier gradients the running could be faster, and it was significant that when a comprehensive series of dynamometer car trials was conducted with one of the enormous 'H 8' class $2-6-6-6$ locomotives in 1943, the ultimate development of C. & O. steam power, the maximum draw-bar horsepower registered was at a speed as high as 46 m.p.h., with a train load of 13,650 tons. But the evolving of a locomotive design of such calibre does not just happen, and some reference must be made to the lead-up to it. The Brobdingnagian loads that came with the modern diesel age were no new thing on the Chessie! Although the railroad had taken delivery from Alco of the series of $4-8-2$ locomotives in 1911, mainly for passenger service, it was a time when most other American lines were introducing slow, heavy haulers for freight. The C. & O. '316' class had leading bogies and were evidently intended to get their hauls quickly over the ground. A class of big $2-6-6-2$ compound Mallets came in 1915, mainly for pusher duties; but in 1924 the C. & O. really broke new ground in American locomotive history by introducing the first locomotives of the articu-lated Mallet type, non-compound, for main line running. These great engines, which were referred to briefly in the previous chapter, can be appreciated in their colossal size from the dimensions on page 20. In 1930 a new, non-articulated giant took the road, in a class of $2-10-4$s, with a tractive effort of 91,600 lbs, but the culmination so far as freight power was concerned came with 'H 8' class, and in the summer of 1943 a fascinating series of dynamometer car trials took place on the two sections where the heaviest demands were made upon locomotive power with loaded coal trains.

On the Allegheny sub-division, from Hinton up to the Allegheny summit, and thence downhill to Clifton Forge, seven test runs were made. Of these, three were with so-called 'single' trains made up to between 70 and 76 cars, with an average gross trailing load of 5790 tons. The so-called 'double trains' had between 141 and 145 cars, with an average trailing load of 11,570 tons. The double trains in all cases had the assistance of pusher locomotives, in two cases of the 'H 8' class $2-6-6-6$s. Westbound over the Allegheny sub-division, the test locomotive made five runs on which the average load up the bank from Clifton Forge was 131 cars (128 of them empty) with a gross trailing load of 2986 tons. The locomotive had to be worked

19

extremely hard on all tests, at times absolutely 'all out'; but this condition of service is a feature of design of American steam locomotives, and a thermal efficiency approaching that of the best British and French locomotives was shown. The coal used was naturally that mined locally, and had a calorific value equal to that of the best British grades from South Wales or the South Yorkshire fields.

On two of the eastbound test runs with double trains the 'pusher' was an 'H 7' class 2−8−8−2, of the celebrated class that pioneered the use of simple rather than compound propulsion on large articulated locomotives. It is interesting to compare the proportions of the 'H 7' and 'H 8' classes, thus:

C. & O. Articulated Locomotives

	'H 7	'H 8'
Class		
Type	2−8−8−2	2−6−6−6
Year introduced	1924	1941
Cylinders (4) dia. in.	23	22½
stroke in.	32	33
Coupled wheel dia. ft in.	4−9	5−7
Boiler pressure lbs/sq. in.	215	260
Total evaporative heating surface sq. ft	6580	7240
Superheater sq. ft	1849	3186
Grate area sq. ft	112·2	135
Adhesion weight tons	220	210
Total engine weight tons	253·5	324
Tender weight tons	94·8	195·5
Tractive effort lbs	108,550	110,200

In slow speed working on a heavy bank the 'H 7' would be roughly equivalent to an 'H 8', but the latter would have all the advantage on the faster sections of the line.

During the tests on the Northern sub-division the 'H 8' locomotive performed some of its most spectacular work. On only one out of the five test runs from Russell to Columbus was it necessary to take a pusher over Limeville Bridge. Why this should have been necessary is not apparent from the test reports. On the fastest of the northbound test runs the 109¾ miles from Russell (Kentucky) to Columbus

(Ohio) were covered in 4 hrs 11 min. inclusive of a delay amounting to 27 min. The running time of 3 hrs 44 min. showed an average speed of 29·4 m.p.h. and of this time the engine was coasting for no more than 26 min. During the 'working' time the regulator was full open throughout and steam was being cut off on an average at 59 per cent of the piston stroke. The actual working varied between 44 and 82 per cent — the latter being 'all-out'. Although this would be considered exceptionally severe driving on a British steam locomotive, the performance showed high economy in fuel. On all these runs from Russell to Columbus the coal consumed per hour for each horsepower exerted on the drawbar was a little over 2·9 lbs. In Great Britain a figure of 3 lbs was considered the hallmark of a well-designed locomotive working such trains as the 'Flying Scotsman' or the 'Cornish Riviera Express', and to achieve comparable figures in such 'all-out' conditions of working bespeaks an outstandingly good design.

It is very interesting also that when further freight locomotives were required by the Chesapeake and Ohio in 1949, they purchased 2−6−6−2 Mallet compounds — a modernised version of the design introduced in 1915. The later engines have an interest that is both historic and nostalgic, in that they were the very last steam locomotives built by Baldwins. Two of them are preserved, one at Mount Clare, Baltimore, and a second at Huntington. I was able to climb around the latter, and in the cab could appreciate the excellent arrangement of the controls. Needless to say, they were stoker fired. Again it is interesting to see how their proportions differed from the original compound 2−6−6−2s of 1915.

The basic dimensions were thus almost identical though the later engines had an improved valve gear that gave better steam distribution. The tenders of the later engines were also much larger. But the striking correspondence with a design dating back as early as 1915 is remarkable. These latter engines were built by Alco.

Today, when the one Amtrak train slips unobtrusively through the night, one hardly thinks of passenger locomotives on the pleasant route through the Appalachians. Strange though it may now seem, however, passengers were a major consideration in the early days of railroad construction in these regions. The Chesapeake and Ohio,

21

C. &. O. 2-6-6-2 Mallet Compounds

Year introduced	1915	1949
Cylinders:		
H.P.　dia. in.	22	22
L.P.　dia. in.	35	35
Stroke in.	32	32
Coupled wheel　dia. ft in.	4-8	4-8
Boiler pressure　lbs/sq. in.	210	210
Total evaporative heating surface　sq. ft	4900	4830
Superheater　sq. ft	975	991
Grate area　sq. ft	72·2	72·2
Adhesion weight　tons	163	163·5
Total engine weight　tons	194	194
Tender weight　tons	75·4	97·2
Tractive effort　lbs	76,100	76,000

unlike its great partner to the north, began in a very modest way with a little track from Louisa, on the Kentucky side of the Ohio River, and only twenty-two miles long to where this branch now joins the main line west of Huntington. This first venture indeed dates back to 1836, and later became the Virginia Central; and there was another line chartered, but not built, called the Covington and Ohio. There was a rival project for a canal, with a tunnel nine miles long under the Allegheny ridge, but none of these proposals had really got off the ground by the 1850s. The passenger interest centered upon the attractions of the mineral springs of White Sulphur. With the fame of European spas like Bath, Baden-Baden and Spa, in Belgium, well-established, one finds a Lewisburg newspaper commenting in 1852: 'With a railroad, hundreds drawn by its romantic and beautiful scenery, shaking the dust of the city from their garments and its cares and dissipations from their minds, would flock thither'.

Maybe so, but wealthy tourists, 'flocking' to take the waters at White Sulphur Springs would not pay for a railroad, and even with the prospect of tapping the mineral resources of east Kentucky and the Ohio Valley, progress westward from Richmond, Virginia, was very slow. Then came the Civil War. Although the tide of battle surged up and down these lovely valleys of West Virginia, the unfinished railroad did not present the same targets for sabotage, nor facilities for military transport, as the main line of the Baltimore and Ohio did further north. All the same it was no time for further construction, and properties around White Sulphur Springs were heavily damaged. Recovery afterwards was at first very slow, and it was more than two years after General Robert E. Lee's surrender at the Appomattox Court House in April 1865, and the assassination of Abraham Lincoln five days later, before a railroad conference was convened in West Virginia. It was to the scene of this conference, at White Sulphur Springs, that Tom Johnson was now taking me, in a delightful day-long drive by road from Cumberland, nearly 200 miles to the north. It was at The Old White Hotel, which served the patrons of White Sulphur Springs for more than sixty years, that the conference was held. Arrangements to raise more money were made, work on the line restarted, and in 1869 the first trains from Richmond steamed into White Sulphur Springs. But the track was still temporary, and it was not until the great Connecticut tycoon Collis P. Huntington became interested, and was named president, that construction moved towards completion. In 1873 the last spike was driven in the line linking tidewater of Chesapeake Bay to the Ohio River; White Sulphur Springs was on the main line.

'The White', as the hotel site of the 1867 conference was known, was bought by the Chesapeake and Ohio Railway in the 1890s, and it continued as a centre of fashion with every manifestation of business opulence. A new boom was beginning in private railroad cars. Railroad presidents began it all, for how else would one arrive at White Sulphur but in 'private varnish', as the saying went? It might be Scott of the Pennsylvania, Reinhart of the Sante Fe, King of the Erie, while W. K. Vanderbilt of the New York Central owned two! But there was a tiny cloud on the otherwise serene sky when money, not tradition, made it a heady era. In 1900 the first 'horseless carriage' arrived at White Sulphur, by rail, in a Chesapeake and Ohio freight car. The formidable competitor of the twentieth century had been born. In 1913 the 'Old White' was joined by the magnificent new 'Greenbrier', described by one enthusiastic guest as a 'gorgeous hostelry which to my mind was like a fairy palace set amid the lights and shadows of the Allegheny hills.' And it was to stay at Greenbrier that Tom Johnson brought me in May 1977. The thought occurred to me that few, if any, of those who come to enjoy the golf or other sporting facilities in its glorious private parklands, or even to drink the waters at the beautiful little spring house, would give even a passing thought to the railroad affiliations of the place, any more than visitors to Dornoch, Gleneagles or Turnberry do in Scotland.

After the financial disaster of 1929 some recovery in passenger business had begun by the mid-1930s, and this prompted the C. & O. to introduce new locomotives particularly for working the mountain sections. The 4−8−4 type was then becoming popular in the USA for operating over routes that included a mixture of fast uninhibited running and severe climbing, and in 1935 delivery was taken from Lima of five tremendous engines with 27½-in. by 30 in. cylinders, 6 ft diameter coupled wheels, a combined total heating surface of 6881 sq. ft and an enormous stoker-fired grate of 100·3 sq. ft. In running the Washington-Chicago service, the C. & O. was to some extent in competition with the Pennsylvania, although the two routes served widely dispersed areas intermediately — Pittsburgh on the one hand, and Cincinnati on the other. West of Huntington there was every need for fast running; and there, as also on the northward run through Columbus to Toledo, the 'F 19' class of 'Pacifics' dating from 1926 were holding the fort. With the increase of traffic on account of the second world war, which was amply evident even before the USA became directly involved, larger locomotives were needed for the more level routes, and so came the eight 'L 2' class 'Hudsons' of 1942, from Baldwins. The basic dimensions of these three classes of passenger locomotive are shown in the facing table.

The northward run from Russell Yard to Toledo, so important in the transport of coal for shipment on the great lakes, leads on to another important phase in C. & O. history. By the 1940s the railroad was working in close association with two others in the north, the New York, Chicago and St Louis, popularly known as the Nickel Plate, and the Pere Marquette. The C. & O. had financial interests in both, and at one time there was also talk of a closer affiliation with the New York Central and its allies. Such a combination, extending clockwise from Washington to St Louis and Chicago, embracing the whole of the state of Michigan, both sides of Lake Erie, and then round to

C. & O. Express Passenger Locomotives

	'F 19'	'L 2'	'J 3'
Class			
Type	4−6−2	4−6−4	4−8−4
Year introduced	1926	1942	1935
Cylinders dia. in.	27	25	27½
stroke in.	28	30	30
Coupled wheel dia. ft in.	6−1	6−6	6−0
Boiler pressure lbs/sq. in.	200	255	255
Total evaporative heating surface sq. ft	4239	4233	4343
Superheater sq. ft	1213	1810	2058
Grate area sq. ft	80·3	90	100·3
Tractive effort			
main engine lbs	47,500	52,000	68,300
Booster lbs	none	12,600	12,400

Montreal, Boston and New York, would have meant the virtual encirclement of two other giants, the Pennsylvania and the Baltimore and Ohio. It would seem that at that time it was the C. & O. from its exceptionally strong financial position that was calling the tune, while that of the New York Central was not quite so happy. The immediate outcome, in 1947, was that the C. & O. relinquished its financial interests in the Nickel Plate, but took over completely the Pere Marquette. Its acquisition added nearly 2000 route miles to the Chesapeake and Ohio system, and gave it two separate entries into Canada, at Sarnia, and Windsor, Ontario. The Pere Marquette was named after the Jesuit priest who had set up a mission at Sault Ste Marie, and who accompanied the explorer Joliet in an attempt to find the great river that would lead them to the Pacific Ocean. They found the Mississippi, but it went the wrong way!

The Chesapeake and Ohio is above all a transporter of coal, and in round numbers the traffic requires about 70,000 cars. Clearly the maintenance and replacement of such a fleet requires to be highly organised, and until the 1920s it was spread between works at seven different locations ranging from Newport News, on Chesapeake Bay, to Peru, Indiana, about half-way between Cincinnati and Chicago. This was not economic, and it was decided to concentrate the work at one large plant at which repair work could be organised on a production line basis. A site where space was virtually unlimited was chosen at Raceland, Kentucky, near to Russell Yard, and the new shop covering eighty-four acres was brought into service in October 1929. In 1947 fabricating facilities were added, followed in 1955 by a new reclamation plant, and by that time also new cars were being built at Raceland. These, in keeping with the predominating traffic on the railroad, were mainly open-top coal hoppers, and gondola cars. The repair organisation was also extended to deal, on a flow-line basis, with covered hoppers, pulpwood cars, box cars, and cabooses. Alongside this the production of new cars at times reaches astronomical proportions. During 1969 for example, Raceland was turning out sixteen 100-ton coal hopper cars *per day*, not to mention six 100-ton gondolas at the same time. When I visited the works they were turning out eight 100-hoppers a day.

At Huntington, not many miles away on the opposite side of the Ohio River, the diesel-electric locomotives taking the bulk of today's traffic are maintained, but the shops have an interesting record in steam locomotive maintenance and construction. I have referred earlier to the development of C. & O. passenger power from the 'Pacifics' of 1926 to the 'Hudsons' of 1942, but when visiting the Railroad Museum at Baltimore I was shown a streamlined 'Hudson' locomotive that seemed outside the general line of development, the '490'. In the post-war years when the great transition from steam to diesel power was sweeping across the USA, the C. & O. at first remained an entirely steam line, like its neighbour to the south, the Norfolk and Western. To meet the requirements of the passenger traffic between Washington, Cincinnati and Chicago, which was then growing in importance, it was decided to modernise some of the 20-year old 'Pacifics', and at the same time to bring them into line with popular trends by streamlining and the addition of a distinctive livery. The reconstruction work was done at Huntington shops, and involved changing the wheel arrangement from 4−6−2 to 4−6−4, and adding a booster to the hind wheels of the four-wheeled trailing truck beneath the firebox.

Although the cylinder dimensions remained the same, namely 27 in. diameter by 28 in. stroke, new cylinders were fitted, equipped with Franklin type poppet valves. The boiler barrel and firebox remained the same, but there was a re-arrangement of the tubes, and inclusion of a superheater of the 'E' type provided 2001 sq. ft of heating surface against the former 1213 sq. ft. The nominal tractive effort of the main engine was increased only in proportion to an increase in boiler pressure from 200 to 210 lbs per sq. in., but the capacity of the locomotive for acceleration, and in making a high transitory output in climbing a heavy gradient was notably increased by the addition of the booster, accounting for an extra 12,000 lbs of tractive effort. The original tenders of the Vanderbilt type had a capacity of 15 tons of coal, and 12,000 gallons of water. The new tenders styled to match the streamlining of the locomotive weighed no less than 159 tons in working order, with 25 tons of coal and 18,000 gallons of water. In their silver-grey livery, with a broad yellow band extending from front to rear, the general effect is striking. It is good that the first of these notable rebuilds has been preserved and is on permanent display at Mount Clare.

Despite the prevailing trend towards non-steam forms of motive power, the Chesapeake and Ohio, ever mindful of the fact that 90 per cent of their freight revenue was derived from the conveyance of coal, worked out a design for a steam turbine electric locomotive, in collaboration with the Baldwin Locomotive Works, and the Westinghouse Electric Corporation. Delivery of the first unit was taken in 1947. This remarkable machine, which had the distinction of being the largest passenger locomotive in the world, was in effect an electric locomotive on which the self-contained generating plant was powered by a coal fired steam turbine. The locomotive itself was 90 ft long, and it hauled a tender carrying 25,000 gallons of water. The locomotive, which was completely streamlined, had the coal bunker in front, then came the boiler, and the turbine and the generators were in rear. The wheel arrangement was 4−8−0+4−8−4, and every one of the driving axles was directly powered. The driving compartment was between the coal bunker and the boiler. The starting tractive effort was 98,000 lbs and at a speed of 40 m.p.h. the drawbar pull that could be sustained indefinitely was 21½ tons. It was expected that speeds of 100 m.p.h. would be sustained on level track, and that the then-existing journey time between Washington and Cincinnati of 13¾ hours would be cut by two hours. The distance is 599 miles, so that an average speed of 51 m.p.h. was envisaged, including the negotiation of the mountain sections. Today the *James Whitcomb Riley* takes 13 hrs 20 min.

Three of these enormous steam turbine-electric locomotives were built, but they came too late in steam history for their potentialities to be fully developed. In this respect they were like the geared-turbine steam locomotives on the Pennsylvania, and on the London Midland and Scottish in Great Britain. But the Chesapeake and Ohio experiment was a brave attempt to apply turbo-electric drive, while still using the fuel that was so readily to hand.

CHAPTER THREE

The Vortex of New York

Before the jet age nearly all travellers from Europe to the USA arrived by sea at New York. From the deck of a liner entering the bay and passing the Statue of Liberty they were able to appreciate something of the astonishing geographical situation of this uniquely placed city. Today, when arriving or departing by train, one can get no conception of the general layout, and I have not yet seen it from the air. So one must resort to maps, and it can at once be said that so far as main line railroads are concerned, it is now vastly simpler than the situation that existed no more than forty years ago. At the turn of the century there was only one passenger station in the city proper on Manhattan Island — Grand Central — shared by the New York Central, and by the New Haven. All the other railroads serving New York had terminal stations across the Hudson, or North River, in Jersey City, and thence came the Central of New Jersey, the Pennsylvania, the Lehigh Valley, the Erie, the Delaware, Lackawanna and Western, and the New York West Shore and Buffalo. Across the East River, in Long Island City, was the terminus of the Long Island Railroad, the line from which Henry W. Thornton came, in 1914, to be General Manager of the Great Eastern Railway, of England. Later he became President of Canadian National.

Apart from those arriving at Grand Central terminal, all passengers by other railroads had to take ferry boats to reach New York, either from Jersey City, or Long Island City, and the Pennsylvania Railroad had no fewer than three ferry services, two to New York City and one across the East River to Brooklyn. It is interesting to recall that while the transatlantic liner berths of the British and French steamship lines were in New York, just upstream from the Pennsylvania Railroad ferry terminal at the foot of Desbrosses Street, those of the Nederland Line were adjacent to the Pennsylvania Railroad terminal in Jersey City, and the German lines — Hamburg Amerika, and North German Lloyd — had berths farther upstream in the Hudson River, and near to the railway terminals of the Erie and the Lackawanna railroads. It would seem that the aim was to get passengers from the continent of Europe away from New York as quickly as possible!

At the time of the great Columbian Exposition at Chicago in 1893 there were no less than forty-four through trains daily from New York, following, between them, *eighteen* different routes. Of course such a proliferation of service could not last, but even after the great slump of the 1930s through passengers still had the choice of seven routes, and the mention of one of these comes as a supplement to the first two chapters of this book, that of the Baltimore and Ohio. That company worked in partnership with the Reading and with the Central of New Jersey, but it was not until 1926 that the through trains from Washington were brought into Jersey City Terminal by locomotives of the B. & O. Prior to that it was Reading locomotives that worked the B. & O. trains to Bound Brook, and those of the Central of New Jersey that completed the journey. They were of the 'Pacific' type, of very similar proportions, thus:

Railroad Class	Reading G−2−SA	C.R.R. of N.J. '825'
Cylinders dia. in	25	26
stroke in.	28	28
Coupled wheel dia. ft in.	6−8	6−7
Total evaporative heating surface sq. ft	3045	3757
Superheater sq. ft	745	816
Grate area sq. ft	95	94·8
Boiler pressure lbs/sq. in.	230	210
Tractive effort lbs	42,800	42,700

The service was everywhere in strong competition with that of the Pennsylvania, and over well aligned routes both classes of 'Pacific' were called upon for much hard and fast running. In 1910 however, the Pennsylvania established a major advantage over their rivals by the opening of their magnificent new station in the heart of New York City, reached by a tunnel under the Hudson River, and a new line from Kearny Junction. The time-consuming ferryboat crossing of the river was thus obviated. Lehigh Valley trains were also routed into the new Pennsylvania station. Before describing the tremendous engineering work involved in the building of this station, however, and of its approach lines, one may perhaps be forgiven for indulging in a little nostalgia.

The old way certainly had its charms for those who enjoyed travelling for its own sake. The ferry boats of the Pennsylvania that plied across the Hudson River were veritable floating palaces; large, light, and luxuriously appointed, they each had an upper saloon and deck from which a splendid view of the river front and the shipping of New York City could be seen. And what a sight it is! Skyscrapers are so closely clustered on Manhattan Island as to make up that breathtaking skyline that sets New York apart from all other American cities; and as a foreground there is the pageant of shipping constantly in flow along the river. Then, as to the Jersey City Terminal of the Pennsylvania, a guide book of 1892, prepared for visitors to the Columbian Exposition, sets the scene thus:

A great high, wide spreading, graceful arch, through the white glass of which the sunlight filters down over lines of long, sleek passenger cars, made up into trains about to start for various sections of the country. A half dozen surcharged locomotives far away down the vast transparent roofed enclosure are sending up clouds of white steam, the music of which as it comes moaning from the open safety valves mingles with the clatter of hurrying baggage trucks, the distant rattle of whirling ratchet wheels making fast an arriving ferry boat, the sonorous voices of the conductors in blue uniforms and silver buttons, standing at the head of the long lanes of platforms and directing passengers to their soon-to-be-moving trains, and the incessant drone of the newsboys with their daily and weekly papers, the latest magazines, the newest novels, and the inevitable silk travelling caps.

Jersey City Terminal of the Pennsylvania was indeed more like an English station, in the airy pleasant atmosphere on its platforms — a transatlantic Paddington, or St Pancras. But the book continues:

'Philadelphia, Pittsburgh, Chicago and the West!': so booms the voice of the conductor, above the babel of all other sounds. A negro porter takes your portmanteau and your rugs and you hurry forward.

The inconvenience of the ferry crossings of the Hudson, or North River, whatever their interest in other respects, led to the formation of the North River Bridge Company, which projected the building of a great suspension bridge across the river to enable all the railroads then terminating on the western shore to enter New York City at the foot of West 23rd Street. The Pennsylvania gave this project its support by agreeing to pay its share, on the basis of traffic density, for use of the bridge; but it was the only railroad company that did so. Presumably all the others declined on the grounds of expense, and the project was

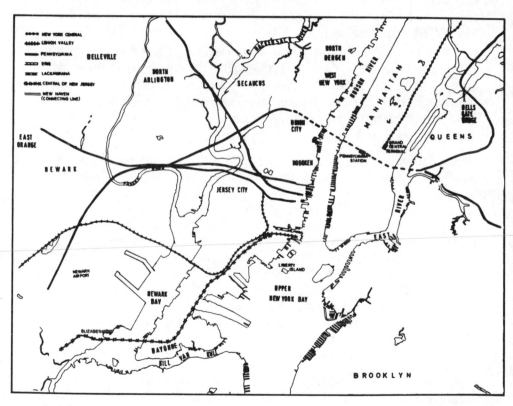

4. New York—the railway approaches

abandoned. In 1900 however, the Pennsylvania had acquired control of the Long Island Railroad, and the great plan was evolved, not only of establishing terminal facilities in New York City for its own large main line business and for local traffic then centred upon the Jersey City terminal, but of connecting through to the Long Island system by a chain of tunnels. It was a tremendous undertaking that involved tunnelling under the North River, the construction of a huge new station in the heart of downtown New York, and then continuing with tunnels under the East River to link up with the Long Island Railroad. The estimated cost of the whole job, including the interchange yards with the existing lines at Harrison, New Jersey, and Sunnyside, Long Island, was $100 m.

The work was organised in five divisions with contracts let to separate contractors. Four of these were started at different times in the years 1903-4, covering the North River Tunnels, the Terminal Station excavation, the Cross-Town Tunnels, and the East River Tunnels. The fifth section, known as the Meadows Division, linking the North River Tunnel section with the Harrison N.J. interchange yard was not started until 1906 and was the least complicated; it involved little more than embankment and bridging. There was a good reason for its late start, because some of the material excavated from the other sections was used in making the embankments. The line itself in the Meadows Division was double-tracked, and ran for six miles across the Hackensack meadows before coming to Bergen Hill. By the time the project was launched sufficient experience had been gained elsewhere with electric traction to enable the Pennsylvania to decide upon this form of traction from the outset, with changeover from steam to electric haulage at the beginning of the new line, at Harrison Interchange Yard.

The first section of tunnelling was under Bergen Hill, a ridge of trap rock forming a southern extension of the famous Hudson River Palisades. The new line was taken through the ridge in two single track parallel tunnels, each just over a mile long, and the most interesting and difficult part of the job began at the eastern end, although in these tunnels a very tough form of rock was encountered, which slowed up the work. When it came to the under river section, there were problems of a different kind. Although there was solid rock on both banks — a bit too 'solid' in places! — the bed of the North River consisted of a deep layer of silt that was a mixture of clay, sand and water. It was necessary to use a shield for driving the tunnel through this somewhat shifty bed, and from trial borings it was determined that the top of the tunnel tube would be about twenty-five feet below the river bed. At one time in the preliminary investigations consideration was given to use of temporary structures or floating plant in the river, but in view of the amount of shipping, including transatlantic liners using the waterway, it was thought essential to conduct all operations beneath the river. As it turned out, the tunnelling under the North River proved a much easier job than that under the East River. The North River tunnels were each single-tracked, descending on a gradient of 1 in 72 (1.4 per cent) from the New Jersey side, and climbing into the Terminal station on a gradient of 1 in 53 (1.9 per cent). It will be appreciated that such gradients would have been quite impracticable with steam traction.

The Terminal station site extended over two city blocks and one intersecting street, and covered an area of eight acres. Because the tracks are from 39 to 58 ft below street level, there was a vast amount of material to be excavated. When finished, an elaborate system of drainage had to be maintained. The work was proceeding at the same time as that of the tunnels on both sides, and these latter could not be used for removal of the spoil. There was an estimated total of 517,000 cu. yards of material to be carted away, and a light railway was constructed to convey dump cars to a specially constructed pier on the left bank of the North River, and extending a distance of 677 ft from the sea wall out into the waterway. This pier was equipped with six derricks, eighteen chutes, and eight telphers for dealing with the various kinds of spoil excavated. Of the total volume about 15 per cent was used in the embankments of the Meadows Division, but by far the largest proportion went in the construction of a large new freight terminal, at Greenville, N.J., adjacent to the Greenville piers of the Pennsylvania in Upper New York bay.

The cross-town tunnels were driven through hard and dry rock, and the excavation was entirely by blasting. Although the rock surface was little more than 5 ft below ground level, and the tunnels were bored at roughly 70 ft below ground, the concussion caused by some of the blasting was severe enough to break glass in neighbouring buildings. Concussion was particularly severe when the working shafts were being excavated. Very great care had to be taken when underpinning of large buildings was necessary, and to avoid disturbances during the night the working hours were confined to two shifts, 6 a.m. to 2.30 p.m. and from then to 11 p.m. Whereas a two-track approach to the new station was considered adequate from the New Jersey side, the addition of the heavy commuter traffic from Long Island made it necessary to have four tracks from the east. These were accommodated in twin-track tunnels in the rock of Manhattan Island, but these had to change to single track 'tubes' under the East River.

The decision to use the shield method of construction for the tunnels under the East River was not lightly taken. The preliminary soundings had shown that beneath the river bed there was a great variety of materials, including quicksand, boulders, sand, gravel, clay and bedrock. There were no precedents to act as a guide, and in view of the difficulties that were anticipated as a result of these surveys consideration was given to other methods of construction. One of these was the freezing process, and an experiment on quite a large scale was made to explore its possibilities. A pilot tunnel 7½ ft in diameter was driven into the river bed for a distance of 160 ft. Circulating pipes were installed in it, and brine at a very low temperature was passed into them until the ground was frozen for a distance of about 15 ft radially around the pilot tunnel. But it was found that the process of freezing the ground was so slow that the idea was abandoned.

The extremely mixed nature of the ground below the river bed led to many troubles during the progress of the shields for tunnel boring. Fissures opened out in the river bed, and led to blow-outs. Some of these had the diverting effect of creating vertical jets of water, like those from a geyser, to rise from the surface of the river, putting navigation at risk. To check the flow of escaping air the bottom of the river over the tunnel had to be continually blanketed with clay. When finished, the tunnels each had an outside diameter of 23 ft, and after lining with concrete the inside diameter is 18 ft. Then outside the iron lining there is a thick layer of concrete grouting, to a depth of 2 ft radially. A concrete bench, the upper surface of which is 1 ft below the axis of the tunnel, was built on each side of the track, within which benches are ducts carrying various necessary electric cables. So the great plan was carried through to a successful conclusion, and by 1912 the new station was dealing with 500 trains a day, with a maximum of 50 during the busiest hour.

Although New York was so intense a focal and concentration point for passenger traffic entering and leaving the United States in the years between the two world wars, it is remarkable that it was handled through no more than five stations. In addition to the new Pennsylvania and Grand Central there were those of the C.R.R. of N.J., also used by Baltimore and Ohio trains; that of the Erie, and the Hoboken terminus of the Lackawanna. From those five stations went the seven competitive services to Chicago. The accompanying map shows the routes they followed, and the distances and fastest times were:

Railroad	Distance miles	Fastest time hrs	min.
Pennsylvania	902·7	16	00
Lackawanna—Nickel Plate	920·4	21	00
New York Central	958·3	16	00
N.Y.C.—Michigan Central	958·6	19	15
Lehigh Valley—Grand Trunk	976·5	21	57
Baltimore & Ohio	989·2	20	28
Erie	995·6	22	05

The 16-hour trains of the Pennsylvania and the N.Y.C. provided Pullman accommodation only and required a supplementary service charge. The fastest trains on both these routes carrying 'coach' class passengers took seventeen hours. Of course, so far as overall time was concerned the Lackawanna, the Baltimore and Ohio, and the Erie all had the additional handicap of intending passengers having to cross the Hudson by ferry before starting on their railway journeys. As can well be imagined by far the greatest proportion of the through traffic between New York and Chicago used either the Pennsylvania or the New York Central route. In 1939 there were 77 Pullman sleeping cars scheduled nightly in each direction between the two cities. Of these no fewer than 42 worked over the N.Y.C., either on the direct line via Cleveland, or north of Lake Erie over the Michigan Central. Another 24 sleepers worked over the Pennsylvania, which left only 11 between the Baltimore and Ohio, the Erie, the Lackawanna, and the Lehigh Valley.

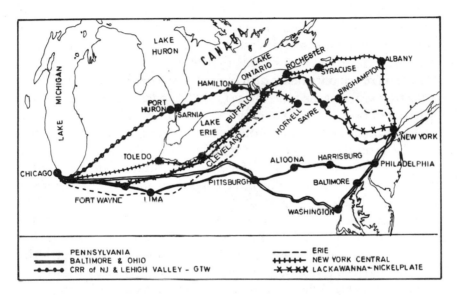

5. Routes from New York to Chicago

The completion in 1910 of the new Pennsylvania station was followed very soon by the complete rebuilding of the New York Central's Grand Central Terminal, and the splendour of this edifice brought forth many eulogies from experienced travellers. As with so many American stations however, the platforms are underground, and somewhat dismal. As passengers are not admitted to the platforms until shortly before departure time, this is perhaps of less consequence than it might be under British methods of working. Grand Central is built on two levels, the upper dealing with long distance trains, and the lower with the suburban. But when built the

37

vast concourses, one for each level, made up for any dismalness that might be felt briefly when descending to the platforms and taking one's seat in the train. The High Level concourse was considered by many to be the finest railway 'waiting room' in the world, utterly dwarfing in size and in magnificence the late lamented Great Hall at Euston. At Grand Central there are three great windows at each end, but what impressed so many discerning travellers was the lightness and brilliance of the decor, with a ceiling in light green; with figures representing the constellations, and the galleries below lit by five great chandeliers. If anyone had time to count the lights in each of these he would find, unless he lost count, that there were 112.

There were separate ticket offices for New York Central, and New Haven trains, and at the time it was built 'Grand Central' was the only departure station in New York for the New England states. The Low Level concourse is spacious enough, but appropriately less ostentatious. The central open space has massive stone supports to the roof above, and the whole area is handsomely lighted, but in a more subdued manner, from semi-hidden lights in the roof. The station itself is in a fashionable part of New York City, flanked by Park Avenue and Vanderbilt Avenue, and within walking distance of the celebrated Central Park. The line is in tunnel for the first 2½ miles out of the terminal, and all trains on the N.Y.C. main line are electrically hauled to Harmon, 32 miles out. At the zenith of railway prestige in passenger carrying, when to ride the Twentieth Century Limited was a status symbol in American business and social life, the daily departure of that train from 'Grand Central' was attended by ceremony as closely disciplined as the changing of the guard outside Buckingham Palace. During the 1920s the train ran regularly in three sections, but at 2·45 p.m. all three moved out simultaneously, with their balconied rear ends exactly in line until they had disappeared into the first tunnel. In the tunnel the first, second and third sections took their places in numerical order and emerged in appropriate succession and space intervals at the outer end.

In the 1920s express train travel from New York was a good deal slower than it became in the breathless, streamlined 'thirties'. In the most highly competitive days before the first world war a time of 28 hours was fixed as the standard between New York and Chicago, by common consent of all the competing railroads, and it was agreed that an extra fare of one dollar (afterwards increased to $1.20) should be charged for each hour less than 28. The basic single fare remained at $32.70. At one time the 'Century' and its rival on the Pennsylvania were making the run in 18 hours, but in the 1920s the time was 20 hours, with a maximum speed limit on the N.Y.C. route of 70 m.p.h. Of course, in addition to the basic fare and the premium for higher speed there were the Pullman charges, which at 1928 levels could be $31.50 for a drawing room with three berths and a separate room with the necessary toilet facilities.

The completion of the new Pennsylvania station in New York in 1910 was the first step towards big changes in the railway facilities to north-east of the city. Until then the terminus of the busy and efficient Long Island Railroad had been across the East River, beside the Newtown Creek, where the present Queens Midtown Tunnel is diving down beneath the river, to pass under Manhattan Island and emerge through the Lincoln Tunnel on the Jersey City side. Connection between New York and the Long Island terminal was necessarily by ferry. The great nine-year project of the Pennsylvania, however, was, as previously mentioned, not only to provide a central city terminus for their own trains from the west, but to bring in all the Long Island commuters, by extending their tunnelling under the East River. In the ordinary way the Long Island would not have been one of the American railroads to receive much attention from British or Continental visitors; but in 1914 — as previously mentioned — to the surprise of the railway world, and to the annoyance of not a few aspiring British railway officers, its General Superintendent, Henry W. Thornton, was appointed General Manager of the Great Eastern Railway, of England. Thornton was an all-round railwayman of outstanding ability. He was trained as a civil engineer, and all his earlier experience in that capacity had been gained on the Pennsylvania. His move to the Long Island, in 1911, was therefore significant of well-established alliance between the great trunk line to the west, and its bustling commuter-working neighbour across the East River.

In tunnelling under the East River the Pennsylvania had been out for bigger game than the Long Island — after all, little more than a glorified suburban system. The New York, New Haven and Hartford had a freight terminal on the Harlem River, and the Pennsylvania launched another great project to connect the approach line to this terminal with the Long Island tracks leading to the tunnel under the East River to their own great city station. This meant crossing the East River at Hell Gate, its narrowest reach, but even so involving a clear span of 1000 ft. The bridge actually built, designed by Pennsylvania Railroad engineers, is of great historical interest. At the time of its construction it was the longest steel arch in the world, but what is of even greater importance is that it proved an exact prototype of the much longer Sydney Harbour Bridge. The Hell Gate bridge was opened in April 1917, and at its centre rises 320 ft above high water mark. Sydney Harbour Bridge, opened in 1932, has a clear span of 1650 ft and a maximum height of 430 ft above high water.

The Hell Gate bridge was not only a splendid piece of engineering; it provided a direct new rail connection between the New England states and the lines to the south-west and west of New York. Hitherto, apart from the platform interchange between the New Haven and the N.Y.C. in Grand Central terminal the only direct connection to the west was by the Boston and Albany, connecting with the N.Y.C. at the latter city. This of course was of no help to passengers bound for Philadelphia, Washington, or the south.

It was over the Hell Gate bridge that I travelled into New York. I had come south from Providence, Rhode Island, by an Amtrak train over the former New York, New Haven and Hartford line. Our last stop had been at Rye, Connecticut, about thirty miles out, and from there briefly on a four-track line we ran fast to the junction of New Rochelle. There the New Haven line goes away northwards to its junction with the New York Central, and so into 'Grand Central'. The commuter trains from the line we had traversed go into New York by this route. After a brief spell at good speed we drew near to the intensely industrialised eastern approaches to the city, slowing down to take the curve on to the Hell Gate bridge. So on to Long Island, the district of Queens, and over Sunnyside Junction.

In the last few miles we had been fairly boxing the compass, and I had begun to lose all sense of direction. We ran, at slow speed, beside the huge Sunnyside yards, which are used for stabling the stock for Long Island commuter trains. There are two nests of sidings *en echelon* on the right-hand side of the line as we were passing, one with 42 and the other with 45 tracks. To avoid conflicting movements with main line traffic a run-round loop burrowing underneath provides access from the east end of the yards to the ingoing track to the terminal station. On arrival in the cavernous depths of the Pennsylvania station I must admit I was not in a suitable frame of mind to appreciate the vast concourse above and its undoubted architectural merits. It was very hot. There were crowds of people everywhere, and I was more concerned in getting a taxi, and driving to my hotel. A few days later, when I was leaving for Philadelphia, I then had time to see what a magnificent station it is.

CHAPTER FOUR

N. & W. — Roanoke and Steam

It was Memorial Day. Everyone was on holiday, and in a pause between the many engagements of a tightly-packed itinerary, I enjoyed a leisurely drive with my friends of the Chessie through beautiful densely wooded upland country southward from White Sulphur Springs to reach Roanoke in the early evening. The Norfolk and Western was one of the last American railroads to stand out staunchly against the floodtide of dieselisation, and recalling the publicity that their magnificent steam locomotives received some thirty years ago, I had looked forward keenly to seeing the works at Roanoke, where they were built and maintained. Using a popular railway catch-phrase one could say that Roanoke was the 'Crewe' of the Norfolk and Western, except that the N. & W. had a real Crewe of their own, farther east. But after dinner that evening, and a stroll down to the line to see the coal trains passing, I fell to thinking of the diverse and exciting history of the N.W. and its constituents before its reorganisation in September 1896, as a railway, rather than a railroad.

Its origin was as modest and unpretentious as that of its neighbour to the north, the Chesapeake and Ohio. When enterprising a railroad nine miles long from City Point, on the James River, to Petersburg, Virginia, the promoters had no thoughts of its development into a great trunk line. It was opened in September 1838, and it was not until sixteen years later that another railroad was opened in this area. This was the so-called South Side Rail Road, running westward from Petersburg to Lynchburg, about a hundred miles, and in due course forming part of the N.W. main line. This was followed, in 1856, by the Virginia and Tennessee, carrying the line westward from Lynchburg to Bristol, and then in 1858 by the Norfolk and Petersburg, taking the line eastward to tidewater at the mouth of Chesapeake Bay, and opposite to the C. & O. Railway port of Newport News. One can smile at contemporary accounts of what the Americans call 'breaking ground', when work on the Virginia and Tennessee Railroad was begun. We read:

Among those present were many of the most distinguished friends and advocates of internal improvement in that State, including Governor Floyd, upon whom, by virtue of his official station, but more by virtue of his liberal and statesmanlike views, and his untiring devotion to the great interests of Virginia, it appropriately devolved to strike the first blow in a work, the commencement of which is justly regarded as a new era in the history of Virginia.

And Governor Floyd having cut the first turf, others seized the spade, and many distinguished guests came forward and took their turn at the job!

Three of the rules of the road are worth quoting:

(a) Passenger trains after being one hour behind time must wait one hour longer for freight trains, unless it arrives sooner and then proceed sending a man ⅓ of a mile ahead with red flag or lantern.

(b) Should two trains meet on the way advantage shall be given to the one which has the greatest distance to run back.

(c) All bridges to be passed at a speed not exceeding 4 miles per hour under any circumstances.

All that was in 1855, before any telegraph had been installed.

Then came the Civil War. With Jefferson Davis, President of the Confederate States, setting up his headquarters at Richmond, Virginia, no more than a hundred miles due south of Washington, the newly opened railroad, or chain of railroads across country was in 'front line' territory. It was not subjected to the dashing raids and guerilla tactics by which Stonewall Jackson harassed the Baltimore and Ohio at Harper's Ferry and elsewhere, but by systematic destruction all along its length, as befitted a lateral railroad extending no more than a few miles in rear of what could be termed the Confederate front line. Lynchburg, Sayler's Creek, Five Forks and Petersburg were all the scene of major battles as the Union forces sought to assail Confederate headquarters from its rear, and Appomattox, the scene of General Robert E. Lee's final surrender in April 1865 lies on the railway just to the east of Lynchburg. In the aftermath of the war the South Side, the Virginia and Tennessee, and the Norfolk and Petersburg were amalgamated to form the Atlantic, Mississippi and Ohio Railroad in 1870. The main line then stretched for some 400 miles from Norfolk to Bristol, and at its most westerly point it was still a long way from the Ohio River, not to mention the Mississippi!

The times were bad, and although the management had high hopes of establishing a lucrative traffic to the south-west, via Bristol, the railroad was thrown into receivership in 1876 and sold at auction. But in 1881 there came the discovery that was to change the entire outlook of the faltering railroad, and eventually to set it on the way to lasting prosperity; this was the discovery of the Pocahontas coalfield in West Virginia. In that same year the railroad itself had been reorganised as the Norfolk and Western Railroad. It was then also that a quiet little village community nestling in a valley flanked by the Blue Ridge and Allegheny Mountains took its first step towards fame. It had the curious name of Big Lick, from its salt deposits that attracted deer and other wild life of the mountains. Big Lick it remained when the Virginia and Tennessee Railroad built its tracks from the east, and its people welcomed the arrival of the new age. There was, however, not yet an indication as to what the future of Big Lick would be. For war came, and the campaigns tore up and down the Shenandoah Valley. It was not until 1881, sixteen years after Robert E. Lee's surrender at the Appomattox Court House, that the citizens of Big Lick raised $10,000 to bring the Shenandoah Valley Railroad into their city, and to link up with the Virginia and Tennessee. Then came the day when Big Lick thought it was time to adopt a more modern name, and in 1882 it became the City of Roanoke, using an Indian name that appropriately enough meant money.

It was a time when other names had been changed too, like the newly established Norfolk and Western Railroad; but at first although numerous branches were opened into the coal-bearing valleys, and the Ohio Extension of the main line was completed in 1892, the financial situation continued to be shaky and it went into a second receivership in 1895. This time however the reorganisation was successful, and as the Norfolk and Western Railway, from September 1896 the N. & W. steamed into the twentieth century in great style. The coalfields of West Virginia tapped by the N. & W. have proved some of the most productive in all the United States, and the railway became a coal carrier second to none. From Bluestone the main line snaked its way to the north-west through this region of fabulous mineral wealth, following the course of the Tug Fork River, throwing off branches to right and left, eventually to cross the Ohio River at Kenova, not ten miles downstream from the Chesapeake and Ohio engineering headquarters at Huntington.

In the buoyant spirit of expansion that gripped the USA in the first years of the twentieth century it is not surprising that the N. & W. monopoly in this area was soon challenged, and so there came the Virginian Railway, to tap the eastern end of the Pocahontas, and to open up a new coalfield, to be known as the Virginian, the deposits of which extended northward to Deepwater Bridge on the Kanawha River. The Virginian was conceived purely as a coal road, and although it was not until July 1909 that regular train operation began, the tonnages conveyed had soon grown to such a figure as to constitute a major problem, not so much in providing tractive power, as in enabling very heavy trains to be safely controlled on falling gradients. Coal from the numerous branch lines in the Virginian coalfield was concentrated at Princeton, and had thence to be conveyed over the 97 miles of the Third District, to Roanoke, whence the N. & W. was intersected. This section included two severe descents: 10 miles of 1 in 67 between Princeton and Kellysville, and 8·7 miles of the same gradient between Merrimac and Fagg. To minimise the number of trains on the Division, which was single-tracked throughout, it was desired to run trains of at least 70 loaded cars, weighing 12,000 tons, and hopefully in due course of trains up to 100 cars. The outcome was two-fold: the introduction in 1917 of some gigantic Mallet compound locomotives of the 2−10−10−2 type with a tractive effort, when working compound, of 147,000 lbs, and a memorable series of trials in 1921 with the double-capacity Westinghouse brakes, on trains loaded to 16,000 tons.

The brake trials proved an epoch-marking stage in the history of freight train operation. The Virginian, like the other coal haulers in the

State, had equally the problem of working lengthy trains of empty cars back to the pits, and the ratio between the loaded and empty weight of the big gondola cars was more than 3 to 1. These had a capacity of 120 (US) tons of coal, with a tare weight of 40 tons, and were carried on two 6-wheeled bogies. The ratio of loaded to empty weight was thus 4 to 1. The problem was therefore that if a brake force was provided that would adequately control the loaded cars, it could be far too great for the empties and could result in locked wheels and skidding. So the conception was evolved of a double brake — one for empty conditions and one for loaded — with a changeover device on each car which would be set in the 'empty' or 'load' position before the start of any particular run. In the trials of 1921 it was demonstrated that a loaded train of one hundred 120-ton loaded coal gondola cars weighing about 16,000 tons could be safely controlled down a gradient of 1 in 57 from one of the 2−10−10−2 Mallet compound locomotives. Thereafter, the 'empty-load' principle postulated by the Westinghouse Brake Company gradually became a standard feature of heavy freight train operation in the USA.

East of Roanoke the Virginian ran roughly parallel to the N. & W. to its point of shipment of the coal, at Sewells Point, at the entrance to Chesapeake Bay. But in those booming years of the 1920s there was plenty of traffic for both of them, and the tonnage of coal that between them was carried through Roanoke was prodigious. The establishment of the Norfolk and Western at Roanoke was perhaps unlike any other in the United States. One thinks of American railroads — even the greatest and most prosperous of them — purchasing large numbers of steam locomotives from one or another of the Big Three of manufacturers. Some, like the Pennsylvania at Altoona, developed their own designs to the stage of home-made prototypes and then placed large orders outside. Others like the Baltimore and Ohio, at Mount Clare, or the Chesapeake and Ohio at Huntington built their own locomotives up to the medium sizes, but went to Baldwins, Lima, or Alco, for the real giants. By contrast the Norfolk and Western built all its own locomotives at Roanoke, and the Class 'A' and Class 'Y 6' articulateds weighed, with their tenders, more than 400 tons. As early as 1917 the N. & W. was building 4−8−2s for passenger work. The principal run was from Norfolk to Cincinnati, and this involved some heavy grade work where the line makes its sinuous way through the colliery areas. Connection with Washington, from the opposing capital city of the Civil War, was made by the Richmond, Fredericksburg and Potomac, once called 'the biggest little railroad in the country'.

Little railroad it may have been with a main line only 116½ miles long, but it had some mighty big steam locomotives, and it has the proud distinction of retaining its title unchanged from the date of its original charter in 1834 down to the present time. One can quite imagine also what things were like during the Civil War, when that 116½ miles connected the two rival capitals! When things returned to normal it became a major north to south link, to the Seaboard Coast line and all its ramifications south of Petersburg. Its great 4−8−4 passenger locomotives bore the title 'Richmond-Washington' on their tenders, surmounted by the words 'Capital Cities Route'. There were no half measures about the R.F. & P., and these locomotives were designed as though they had to work half across America instead of a mere 116½ miles. They had a tractive effort of 66,500 lbs, and with coupled wheels 6 ft 5 in diameter they were intended to run fast. They were named after Governors and Generals — of both sides! — in the Civil War, and the locomotive chosen for the official photograph was the *General T. J. Jackson* — Stonewall Jackson. Nevertheless, we in Great Britain did not hesitate to have locomotives named *King Charles I* and *Oliver Cromwell*.

After this brief digression on to the splendid 'little' R.F. & P., and its not so little steam locomotives, I must return to Roanoke and its products. It is as much a railroad town as Crewe, of the ever-famous London and North Western, and for many years after 1882 when the picturesque name for the settlement was changed, railroading was almost the sole activity, even more so than Crewe, in England; for Roanoke was not only a great junction and centre of engineering activities, it was the administrative headquarters as well — Crewe and Euston rolled into one, as it were. With the passing of the years Roanoke has emulated its English counterpart by adding many other industrial activities to those of railroads, and today its population is 105,000. In walking round the works, and having constantly in mind the great steam locomotives that were built there, I was deeply im-

47

pressed by the way in which manufacturing facilities had been adapted to the needs of the modern railroad. Building 86 ft long box-cars, and 100-ton coal gondola cars may not be such a glamorous occupation as turning out 2−6−6−4 fast freighters; but it is a superb example of modern engineering production. Roanoke is geared to turn out twenty 100-ton gondola cars a day.

The concluding years of the steam age on the Norfolk and Western have become something of a legend. As a coal carrier *in excelsis* the management determined upon the development of the steam locomotive to maximum operating efficiency and maximum utilisation. One of the main arguments of those who advocated a change to diesel traction was that one could obtain far greater daily mileages out of the diesels, because of the time taken to service steam locomotives between successive duties. When later in this book I come to the Santa Fe, I shall be discussing the remarkable feats of performance achieved between La Junta, Colorado, and Los Angeles with the big 4−8−4 locomotives. There it was a case of continuous running over 1234 miles. The Norfolk and Western had no such long-distance workings to their advantage. The total length of the main line between Norfolk and Cincinnati is only 676 miles, a relatively short run for the USA, and it is of course axiomatic that the shorter the run, the less chance there is to secure high percentage utilisation from any kind of locomotive, steam, diesel, or electric.

The Norfolk and Western tackled the job from bedrock fundamentals. The drawing office at Roanoke was set to prepare new designs that would not only give an outstanding performance in hauling heavy tonnages at speed on the open road, but which could be serviced in an absolute minimum of time. The three new standard classes, all built at Roanoke, were each magnificent examples of high capacity steam power, but it is somewhat naturally the Class 'J' 4−8−4 that steal the limelight. Seeing the general trend of steam locomotive practice in North America one could say 'just another 4−8−4', with a different external appearance due to the form of the streamlining; but the N. & W. Class 'J' was very much a locomotive with a difference. For one thing it had considerably smaller coupled wheels than its contemporaries on the New York Central, Union Pacific, Santa Fe and Southern Pacific — only 5 ft 10 in. diameter. While this was in

48

deference to the heavy gradients encountered west of Lynchburg, the eastern part of the main line was straight and level and ideally suited to really fast running. So far as basic dimensions were concerned, the 'J' class were straightforward 2-cylinder simples, and they make an interesting comparison with some other American 4–8–4s as shown in the table on page 51; on the basis of nominal tractive force they were by far the most powerful of all six. They had a mighty boiler, and a firebox to back it up, with a total evaporative heating surface of 5271 sq. ft, a superheater of 2177 sq. ft and a huge grate, for a passenger engine, of 107·7 sq. ft.

One of them was tested in all-out haulage effort, with a trailing load of 15 cars, 1025 tons, on the line between Roanoke and Christiansburg, which section includes an ascent of 1 in 77 for twelve miles. On this gradient a speed of 40 m.p.h. was sustained, requiring a drawbar pull of nearly 50,000 lbs, or more than 60 per cent of the nominal tractive force. This was a remarkable feat for a passenger engine at such a speed as 40 m.p.h. This however was merely 'by the way'. The really notable part of the working of these locomotives was the way in which the purely basic dimensions were backed up by a most comprehensive 'bank' of refinements in design, to link in with the most highly organised arrangements for servicing. The introduction of the new locomotives of Classes 'J', 'A' and 'Y 6' was accompanied by a complete redesign of the depots. On the N. & W. there was no question of a steam locomotive going 'on shed' after a long run. The depots were more like roadside filling stations, at which the largest locomotives were inspected, lubricated, washed, loaded with coal, water and sand, and had their fires cleaned in less than one hour! The engine washing platform at a place like Shaffers Crossing locomotive terminal, Roanoke, was so designed that cleaning, tank filling and fire cleaning could be done simultaneously. The motion was sprayed with a paraffin-base engine cleaning oil. After that the engine passed into a building called the lubitorium, where oil and soft greases were piped under pressure direct from supply tanks to the various points needing lubrication. A multitude of long flexible hoses was provided so that the different grades of lubricant could be pumped to the locomotive simultaneously. The ash was removed hydraulically.

On the through express trains between Norfolk and Cincinnati engines were changed at Roanoke, thus dividing the journey into stages of 252 miles, from Norfolk, and 424 miles. The 'J' class 4−8−4s were used on both stages, and it was the link of four working at the western end that underwent the most intense utilisation. Each of the locomotives made three return trips every four days, covering a total mileage of 2544 with only 16 hrs 5 min. standing time between 8.20 a.m. on the first day of the cycle and 11.15 p.m. on the fourth day — only 16 hrs 5 min. not running in a cycle time of 87 hours. The utilisation was thus nearly 82 per cent. The intervals between successive 424-mile runs were 2 hrs; 2 hrs 35 min.; 6 hrs 15 min.; 2 hrs 30 min. and 2 hrs 45 min. After this marathon cycle there was a spell of 9 hrs 5 min. for more extended examination before the next cycle began. The fastest train between Norfolk and Cincinnati was then the *Powhatan Arrow*, which made an inclusive average speed of 43 m.p.h. throughout the 676 miles, intermediate stops and engine changing included.

Some of the passenger trains worked were very heavy, totalling up to gross trailing loads of more than 1000 tons. Normally the schedules east of Roanoke did not call for speeds of more than about 80 m.p.h. on level track; but on one occasion, for test purposes, one of them was really opened out on the fine straight track between Petersburg and Suffolk, and with a trailing load of 1025 tons the remarkable maximum speed of 110 m.p.h. was attained. Dynamometer car test runs showed that these engines could sustain a drawbar pull of more than 5 tons at 100 m.p.h. while at 70 m.p.h. the pull was 10 tons. Students of British locomotives will always remember the famous target set by G. J. Churchward of the Great Western Railway of a drawbar pull of 2 tons at 70 m.p.h. That was in the early 1900s, and the development of his famous 4-cylinder 4−6−0, the 'King' class of 1927, developed about 3 tons at 70 m.p.h. The 'King' had a tractive force almost exactly half that of a Norfolk and Western 'J', but of course the English boiler and firebox were much smaller in relation to the cylinder volume than those of the Roanoke 4−8−4.

The high speed performance of the 'J' class, despite its relatively small wheel diameter of 5 ft 10 in., is of outstanding interest in view of some trials carried out under the auspices of the Association of American Railroads in 1938. The aim was to secure details of performance, evaporation, coal consumption and such-like in the haulage of a passenger train of 1000 tons at a speed of 100 m.p.h. on level track. The same set of coaches and dynamometer car was used throughout, but it was hauled, on their own roads, by locomotives of the Pennsylvania, the Chicago and North Western and of the Union Pacific. The locomotives used successively were a 'K 4' Pacific, an 'E 4' class streamlined 'Hudson', and one of the 'FEFI' class 4−8−4s of the Union Pacific. The Pennsylvania Railroad had fallen behind somewhat in first-line express passenger power during the 1930s, and although the 'K 4' was a splendid engine in itself, it had neither the tractive power nor the steaming capacity to get anywhere near such a target of performance. The nominal tractive force was only 44,000 lbs. The C. & N.W. 'Hudson' was more powerful, and gave a drawbar pull of 9830 lbs at 90 m.p.h. against 6780 lbs by the Pennsylvania 'K 4', and in the event it was only the Union Pacific 4−8−4 that closely approached, though not actually attained the target.

From the dynamometer car tests carried out with Norfolk and Western 'J' class locomotives from Roanoke in 1946 it would seem, to use a colloquialism, they could have 'walked away with it'!

Drawbar Horsepower of Four Locomotive Classes

Railroad	Pennsylvania	C. & N.W.	Union Pacific	Norfolk & Western
Type	4−6−2	4−6−4	4−8−4	4−8−4
Class	'K 4'	'E 4'	'FEFI'	'J'
D.B. horsepower				
at 70 m.p.h.	2260	3100	4050	4350
80 ,,	2000	2840	3820	4000
90 ,,	1620	2350	3500	3650
100 ,,	−	−	3040	3200

The graph of performance showed some falling off above a speed of 80 m.p.h., which was no more than natural from the high rate of revolutions per minute with coupled wheels no larger than 5 ft 10 in., and the 'J' class reached its optimum output of drawbar horsepower at about 40 m.p.h., when it was most needed for the heavy gradients west of Roanoke.

As early in its history as 1884 the Norfolk and Western, then carrying the title of 'railroad' was advertising itself as 'The Great Trunk Line to the South and Southwest, via Lynchburg and Bristol'. It claimed to be the quickest and most direct route to all Texas and Trans-Mississippi points, via Memphis and Texarkane, or via New Orleans and Houston, and that Pullman Palace Sleeping Cars were run between Lynchburg and New Orleans. In the 1940s the Norfolk and Western was participating in modern express train services in the same vein. Some originated at New York and worked through to New Orleans. The Pennsylvania brought those trains to Washington, with the Southern continuing to Lynchburg. There the N. & W. took over for a run of 209 miles to Bristol. The 'J' class 4−8−4s took a hand in this service, though the opportunities for hard running were less. From its point of divergence from the main line at Walton the line to Bristol is single-tracked for 100 miles, and controlled by C.T.C.

The second of the standard classes of the 1940s was the 'A' 2−6−6−4, primarily intended for fast freight, but also used for heavy passenger duty. These huge engines had a tractive force of 114,000 lbs, and on dynamometer car tests gave a sustained drawbar horsepower of 6300, at 45 m.p.h., against 5000 at this speed by a 'J' class 4−8−4. These locomotives belonged to the later generation of American articulateds that were so well balanced that they could be run safely at passenger train speed. During the war years they were used on very heavy troop trains, and they used to attain speeds of around 70 m.p.h. on the straight and level stretches east of Lynchburg. So many modern features of design had been packed into them that although their size and tractive force was so much greater than that of the 4−8−2 freighters they replaced — 114,000 lbs against 68,880 lbs — their maintenance cost per mile was no greater, and in relation to the work they did their maintenance costs were more than 30 per cent less.

But perhaps the most striking achievement of all in the steam locomotive history of Roanoke was the production of the 'Y 6' heavy freighter. The N. & W. already had a class of 2−8−8−2 Mallet compounds, 'Y 5', of precisely the same basic dimensions, and conse-

American 4−8−4s of the 1940s

Railroad	New York Central	Southern Pacific	Union Paciffic	Santa Fe	R.F. & P.	Norfolk & Western
Class	'Niagara'	'Daylight'	'815'	'3776'	'General'	'J'
Cylinders						
dia. in.	25½	27	25	28	27	27
stroke in.	32	30	32	32	30	32
Coupled wheel						
dia. ft in.	6−7	6−1½	6−8	6−8	6−5	5−10
Boiler pressure						
lbs/sq. in.	275	250	300	300	275	300
Tractive force lbs	61,500	62,200	63,800	66,000	66,500	80,000

53

quently the same tractive force, and it was interesting that when the whole programme of modernisation was launched that compound propulsion was retained, in contrast to the general trend of development elsewhere in the USA. Roanoke took the 'Y 5' and gave it a complete 'face-lift', as the saying goes. The 'Y 6' had one-piece cast steel bed frames, roller bearings to all the locomotive axles, needle roller bearings on the valve gear, and mechanical lubrication to a total of 213 points. The coupling and connecting rods remained of conventional design, unlike those of the mixed traffic 'A' class, which were of Timken light-weight type; but the transition from 'Y 5' to 'Y 6' effected a reduction of no less than 37 per cent in maintenance costs. The 'Y 6' stands out as the ultimate development of the classic Mallet compound articulated locomotive.

During the difficult and changing times of the early 1950s, when dieselisation was sweeping across the USA, the Norfolk and Western remained solidly a steam railroad and in 1956 it still had 427 steam locomotives in service, against no more than eight diesels. But at last the writing was on the wall, and at that time the company had 75 new diesels on order from General Motors. By that time the neighbouring Virginian Railway had retired all its steam locomotives, but that railway had, in 1925-6, electrified 134 miles of its heavily graded line west of Roanoke, where there are some 1 in 50 gradients. The system of electrification was the same as that introduced on the Norfolk and Western itself some ten years earlier on the Elkhorn Grade section, from Bluefield to Vivian — thirty very difficult miles, where previously three Mallet locomotives had been needed to work coal trains of 3250 tons up the 1 in 50, 1 in 75 gradients to Elkhorn Tunnel. The system of electrification used was 11,000 volts single phase alternating current at 25 cycles per second.

CHAPTER FIVE

Down the N. & W. Today — Huge Coal Exports

When I was at Roanoke in May 1977 Amtrak were running 'The Mountaineer' between Norfolk, Virginia, and Tri-State station at Catlettsburg, Kentucky, providing connections at the latter place to Cincinnati and Chicago. In some curiosity I went down to the station at Roanoke to see the westbound train come through, at about seven in the evening, because I was leaving at noon next day on the corresponding eastbound train for Norfolk. With thoughts of 15-car trains of 1000 tons and 'J' class steam locomotives thundering along at more than 70 m.p.h. I was rather taken aback when the 'Mountaineer' did turn up — one Amtrak diesel locomotive and two cars! It needs no further comment from me upon the shattering change that has come over passenger travel in the United States in the last two decades, a change that becomes more pronounced as one moves away from the heavily industrialised areas of the north-east. But at Roanoke the freights were rolling through to some purpose and it is now time to look at operations eastward.

Merger with the Virginian Railway took place in 1959 and was followed by some rationalisation of the workings east of Roanoke. The two roughly parallel routes to the coast are shown in the accompanying map. The difference between them is firstly that the Norfolk and Western, built up of the one-time Virginia and Tennessee, the Norfolk and Petersburg and their predecessors, was originally a socialising line, enterprised to connect up centres of population and such local industry as there was; in consequence it made a rather meandering course passing through hilly country at its western end. The heavy gradients through the Blue Ridge Mountains were a prob-

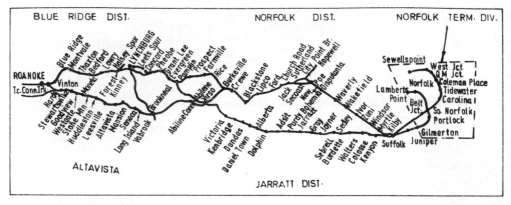

6. Norfolk and Western, and the Virginian, east of Roanoke

lem when the entire east-west mineral traffic of the Norfolk and Western had to follow this route, and was steam hauled. The freights in particular made slow progress, and to avoid having to side-track them to allow express passenger trains to go ahead, the double-tracked line was signalled to permit of both direction running on both tracks. Thus an express could make a running overtake of a heavy freight — both going at the maximum speed possible when climbing the gradient. By contrast the Virginian Railway had no such problems. In the first place it had the distinction of being one of the few relatively large railroads to be constructed by the enterprise and sponsorship of one man, Henry H. Rogers. In the early months of 1903 he initiated and financed surveys which showed that a line of moderate grading was possible east of Roanoke. It was, above all, to be a coal road, and what it was soon carrying has been described in the previous chapter. After the merger of 1959 its easier gradients and excellent alignment made it eminently suitable for maximum tonnage eastbound coal trains, and the bulk of the loaded traffic from both N. & W. and Virginian lines west of Roanoke is now routed over it. On trains travelling east via Altavista the six-axle 3000 horsepower diesel-electric locomotives have a tonnage rating of 10,000 whereas on the original N. & W. route, via Blue Ridge and its steep gradients, it is only 2825.

As on the previous day, the 'Mountaineer' had only two cars; but while this provided no interest from the viewpoint of locomotive haulage effort, the pleasant company of Frank W. Collins, Divisional Road Foreman of Engines, and the privilege of riding in the locomotive cab from Crewe eastwards, gave me a fascinating insight into operation on the line in general and to its topography. At first we were passing through the beautiful hill-country of the Blue Ridge Mountains, on double-track for the first twenty miles over the ridge; then we passed on to single-line which continues for just a hundred miles on to Burkeville. The whole line is equipped with automatic block signalling, and I was interested in the use of a type of signal unit that to my knowledge has not been installed anywhere outside the USA. In general principles the railroads in North America use the 'speed signalling' system, as distinct from the geographical, used in Great Britain and in numerous variations on the continent of Europe; but in the USA there are four variations of the actual signal unit. The most common is the 'searchlight' type, which has a three-position relay mechanism in the signal head, enabling a red, yellow or green aspect to be shown, according to circumstances, from the same lens unit. Then there are the ordinary daylight colour light signals, with a separate lens unit for each aspect, as used in Europe, and first used on Brooklyn Bridge, New York City in 1908. Soon afterwards, as described in Chapter Three of this book, this type was used in the approaches to the Hudson River tunnel and the new Pennsylvania station in New York.

With the electrification schemes being developed on the Pennsylvania, however, an entirely new form of light signal was introduced. This arose from the serious situation that sometimes occurred when the electric headlights on locomotives reflected in the signal lenses, and gave the impression that *all* the colours of a day colour light signal were alight at once. This naturally caused great confusion and danger. The standardisation of the day colour light signal on British Railways, with its separate lens units, has been possible because powerful headlights are not used. On the Pennsylvania, through the efforts of that great signal engineer A. H. Rudd, the so-called 'position light' signal was introduced, which gave the necessary indications by rows of three white lights: horizontal for stop; inclined for caution, and vertical for clear. They were first installed in 1914, and by 1935 the Pennsylvania had more than 11,000 of them. Certain railroads, however, the Norfolk and Western among them, favoured a combination of the two systems—*colour* position lights. These display two horizontal reds for stop; two yellows inclined for caution, and two greens vertically for clear. These basic indications are supplemented by various additional aspects given by supplementary units below the main units.

Fifty miles east of Roanoke we drew in to stop at Kinney. This is the passenger station for Lynchburg, which is a city with many memories of the Civil War. Here connection is made with the Southern Railway, and at one time in the planning of my itinerary there was a suggestion that after seeing the port installations at Norfolk I should return to Lynchburg and continue south by the 'Southern Crescent'. This had the attraction that five hours of connecting time, albeit in the late evening, would have given me an opportunity to look round the historic city. Unfortunately this idea did not work out conveniently, because it so happened that the day I travelled from Roanoke was the very last on which the 'Mountaineer' ran through to Norfolk. After that day it turned north at Petersburg and terminated at Richmond, which city had previously been served by a 'Greyhound' coach on the highway. It then became Norfolk's turn to be served by nothing more than a coach on the highway. The 'Southern Crescent', coming down from Washington and leaving Lynchburg at 11.06 p.m. would have landed me in Atlanta at 8.50 a.m. next morning. Continuing eastward on my own journey we passed Appomattox, where the surrender of General Lee ended the war, and then at Pamplin came to the junction of the Farmville Belt Line. This makes a 37-mile long detour to the south, and links up with the former Virginian main line at Abilene and Virso; but another of its important advantages is that it provides a route for heavy trains that would be precluded from taking the original main line.

Near Farmville is the celebrated High Bridge dating back to the mid-1850s, and having a length of 2500 ft. It was carried on twenty-one brick towers, with a maximum height of 129 ft, and the girders were of latticed timber, one million feet of it in all. As a vital link in Confederate communications it was a sitting target for Union raiders, and sure enough it was burned down during the war. It was rebuilt afterwards as a wrought-iron bridge, but today it is limited to loaded

58

cars having a maximum weight of no more than 55 tons. This of course would be no good for modern N. & W. traffic, and so the Farmville Belt Line is invaluable as a relief route. We stopped at Farmville, from which the coach connection then ran to Richmond, and then having passed Burkeville, where the Farmville Belt Line rejoins, we came to Crewe, where my authority to ride on the locomotive began. I must admit that on mounting this Amtrak diesel my thoughts went back to the many times I have climbed aboard steam, diesel and electric locomotives at Crewe, England, for runs both north and south, and for a moment nostalgia overtook me. I felt I had come to the Norfolk and Western too late. How grand it would have been to mount a 'J' class 4−8−4 and thus been able to compare the impressions with those gained on 'Royal Scots', 'Lizzies' and 'Duchesses' that I had ridden from our English Crewe! But there is nothing to be gained from trying to put back the clock, and we were no sooner away from Crewe, Virginia, than I was completely fascinated by the vivid manifestations of the American railroad scene. This was the first time I had been in the cab of an American locomotive at speed.

We were soon running at a steady 65 m.p.h. over track with the standard American arrangement of staggered joints. The rails themselves are 39 ft long, and several times during my tour I became involved in discussions as to why we in Great Britain lay track with the rail joints opposite to each other. On a finely maintained road like the Norfolk and Western the staggered arrangement certainly gives a very smooth ride, but later in my tour I was to see other roads on which the track was not in such good shape, and with badly packed joints the rocking of heavily loaded box cars, first to one way and then to the other, was rather alarming to see.

Then came the approach to Petersburg. The junction comes at Jack, where the double-tracked Petersburg belt line goes straight ahead, and we were to take the single-tracked 'old line' into the passenger station. The first warning of the speed restriction involved at the turnout was the 'advance approach' signals: the colour-position-light showed the yellow diagonal, with two yellows vertically below. Then at the actual bifurcation the main signal showed the two reds horizontally, with two greens vertically below. This indicated that the diverging

59

road was clear, but a speed of 30 m.p.h. was needed over the junction. Just before reaching Petersburg station we ran beneath the main line of the Seaboard Coast Line, coming up from the south and heading for its end-on junction with the Richmond, Fredericksburg and Potomac at Richmond itself.

From Petersburg, after joining the Belt Line at Poe, the main line is straight for some fifty-five miles, through level farming country, and we ran steadily at the maximum line speed of 65 m.p.h. This may not appear very fast, but on this stretch the same speed is run by the heavy freights as well as by this now-withdrawn passenger train. For part of the way this double-tracked line is signalled for running in either direction. Near Waverly we passed a westbound freight with 150 cars, hauled by two diesel locomotives, but of course the bulk of the freight would be flowing on the former Virginian line. This latter line is equipped with Manual Block Signalling. I should explain, however, that in the USA the term does not mean the same as it does in Great Britain. It is nothing more nor less than the ordinary telegraph or telephone block, where an operator at one station is free to clear his signal at any time without any electrical or mechanical check from any other station. The signals are given by train order boards, which stand in front of the station building, or tower as shown in the accompany-

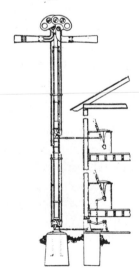

ing drawing. One signal arm is controlled by the upper lever, and the other arm by the second lever.

On the former Virginian main line, which is single-tracked throughout, the Manual Block System rules are comprehensive. The normal position of the train order signal is at STOP when there is an operator on duty. It is changed to PROCEED to permit a train to pass when there are no orders on hand for trains in that direction and the block is clear. But it should be added that the term 'clear block' is used only in reference to trains moving in the same direction. Movement of trains in opposite directions is governed by timetable or train order authority. If a train is stopped as a result of the train order signal being at STOP, it is not allowed to proceed without a Clearance Card, handed to the driver by the operator in the station or the tower. More detailed reference to the Train Order System of working is made in the next chapter.

On the long straight of the N. & W. we made good time, and at 5.30 p.m. came to Suffolk, the 'Peanuts Capital of the World'. Here the N. & W. proper, and the former Virginian lines intersect and change positions, as can be seen from the map. We ourselves had covered the 59 miles from Petersburg in 59¼ minutes and, as we were leaving on the last stage of the journey, we passed another heavy westbound freight hauled by four diesel locomotives. We had made a brisk start, passing Milepost 7, 15¾ miles from Suffolk in just over 16 minutes, but by then we were entering the Norfolk Terminal Division, where the line crosses navigable waterways. The first comes at Drawbridge 7, over which there is a speed limit of 30 m.p.h.; but an important operating consideration there is a section of track connected with the drawbridge working which is dead in relation to the automatic signal system. If anything were left standing on such a dead section, it would be unprotected by the signalling; so, if any vehicle had to be detached or left in the area train crews are warned to leave it clear of the dead section. If this were not possible, arrangements would have to be made for it to be protected by a flagman, and the Bridge Operator notified accordingly.

Beyond Portlock, where there is a large yard reserved for grain traffic, we crossed, almost at right-angles, the former Virginian line which went round to Sewells Point, nearer to the mouth of

61

Chesapeake Bay than Lamberts Point, the original Norfolk and Western coal port. Travelling very slowly now, over road crossings where
city ordinance prohibits whistling, we passed over a second drawbridge, and so came into Norfolk passenger terminal, slightly ahead of
time. It would have been a poignant experience to ride in the locomotive cab of the last passenger train to enter Norfolk if this had been a
symbol of a railway declining towards its eventual collapse and closure; but in 1975, in *Modern Railroads*, the Norfolk and Western was
voted 'Railroad of the Year' on its fourfold showing of 'coal, cash,
costs, and credibility'. It is indeed paying a handsome dividend to its
79,000 shareholders, and my first sight of the Lamberts Point coal
yard, as we rode into Norfolk, was a confirmation of the colossal
business the railway has in coal. It was a beautiful evening, and across
the entrance to the James River I could see the rival coal port of the
Chesapeake and Ohio, Newport News, prompting me to turn up
some statistics relating to the huge coal exports of that railroad. So far
as the Norfolk and Western is concerned a 'modest' total of 2¼ million
tons had been exported from Lamberts Point in the month just prior to
my visit; and that represented only about one-third of the total tonnage of coal conveyed on the railroad as a whole.

Next morning Allen B. Childress, Assistant Superintendent of
Norfolk Terminal, called for me, and we went to see the coal loading
plant at Pier 6. On the way it was explained to me that in the
preliminary reception yard at Lamberts Point there would usually be
about 7000 loaded coal cars on hand, representing about 580,000 tons
of coal. This would belong to no fewer than 950 different classes,
though some of these did not represent a very large volume. Generally
speaking, about 400 different classes had to be dealt with regularly.
We went to the top of one of the loading towers on Pier 6, from which
there was a wide panoramic view over the whole area. A little way
inland is the Barney Yard, where loaded coal cars are assembled before
the contents are dumped into what are termed 'blending bins'. The
Barney Yard has 17½ miles of track and can hold 1200 cars. It is a
specialised kind of marshalling yard in which the railway itself sorts
the cars containing different classes of coals, as a first step towards the
more specialised blending required by different customers. Trains of
cars are propelled from the Barney Yard to a retarder installation,

which slows down each car as it rolls towards the weighing station. It is essential that no car passes over the scales at more than 5 m.p.h. The speed is measured by radar, and if any adjustment is required the necessary data is relayed electronically to the retarder and the speed of the car controlled accordingly.

In the Scale Office each car is weighed, and its weight recorded automatically. In this office there are two scales, each with a maximum capacity of 400 tons. The next stage in this highly automated procedure came as a surprise to me, because the cars next pass through a thawing shed. Although Norfolk itself has a mild, ice-free climate that permits of loading of ships all the year round with few delays from adverse weather, conditions are not so mild in the mountains of West Virginia and Kentucky where the coal traffic originates; in winter cars arrive at Lamberts Point with their contents frozen solid. Special arrangements have to be made to thaw them out, otherwise the coal could not be dumped easily. The thawing shed is equipped with electrically-powered infra-red heating elements, working at the high temperature of 1550°F. They are grouped on each side and beneath the cars, and in a carefully controlled slow passage through the shed, in six to nine minutes the coal is fully thawed out. On leaving the thawing shed the journey by railroad for the coal is virtually ended, though it still remains in the care of the Norfolk and Western. For now the cars come to the rotary dumpers. The dumper mechanism which has an automatic chain drive pushes each car into position, locks it there, rotates it through 165° and, after the load has been discharged, turns it upright again and releases it. The dumpers work very quickly and can deal with 252 cars per hour — 46 a minute between them. The dumped coal then falls into the blending bins.

There was a time on the steam railways of Great Britain when special grades of coal used to be specified for the most important passenger duties; but then, in the difficult conditions that developed in the second world war, the railways had to take what they could get — often with indifferent results in train running. With the facilities now developed, however, the customers of the Norfolk and Western are able to specify a far greater precision in the nature of the coal they require than ever any pre-war British railway was able to demand for its locomotives. Customers of the N.W. now require not merely coal

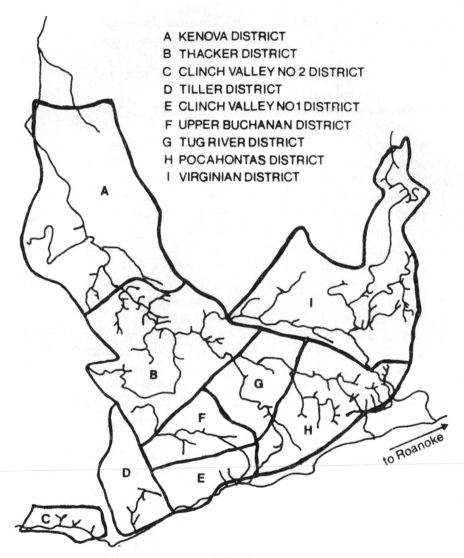

A KENOVA DISTRICT
B THACKER DISTRICT
C CLINCH VALLEY NO 2 DISTRICT
D TILLER DISTRICT
E CLINCH VALLEY NO 1 DISTRICT
F UPPER BUCHANAN DISTRICT
G TUG RIVER DISTRICT
H POCAHONTAS DISTRICT
I VIRGINIAN DISTRICT

7. The Norfolk and Western coal districts

from one particular pit, but clearly specified percentage blends from several, and this is done at the Custom Blending Station. This is located at the water's edge adjacent to one of the older piers. In this building where the processes are electronically controlled, blending

64

ratios of up to 7 to 1 can be present at each of the three blending points. Coal falls from two bins, at rates that are automatically varied, on to the moving shuttle conveyors, while a third control further varies the blend proportions by presetting the relative speed at which the two shuttle conveyors deposit coal on to the main transfer conveyor belt. This runs roughly at right-angles to the line of the pier, and at the Transfer House the coal is directed on to the pier conveyor belts.

Pier 6 is a remarkable example of mechanised handling of coal in bulk. It can accommodate four of the largest sea-going colliers, and the two loading towers which stand 192 ft above water level are designed to travel the length of the pier, can be positioned so as to load two ships at once, or both can concentrate on one ship. They have retractable booms which can reach down 120 ft and they include telescopic chutes, by means of which the coal can be rapidly and evenly distributed into the hold of a ship. Childress took me to the top of one of these towers, and I was able to watch and photograph the process. On the day I was there ships were being loaded with coal for Brazil, Canada, Japan, and also for Belgium, Holland, France, Germany and Italy. The integration of the port working with the railway at Norfolk, which of course has its counterpart across the bay at Newport News, is an interesting and vastly enlarged modern development of the activity that used to prevail at the South Wales ports in the years before the first world war. The Norfolk and Western takes more coal direct from the mines than any other single operator in the USA and this amounts to the high total of between 65 and 75 million tons every year.

So far I have written only of the original Norfolk and Western and of its neighbour and constituent, the Virginian; but in 1964 five other railroads were merged with it, namely the Wabash, the Nickel Plate, the Pittsburgh and West Virginia, the Sandusky Line of the Pennsylvania, and the Akron, Canton and Youngstown. The last three were relatively small concerns, but the incorporation of the Wabash and Nickel Plate completely changed the situation respecting all three lines, and resulted in a new 'Norfolk and Western' with a route mileage nearly three times that of the original. Although I did not travel over any part of them the accompanying maps and brief notes on their past history are of interest in showing something of the great

65

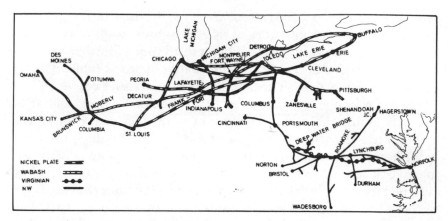

8. The greater Norfolk and Western system, after the mergers of 1964

'hinterland' behind the famous artery from Roanoke to Norfolk on which I travelled.

Since 1964 the Norfolk and Western can no longer be classed primarily as a coal carrier. With the Wabash contribution the N. & W. moved into a leadership position in transport of cars and automobile parts, and by its western extensions into the states of Kansas and Nebraska it secured a gateway to the grain states of the Middle West, not to mention a main line into Canada. With the Nickel Plate it needs no more to be said than that the cities of Buffalo, Cleveland, Toledo, Chicago and St Louis were now on Norfolk and Western main lines. The Wabash originated as long ago as 1838 in a little road built by the State of Illinois, called the Northern Cross Railroad, and which was in danger of failing altogether after a relatively short time. A financial rescue operation, and a merger with the Lake Erie, Wabash and St Louis put things on a more solid foundation, and the line eventually prospered and extended from Kansas City and Omalia in the west to Buffalo in the east. Its headquarters were at St Louis, Missouri.

The Nickel Plate had a much more chequered career. It was organised in New York in 1881 under the name of the New York, Chicago and St Louis. Initial construction was rapid, because within two years no less than 523 miles of line had been opened, between Buffalo and Chicago. But it never reached New York, and in the vigorous 'empire building' activities of the great Commodore Vanderbilt it came under the control of the New York Central. In 1914, however, this arrangement was ended and it was sold to the Van Swerigen brothers of Cleveland, Ohio. After the first world war an attempt was made to amalgamate it with five other railroads under the same control, including the Chesapeake and Ohio, but although this merger did not materialise the Nickel Plate remained under C. & O. control until 1947. It then became independent, until the merger with the Norfolk and Western in 1964.

CHAPTER SIX

Atlanta — nerve centre of the Southern

Saturated with statistics of coal, more coal, and still more coal, and all it means to the Norfolk and Western, I left Pier 6 and went with Allan Childress for an early lunch. The dedicated railroadman is an international character. It matters not whether the scene be set in Norfolk, Virginia, in Toronto, Kanazawa, or Bangkok; in de Aar Junction, Sydney, or Invercargill; in Vienna, Amsterdam, in Crewe (England) or in Aberdeen. By the sheer force of his enthusiasm, his expertise and his pride in the job, he channels one's thoughts on to a single track, and I am inevitably caught up in the stream and carried happily along with it. But over lunch that day I recalled that bed for me that night was in New Orleans, just about 1000 miles away, and that I had to 'do' the Southern Railway in the meantime! I began to feel like the most superficial of tourists, and at the airport awaiting the call to board, I looked at an old brochure which told me that the Southern Railway System of today embraces no fewer than fifteen railway companies. Of these only two, the Southern itself, and the Central of Georgia are of any size, with route mileages of approximately 6290 and 1765 respectively. Four others are:

Cincinnati, New Orleans and Texas Pacific	336 miles
Alabama Great Southern	326 miles
New Orleans and Northeastern	203 miles
Georgia, Southern and Florida	475 miles

It would seem that against this network of 10,000 miles there would be no room for anything else in this south-eastern region of the USA, but on a railroad map on which the lines of the Southern were heavily accentuated, there was a criss-cross pattern of finer lines indicating many other routes. The railroads of the region seemed as closely interwoven as those in the North-East Corridor; but the call to board the aircraft had come, and I put the map away. The weather had become heavy and humid over Norfolk and thundery clouds were piling up, but it cleared beautifully as we flew south. At Wilmington, at the mouth of the Cape Fear River in North Carolina, where we called briefly, the prospect over the sea was delightful. In little more than another hour we were at Atlanta.

The feeling of inadequacy on my part at the prospect of 'doing' the Southern Railway System in a single afternoon and evening was still very much with me when I reported at the Control and Computer Center in Atlanta; but it was soon dispelled under the kindly guidance and enthusiasm of my new friends, who little by little unfolded before me the ramifications of the entire system on one control panel after another. It was a marvellous exposition. They made no attempt to swamp me with statistics. Instead we had a leisurely walk round the various control rooms for informal talks with the dispatchers, and other officers, from whom I had to answer many questions about British and European railway practice. This made it all the more enjoyable. But the point that will already be uppermost in the reader's mind is how the minute-by-minute operating situation on the entire system is presented to the one control centre. The answer lies mainly in the magic letters C.T.C.

Until about fifty years ago operation on an overwhelming proportion of American railroad mileage was regulated by timetable and train orders. Communication between control points was by telegraph, both in the issuing of instructions to trains and in receipt of information at headquarters on the traffic position on the line. The key operating man on any division or sub-division of the railroad was the dispatcher, who telegraphed instructions to those stations and signal towers on the line where there was an operator on duty. Conversely, the operator had to telegraph back an acknowledgment of receipt of the order, giving his initials and the office call code. It was the operator's duty to translate the instruction received by telegraph into a written order, and then to stop the train to which it was addressed and hand it personally to the enginemen. On most American railroads and particularly those carrying light, or relatively slow traffic, there were no fixed signals, and operations were regulated entirely by the issue of written train orders.

The train dispatching system needs more than a passing mention in order that the full significance of recent developments may be fully appreciated. The fundamental element is the timetable for the line, issued over the authority of the superintendent, containing the schedules of all regular trains and providing for their safe working. It is important to emphasise the difference between regular and extra trains. The former, by the fact of their schedules being printed in the timetable, have definite authority to use the track at those times, and to proceed, whether there are any signals at the entrance to a section or not. On a single-tracked railway, for example, Westbound No. 45 might be scheduled to run from A to B, and at the latter station to cross Eastbound No. 201 before proceeding from B to C. Train No. 45 would wait at B until No. 201 arrived. But No. 201 might be running very late, and then train orders would have to be issued by the dispatcher to arrange a different crossing station. Extra trains, which on some railroads include all freight trains, have no timetable authority and their movements are regulated entirely by train orders. In telegraphic communications and out on the line 'extras' are designated by the number of the locomotive, prefixed by a letter 'X'. If the train should be multiple-headed, as in the case of the majority of heavy freight trains today, the number of the leading unit is used for recognition by opposing trains and by the operators at stations.

Next to be explained are the various classes of trains, which amount practically to rank, with some established as superior to others by their class — first, second or third. On single lines superiority is laid down according to direction. In the case of two trains of equal class travelling in opposite directions, it will be recognised on the particular line that the westbound is the 'superior' direction, and that the westbound train would have preference over the eastbound. If the dispatcher should find it necessary to change any of the timetable arrangements by train order, he confers what is called 'right' on certain trains, and this makes them superior to certain others, within the terms of his order. The governing principle of the dispatching system is that a superior train has the right of way, and inferior trains must keep off its schedule.

This means that the superior train has a right to proceed against those inferior to it — as long as its schedule is in force. As soon as a train becomes twelve hours late, however, it loses all the authority derived from the timetable and can then be run only as an extra, on train orders.

It will be appreciated that the regulation of traffic by the train dispatching system, and nothing more than communication by tele-graph or telephone, is not a very rapid process. Furthermore, with the human element taking so prominent a part in the transcription of messages and so on, mistakes are liable to occur, sometimes resulting in collisions on single-line. But it was the thoroughly established method of working on North American railroads for very many years. All grades concerned with the running of trains had grown up and lived all their working lives with it, and it was indeed an ideal and economical system for the relatively light traffic conveyed on many lengthy stretches of line. On the Central of Georgia, for example, before its incorporation in the Southern Railway System, out of a route mileage of about 1770, all except about 520 miles had no block signals, and traffic was controlled entirely by train dispatchers and written train orders.

From this reference to the Central of Georgia a look at the whole Southern Railway System of today follows naturally, with the help of the accompanying map. The system includes two main routes from the north, from Washington and from Cincinnati, which converge at Birmingham, Alabama, and continue south-westwards to New Orleans. The second of these two trunk routes was originally made up of three railroads. From the northern end there was the Cincinnati, New Orleans and Texas Pacific, which despite its long name extended no further south than Chattanooga, 336 miles. Then came the Alabama Great Southern extending another 240 miles, to York, and finally the New Orleans and Northeastern, which did actually bring the tracks into New Orleans itself. At a later stage the N.O. & N. was brought into the operating area of the Alabama Great Southern. From Washington the line was Southern all the way.

The Central of Georgia, with its headquarters at Savannah, was a line with a history. It was chartered in 1833, to build a line from the coast into the interior of the State, and when construction started two

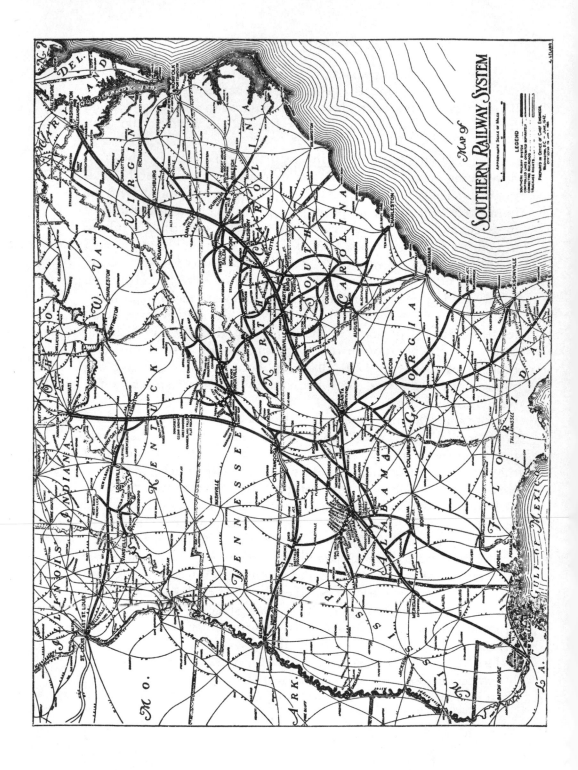

years later the 5 ft gauge was chosen, irrespective of anything that was going on in the north. It was fought over and badly smashed up during the Civil War, and eventually rebuilt as a standard gauge line. Its ultimate extent is shown on the map, and today it is still operated as three separate divisions — Alabama, Georgia and Coastal. Macon, Georgia, is a general junction from which seven lines radiate. One of these is the main line of the Georgia Southern and Florida, leading south to Valdosta and Jacksonville, while there is a parallel line northward to Atlanta of the Southern proper. Both of these have regular timetabled trains.

The Southern itself included the line on which the first-ever scheduled service in the USA began, on Christmas Day 1830, on the South Carolina Canal and Rail Road. Its motive power included the first locomotive built in the country for service on a railroad, the *Best Friend*, usually having the words *of Charleston* appended, in recognition of the starting point of the railroad. The extent of the South Carolina Railroad is now marked by the Carolina Division of the Southern, going north-westwards to cross the main line at Blacksburg and continuing to Marion to make junction with the west to east line from Murphy, through Asheville to Salisbury. It is curious that Weissenborn's engraving of 1871, purporting to show the *Best Friend* on an excursion train in 1831, should show troops with the 'stars and stripes' on the leading open truck, when the sentiments of the Carolinas, both north and south, were so strongly anti-Union in years before the Civil War.

The Southern includes another important 'first' in American railroad history in that its constituent of the far-reaching name, the Cincinnati, New Orleans and Texas Pacific, was the first American railroad to be completely protected by automatic signals. Together with three short branches the main line of the C.N.O. & T.P. now forms the Kentucky Division of the Southern, and mention of automatic signalling brings me back to the positive transformation in train operating that has been wrought by the introduction of C.T.C. It is appropriate that detailed reference to it should be made in this chapter, because it was on a line used by the Southern that signalling

9. The Southern Railway system—a map prepared in 1942

providing for the movement of trains in either direction on single-track, without train orders, was used as early as 1882 at Louisville Bridge, Kentucky, across the Ohio River. The actual installation was made by the Pennsylvania but the bridge was used also by the Baltimore and Ohio, and it lies on the Western Division of the Southern from Lexington (Kentucky) to St Louis. Although the modern concept of C.T.C., as a method of operating trains without train orders, dates from the mid-1920s, it is based upon long-established fundamental safety principles, except that an immeasurably more efficient means of communication is put into the hands of the dispatcher.

Panel signal boxes are nowadays an established feature of most modern railways all over the world, in many instances eliminating a large number of small wayside signal boxes necessary for manual block working in the British style; but in the USA the first C.T.C. installations were made on lines that previously had no block signals at all and were regulated entirely by timetable and train order. C.T.C. enabled the regulation of train movements to be made by signal indication alone. The dispatcher did not have to wait for telephone or telegraphic advice of the position of trains; he had an up-to-the-minute picture of exactly what was happening on his division, by indication lights on his control panel. Conversely, by actuating the appropriate thumb-switches on his panel, he could clear signals, or operate points that might be anything up to 50 or 100 miles away, and so regulate the movement of trains.

It might at first sight be imagined that a vast amount of cabling would be necessary to enable this remote control and indication to be carried out, but actually only two or three line wires are used throughout an area operated from a C.T.C. panel. The controls are coded, as in an automatic telephone system. If to clear the westbound starting signal from station X the dispatcher turns the appropriate switch, in effect he 'dials the number' of that signal, and conversely the movements of trains on the line, which are noted by the occupancy and clearing of successive track circuits, are relayed back by the track circuit apparatus dialling their number back to the dispatcher and registering the situation by coloured lights on his panel. Just as with automatic telephone switching the sending of a code, either a 'control' from the dispatcher or an 'indication' from somewhere out on the line, takes a measurable time of about four seconds; but this is, of course, of no consequence on a line where the traffic is not very heavy.

In the control centre at Atlanta, for example, I saw the C.T.C. panel covering the 148 miles northward to Chattanooga over which there were then seven first class, and two second class scheduled trains in each direction during the 24 hours. The running time over the 136¼ miles between Summit and Inman Yard (Atlanta) was 4 hrs 38 min. southbound, and 3 hrs 25 min. northbound for the first class trains. The northbound is the superior direction. The second class trains took roughly an hour longer in each direction. The northbound first class trains were scheduled to make an average speed of 40 m.p.h. over this section. Except for a short length of double-track towards the southern end of this section speed is limited to 55 m.p.h. by all trains. Faster running is permitted with passenger trains on the main line northeastwards from Atlanta, and generally the limits are laid down as follows for American railways as a whole:

Lines equipped with C.T.C.   79 m.p.h.
Lines with automatic block signalling (non–C.T.C.)
                                                          59 m.p.h.
Train Order (Dark Territory)   49 m.p.h.

Over the Southern System there is now only one passenger train, the 'Southern Crescent', which runs nightly between Washington and Atlanta and three times weekly between Atlanta and New Orleans. It conveys through cars from New York to Washington by Amtrak, which organisation also provides connection at New York from Boston. On days when the service south of Atlanta operates the total time for the 1610 miles from Boston to New Orleans is 34 hrs 20 min., an average speed of 47 m.p.h. Before the major post-war recession in passenger business the Southern operated luxury trains on a number of routes. The brochure of 1966 recommended intending passengers to

. . . see *all* of America at ground level and stop over at each historical, scenic, or educational point that has intrigued you for years! Hundreds of bonus, explorable miles are yours, for example, on a round trip from New Orleans to Washington you can see Stone Mountain and the cyclorama at Atlanta, GA., in one direction and visit the Smoky Mountains via Asheville, NC., and Knoxville, Tennessee, and the wonders of Chattanooga in the other; or even return via Florida, thence fascinating Savannah — all at the regular low fare applicable via the direct route.

Alas, these tempting offers did not save the passenger service on all except the one main line. The one train that has survived, the 'Southern Crescent', is one of the very few truly luxurious services remaining in North America. There are sleeping cars between Washington and Atlanta, New York and New Orleans, and one between New York and Los Angeles. This latter is transferred to an Amtrak service at New Orleans. The stop-over time extends to many hours and through passengers occupy the sleeping car during this time. Between Washington and Atlanta the 'Southern Crescent' provides what is termed a Master Room accommodation. For daytime travel the room has two armchairs and a sofa, while adjacent is a private shower-bath. Two lower berths and one upper provide secluded travel for a family of three, and this sleeping car is always marshalled next to the Tavern Lounge car. There is also a dining car with full restaurant facilities running between Washington and Atlanta or New Orleans depending upon which day of the week the train is travelling.

Although the present diesel-hauled 'Crescent' is a beautiful train, both to see and to ride in, connoisseurs of rail travel have affectionate memories of the days when it was steam-hauled. The Southern was one of the few American railroads that did not finish their locomotives in black. Green and gold was the colour, magnificently captured in one of Fogg's inimitable paintings, and preserved for posterity to see in the 'Pacific' engine No. 1401 now restored and on display at the Smithsonian Institute in Washington. The Pullmans of the 'Southern Crescent' were green to match the locomotives. These fine engines were introduced in 1923. The train makes fast time today over some sections, as it must to cover the 397 miles from Danville to Atlanta in 514 minutes with 12 intermediate stops. Some of the station to station runs are performed at little less than 60 m.p.h., such as Reidsville to Greensboro, 24 miles in 25 minutes; Salisbury to Concord, 22 miles at a level 60 m.p.h. and Greenville to Clemson, 30 miles in 33 minutes. Some of these stops are conditional only, to take up or set down revenue passengers.

76

While the 'Southern Crescent' is in every way a prestige train, and accorded all the priorities due to it, the present-day business of the Southern is freight. Down here, in the deep south, one is naturally curious to know what the traffics are, in a land so far from the heavy industrialism clustered along the Great Lakes, or the teeming commercial rat-race of the North-East Corridor. I saw vast fields of tobacco, snowy fields of cotton, old plantations, and I was not surprised to learn that the Southern is the largest carrier of cotton and of cotton textile products in the world. This is not to say that the area is devoid of engineering industry. That line to the north, the old Cincinnati, New Orleans and Texas Pacific takes train-loads of supplies to Ford and General Motors, and brings those gigantic 'trailers' that are so astonishing to English eyes, carrying fifteen cars on three tiers — five cars on each. They load up to a height of 18 ft and are 89 ft long. The whole philosophy of freight on the Southern is a rapid turn round of cars. There are no long waits in sidings or freight terminals. As one dispatcher said to me: 'The folks down here manufacture out of box cars'!

The Southern was one of the many American railroads that had re-switched and greatly stepped up its operations during the second world war. Before the war oil and cotton was sent north from Galveston and other ports on the Gulf of Mexico by coastwise shipping; but U-boats, operating very far from their European bases, were soon taking such a heavy toll off the coast of Florida that this traffic had to be transferred to rail, and to reach the North-East, the Southern was the only way. The South was chosen for a leading part in the nation's war production programme: army training camps, airfields, aircraft factories, powder plants, ammunition depots — everything one could think of to supply the armed forces. To get all these into production brought an enormous increase in railway traffic of all kinds, both materials and personnel. So far as troop movements were concerned, the trains required for moving a whole division make one think! An American division consisted of 15,000 men, each one of whom required eight tons of equipment — 120,000 tons. An armoured division required seventy-five trains to transport it! — and from what I have written already in this book American freight trains are no lightweights.

Mention of some of the great tasks in war transportation carried by some of the railroads of the South in 1942-5, inevitably brings a reminder of what happened in 1861-5. After the final surrender at Appomattox the railroads of the South were in as crippled and defeated a condition as the armies they had worked to support. As one writer has expressed it:

Twisted rails, burned ties, gutted depots and freight houses, destroyed bridges, and lost or dilapidated rolling stock scattered from Louisiana to Virginia was the heritage of the average southern railroad as peace finally came in the spring of 1865.

An English traveller, John H. Kenneway, described his arrival in Atlanta, in November 1865:

The train stopped, and we were landed among an inextricable labyrinth of rails that centered in what had once been the station; whence, under the guidance of a coloured man, and with the help of a lantern, we picked our way as best we could through the deep and sticky mud . . .

Atlanta indeed: the present nerve centre of the Southern!

At the beginning of the second world war the Southern had about 1600 locomotives of which only 18 were diesels. The main line steam fleet included 290 passenger engines and 1009 freighters. This did not include the stock of the Central of Georgia which was then an independent company. After the war, with oil resources so close at hand in Texas, it was only natural that the Southern should have been among the earliest of American railroads to complete the changeover to diesel traction, and today the traffic of the enlarged system with a route mileage of 10,500 is operated with 1300 diesel–electric locomotives. While there are numerous variations in the maximum loads the different classes of diesel are allowed to take over different parts of the system; generally speaking the limits for the largest 6–axle units range between 2400 and 3800 tons, according to gradient. The regulations do not permit of coupling more than three 6–axle units in multiple, nor more than four of the 4–axle type. This means that the maximum load of freight trains is around 11,000 tons.

I saw the departure of the northbound 'Crescent' at 7 p.m. on one of the panel diagrams, and then it was time to take a taxi back to the airport. The 'Crescent' itself covers the 521 miles down to New Orleans in 10¾ hours, entirely a daytime run that I was sorry not to be able to make myself. But time was not on my side and that evening, soon after darkness had fallen, I was looking down from the air on the glittering spectacle of New Orleans. Knowing its nearness to the Gulf of Mexico, I was at first surprised to see a dazzling waterfront facing *north*, until I realised that the water below was not that of the Gulf but of Lake Pontchartrain. Although all my railway associations with New Orleans are described in the next chapter, which includes a map on page 82, the entry of the Southern into the city may be pointed out. It is the line of the Alabama Great Southern, which name appears on at least one of the modern tourist maps of the city. The line runs right along the waterfront of Lake Pontchartrain, at the eastern end of which it is joined by that of the former Gulf, Mobile and Ohio, now merged with the Illinois Central.

Once again I was satiated with sightseeing and note-taking. As the aircraft began to descend I recalled that only that same morning I was watching coal loading at Pier 6 Lamberts Point, and that the Southern had later taken me for a tour of their entire system. Now I was landing into the warm fragrant air of the South, with the Mississippi close at hand, and the French atmosphere immediately noticeable. It is a longish drive from the International Airport to the city; time for no more than a late evening stroll, and then, with the prospect of another long day ahead of me, bed.

CHAPTER SEVEN

Northward from the Gulf— saga of the Illinois Central

For decades before the Civil War New Orleans was not really interested in railroads. The Mississippi River was a broad, unique artery of traffic for the vast trade in cotton, and at the point where its waters mingled with those of the Gulf the Crescent City had grown and prospered. Its merchants and business men felt they had a continuing and indestructible hold upon the waterborne traffic, and seemed anxious that no new-fangled ideas of transport favoured in the North should intrude upon their monopoly. So successfully were railroad projects given the cold shoulder that by 1850 less than a hundred miles of line had been opened in the State of Louisiana. In the previous year something of the complacency of New Orleans had been shaken by Congress giving consideration to a bill to promote a great railroad that would extend from north-western Illinois to Mobile, Alabama, and the threat of a rival port on the Gulf of Mexico stirred some of the more far-seeing traders to action. Quite apart from this unwelcome project the trade of the city was declining, and shrewd observers began to realise that existing means of transport would soon be inadequate. As quickly the pendulum swung the other way, though it was perhaps significant that the main drive and enthusiasm was generated by a young banker-businessman from the North, one James Robb; and he was soon pushing the Louisiana legislature towards State financial help for the construction of railroads. So, in the spring of 1852 the New Orleans, Jackson and Great Northern Railroad was chartered in both Louisiana and Mississippi, with James Robb as president.

It was a formidable task that these pioneers of the South had undertaken; formidable in quite a different way from the task that faced those who crossed the Alleghanies, or who struck out across the prairies of the Middle West. In Louisiana there may not have been rugged mountain ranges, and attacks from Indians, but as Julia Bishop of New Orleans once wrote:

Fancy wading into the trackless wilderness when the depth of the slimy water or the treacherous mud were wholly unknown. Fancy the alligators and poisonous snakes and the swarms of insects that made life a horror, while these first men were finding a way for the present generation to travel in ease and comfort!

A noted military engineer, Captain Grice, who spent a considerable time surveying possible routes, was so intimidated by the conditions that he proposed the line should terminate on the north shore of Lake Pontchartrain, and that connection across the lake to New Orleans should be made by steamboat. In full knowledge of the way unstable ground had been successfully crossed in England by George Stephenson at Chat Moss, and in Holland by Conrad, the lack of a solid foundation through the dense forests, across the seemingly bottomless marshes (or bayous as they are known hereabouts), not to mention the 'trembling prairies', gave no hope to some that a safe and substantial railroad could be built. As ever in railroad promotion, however, there were more optimistic views, and Colin Tarpley, with almost evangelical fervour, urged that the line must be taken round Lake Pontchartrain and right into New Orleans. Not to do so would, in his view, be shirking one of the primary objects of the whole enterprise. He described the plight of an ox-team fighting its way through mud, the wagon with its wheels mired to the hub, as it was dragged on its way to the river landing, with the few bales of cotton it carried plastered with mud. Tarpley's oratory carried the day, and the circuit to the west of Lake Pontchartrain was agreed upon.

With iron and credit from England construction went ahead more rapidly than had been expected in the relatively flat country to the north; and in the early spring of 1858, the line was completed to Canton, Mississippi, 206 miles from New Orleans.

The arrival of the first train in Canton was made the occasion for a remarkable demonstration. It was on 31 March 1858, and a special

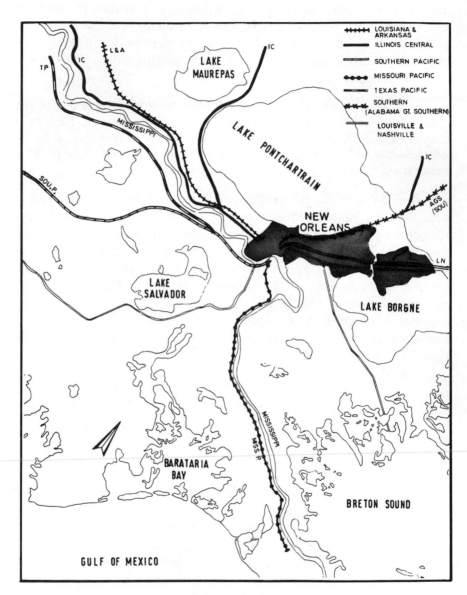

10. New Orleans and its approach lines

train conveying the President of the railroad and many distinguished guests had left New Orleans at 7 a.m. A flat car was propelled ahead of the locomotive, carrying a cannon, and this was fired at frequent intervals all along the route to announce the progress of the train. That progress was naturally not very rapid, and the train did not arrive in Canton until 11 p.m. Then the President of the railroad ceremonially drove the last spike, and the company adjourned thus:

At Canton the barbecue was held in a nearby grove, and the approach of the first train was hailed with genuine joy. Rumbling of this first through train from New Orleans was as the rattling of the keys of freedom in the ears of a jailworn prisoner. Southern and Central Mississippi now were free of the nightmare of having to haul cotton long distances over bad roads to muddy river banks. No longer would the farmer have to pick his season in which to ship cotton to a Gulf port market. New Orleans could now be reached by rail, and the long tedious journeys to the banks of the muddy Pearl and Yazoo rivers were gone forever. No more would the cotton planters see the cotton factors shake their heads in disgust at bales of cotton caked in mud from having been rolled up and down soft river banks.

By the time the railroad was opened through from New Orleans to Canton it owned twenty-two locomotives, mostly of the basic 'American' 4−4−0 type, all of them wood-burners, with the usual enormous and picturesque 'balloon' smokestacks. They were all named after stations on the line, classical titles, and notably *James Robb*, while further units added after the opening to Canton savoured somewhat of broad gauge days on the Great Western, in England, with *Sultan, Rover, Corsair, Dragon*, with a touch of Old Crewe in the days of Francis Trevithick: *Lion, Messenger, Mercury* and *Atlas*. As to running the trains, while African railways had interruptions from lions and elephants, Canada had bears, and in later years the trains of Thailand would occasionally find a water buffalo asleep on the line, in the densely forested bayou country of Louisiana engine crews had to keep a sharp look-out for alligators. They would crawl out of the marsh, climb up the railway embankment, and drape themselves across the track for a sunbathe. On coming across such an obstruction the enginemen would stop, go forward, wake the reptile, and usher him out of the way!

There was good reason for this strong direct drive to the North, because in 1855 the Illinois Central had reached the north bank of the Ohio River, at Cairo, and connection with that railroad would open the way for the trade of the South to flow towards Chicago. Down in New Orleans I suppose it is no more than natural for me to be writing first of the southern constituents of the Illinois Central, rather than of the parent system, which obtained its charter in 1851 and had completed the 705 miles of line authorised by September of 1856. Certainly I found myself becoming very quickly absorbed and fascinated by the spirit of the South on a day of cloudless sunshine when the thermometer eventually topped the hundred. At the Illinois Central terminus I was greeted by George McCann, who had come down from Chicago to act as my guide, and with him were Messrs Renton and Pieck, respectively Assistant Superintendent and Divisional Engineer.

Outside the station there was waiting an unusual form of 'estate car' which could run either on the highway or on the railroad track. It reminded me of the Ro-Railer vehicles used for track maintenance work on certain lines in Scotland before the second world war, in which the drive from the engine could be changed from the pneumatic-tyred wheels to the railway wheels. This American car was simpler in that the pneumatic tyred wheels were spaced laterally to come exactly over the rails. The drive was through these wheels wherever the car was running, the small railway flanged wheels being lowered to act as a directional guide when on the railroad. Our first visit was southward from the station through a pleasant residential area to the banks of the Mississippi. Here the New Orleans Public Belt Railroad runs, serving a long succession of wharfs, warehouses and railway yards along the water's edge. In addition to the Illinois Central and the Alabama Great Southern section of the Southern, the Louisville and Nashville, Southern Pacific, Texas & Pacific, and the Louisiana and Arkansas come into New Orleans, and this Belt Railroad is something of an exchange route for them all.

One of the most interesting traffics that I saw on this line was that provided by the Piggyback service. The idea of transporting highway-truck trailers on special railroad flat-cars originated in the 1950s and the Illinois Central introduced it on an experimental basis in

84

1955, between Chicago and Memphis. Like many innovations it developed slowly. It was not to the liking of road hauliers, who began losing traffic to the railroads. Furthermore, the transfer operation was a great deal simpler than with 'container' traffic on European railways. Because of the much greater height permissible in the USA, the load did not have to be transferred from the truck-trailer; the entire trailer, wheels as well, could be lifted bodily on to the railroad flat-car. At New Orleans the loaded piggyback traffic is two-way. The inward loads consist largely of imports from overseas, such as coffee from Latin America, olives from Spain, burlap — a coarse canvas from India, used for wrappings — and sisal, a form of hemp, from Mexico. At the time I was there the Illinois Central was running one all-piggyback 'hotshot' freight into New Orleans, and a similar one out every day.

We then made our way, with the 'estate car' on the railroad track, beside one of the wide bends of the Mississippi to the point where the Belt Railroad swings alongside the Illinois Central main line and for a time we were heading north-west. But before leaving the immediate neighbourhood of New Orleans and referring to the map on page 82, I must not forget the second entry of the Illinois Central to the city, round the eastern end of Lake Pontchartrain. I should, strictly speaking, be using the full name Illinois Central Gulf, because that eastern entry was originally that of the Gulf, Mobile and Ohio, using trackage rights over the Alabama Great Southern section of the Southern Railway over the last twenty miles. The G.M. & O. was merged with the Illinois Central in 1972. We came to the end of the belt-line and passed on to the double-tracked main line of I.C.G., running as an ordinary train to colour light signal indications. In swinging round into a northerly direction we came to a grade crossing with the single-tracked line of the Louisiana and Arkansas Railway, a part of the Kansas City Southern Railway.

In view of the early reluctance of pioneers to build railroads through the bayou country it is remarkable how many were eventually built, significant of the positively magnetic attraction exercised by the beautiful and usually prosperous city of New Orleans. One that is now a subsidiary main line of I.C.G. arose out of the great empire-building tactics of that nationwide railway entrepreneur Collis P. Huntington.

With large financial interests in California as well as in the Chesapeake and Ohio he conceived the idea of a transcontinental chain of railroads lying far to the south of the Chicago maelstrom, all under his own control. Construction was proceeding rapidly with the Southern Pacific from Los Angeles through El Paso and Houston towards New Orleans, while westward from Louisville, Kentucky, he had bought up some small railroads that extended his influence from the western end of the Chesapeake and Ohio to Memphis, Tennessee. All that was necessary to complete the chain was a line down the valley of the Mississippi through Vicksburg and Baton Rouge to New Orleans.

So there was launched the line that in 1884 was consolidated as the Louisville, New Orleans and Texas Railroad, though it did not reach within very many miles of either of the extremities in its name. One would have thought that construction almost entirely in a river valley would not have presented many difficulties; but that was not to know the nature of the Mississippi! Huntington's principal partner in the enterprise, Major Richard T. Wilson, confessed afterwards that no-one would have undertaken it if they had known beforehand what they were in for. Yet under the dynamic leadership of a young Georgia graduate of the University of Virginia, Jim Edwards by name, 456 miles of railroad was built through dense forests, and across river swamps, where floods, landslips, quicksands, and washouts on a gigantic scale impeded the progress, in the incredibly short time of two years. While the cities of Memphis and Vicksburg are perched on high bluffs, well above the flood level of the Mississippi, the land between is the Yazoo Delta, an exceedingly rich and fertile land hitherto avoided by railway builders because each year it was turned into a huge lake by the flood waters of the Mississippi and the Yazoo River. The line that Jim Edwards built became part of the Illinois Central in 1892.

But to return to its starting point in the south just beyond that grade crossing of the main line with the Louisiana and Arkansas. Such crossings, 'level crossings' as they would be called in Great Britain, are common in North America, and around Chicago in particular they are very numerous. We stopped for me to examine the massive track work on the actual crossing, which has to withstand tremendous pounding from the passage of heavy trains. The crossing is protected

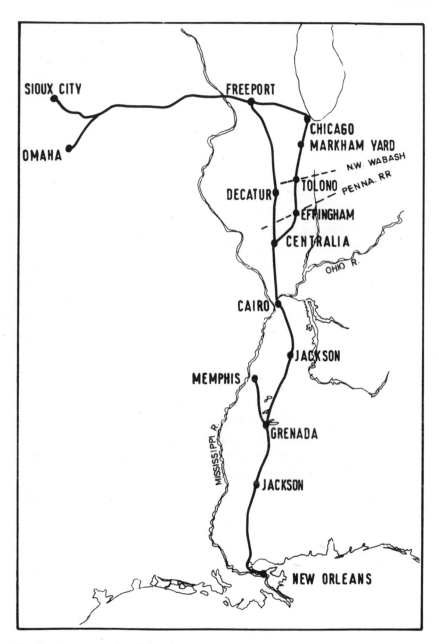

11. Basic network of the Illinois Central

by colour light signals forming part of the New Orleans remote-control area installation. Nearby was the international airport at which the plane bringing me from Atlanta had touched down on the previous evening. We were now heading out into open country on the narrow strip of land between the Mississippi and Lake Pontchartrain. As will be seen from the map there are many lakes in this marshy delta-land bayou country. I was charmed by the profusion of water hyacinths growing wild by the side of the line, and grateful that we did not have to stop to shoo any alligators off the track! We stopped briefly at May's Yard, concentration point for the ordinary freight traffic out of New Orleans, and I saw that one of the train dispatchers was a woman. In Great Britain during the second world war we had many women in mechanical signal boxes, but this was the first time I had seen one as a dispatcher. The outlet from the small Lake Maurepas is by the Pass Manchac, crossed by a single-tracked bascule-type bridge, the operation of which was demonstrated to me. Then we drove on to Ponchatoula, a delightful country township claiming to be the Straw-berry Capital of the World! There are now no passenger trains calling at the picturesque station, but the buildings are in active use as a kind of general market run by the ladies of the neighbourhood for selling souvenirs, and suchlike. Manchac and Ponchatoula were two of the original stations when the line was first built.

In the inspection car we drove northward to Hammond, where George McCann and I were to join the northbound 'Panama Limited', an Amtrak train running through from New Orleans to Chicago. Hammond is another very pleasant station, where I saw heavy freights going through before our own train arrived. I counted 139 cars on one triple-headed general freight going north. We were travelling up the main line from the south, but from Hammond there is a lateral road to the west, joining Jim Edwards's road at Baton Rouge. While this used to pass through a land that breathed the very spirit of the old 'deep south' in its early colonial atmosphere and occupations, and tracts of unexplored land, now, I was told, the whole area between Baton Rouge and New Orleans has experienced such a rapid industrial development that it is sometimes referred to as the 'American Ruhr'. Travelling on the principal main line through Ponchatoula to Ham-mond, through such a smiling wholly rural countryside, it was hard to believe that such a highly industrialised area was so near. One can be fairly sure that C. P. Huntington, Major Wilson, and Jim Edwards never envisaged such a development when they drove the Louisville, New Orleans and Texas Railroad through the swamps with such unrelenting vigour.

The original main line from the south, the New Orleans, Jackson and Great Northern, and the Mississippi Central, did not pass through Memphis but continued almost north to the second Jackson — Jackson, Tennessee, and thence into Kentucky and to the left bank of the Ohio River at East Cairo. Unlike the Egyptian capital, the pronunciation of the last-named city is 'Care-oh'. Our train was routed via Memphis, but it was midnight before we got there, and not a great deal could be seen from the carriage windows. George McCann and I had another 150 miles of travelling before we reached our beds that night. We were riding another part of the emergent American railroad network that played an important part in the Civil War. The lines running north and south were of great strategic value to both sides, both in turn seeking to use the lines, or cripple them. Each army before yielding territory destroyed the track, blew up bridges, burned down the depots, and wrecked watertanks. In his fine book *Main Line of Mid-America*, Carlton J. Corliss has a chapter entitled 'Beating Drums', which in relating plain fact is more exciting than many a carefully written film scenario.

At the time of the Civil War the lines north and south of the Ohio River were unconnected both physically and business-wise, but the well-established Illinois Central, with their southernmost railhead on the north bank of the river, at Cairo, had been anxious to establish regular and reliable communication with New Orleans. In 1855 the railroad sought to enter into an agreement with certain steamboat owners to provide a daily service between Cairo and New Orleans down the Mississippi River. They concluded a mail contract with the Post Office for carrying mail in this way, but when this was known the fat was fairly in the fire. The steamboat operators sent their prices up sky-high, and as the Illinois Central was not prepared to be blackmailed in this manner, the Post Office cancelled their contract and re-advertised for bids. The steamboat operator who won the contract gathered nothing but odium, because of slow and unreliable service, and it was not until 1858 that the Illinois Central established its own line of first-class steamers on the great river. Its fleet included some of the finest steamboats on the Mississippi, and for the first time a regular scheduled transport service, all the year round, was provided between Chicago and New Orleans by railroad to Cairo and thence by steamboat — all under Illinois Central management.

Navigation on the Mississippi was then a picturesque, exciting, and sometimes hazardous business. The steamboats themselves were like nothing else on earth, but those of the Illinois Central Railroad Line gained a very unusual distinction. Two Missouri farm-boys, the brothers Samuel and Henry Clemens, of Hannibal, after gaining a first experience of river life obtained jobs on the I.C.R. steamboat *Pennsylvania*. Sam did not stay long on the job, because he despised the pilot, and transferred to another ship of the same fleet, the *A. T. Lacy*. Had he not done so, the literary world would have been the poorer, because soon afterwards the *Pennsylvania* blew up near Memphis, with heavy loss of life. As co-pilot he would have been on the bridge at the time of the disaster. His brother, Henry, was fatally injured. Sam Clemens became a fully-fledged Mississippi River pilot, but although he always thoroughly enjoyed the life, and piloted the *Crescent City* and the *New Falls City*, he was always scribbling when not at the wheel. His writings were to some purpose, and under his pen-name they became world famous. I wonder what the one-time Mississippi River pilot, Sam Clemens, who served the Illinois Central Railroad Line would have thought had he lived to learn that a great English railway, the London and North Western, had named one of their express passenger locomotives after him, the *Mark Twain*.

At the time I travelled there was only one through passenger train a day between Chicago and New Orleans, operated by Amtrak. In the early fifties there had been a very marked decline in passenger business, but later it was halted, and the year 1966 was the best for total passenger traffic for ten years. A determined effort was made to effect a revival. An intensive market research exercise was carried out to try and find the kind of service the public wanted. New overnight coach services were put on; dome cars were added to the streamliners 'City of New Orleans' and 'City of Miami', while at the same time some trains with marginally low patronage were taken off. By the summer of 1968 less than two dozen daily through passenger trains were serving Chicago, Sioux City, St Louis, Memphis and New Orleans. By 1971 only the 'City of New Orleans' was left, and when the passenger service was taken over by Amtrak the overnight 'Panama Limited' was revived and the daytime 'City of New Orleans' withdrawn. Today the 'Panama Limited' covers the 920 miles between Chicago and New Orleans in 18 hrs 35 min., an overall average speed of 49·5 m.p.h.

Today Illinois Central Gulf is almost entirely a freight operating railroad, and it is done in a big, imaginative and most efficient way. Although one naturally thinks of Chicago as the nodal point of many railroads that serve the city, important though it is to I.C.G. it is by no means the predominating centre of traffic in the north. In fact, as will be told in more detail in the next chapter, Chicago was at the end of a *branch line* in the system of lines authorised by the original charter. Now, some of the newest through freight services enterprised by I.C.G. are deliberately routed to by-pass the congested Chicago area. Three of these services are of particular interest as showing how I.C.G. links up with other major railroads. In all three cases the southern termini are New Orleans and Mobile. The one that comes nearest to involvement in the Chicago complex is that operated in conjunction with the Soo Line, and its Canadian connections. The 'Soo' is the universal abbreviation of the full name of the twin cities on each side of the narrow isthmus between Lake Superior and Lake Huron — Sault Ste Marie, one American, one Canadian of the same name — and the railway that first earned the nickname of the 'Soo Line' was the Minneapolis St Paul and Sault Ste Marie. But now, after a merger with two other railroads the official title is the Soo Line Railroad, and it retains its strong Canadian affiliation. The Soo Line comes within a few miles of Chicago on its own metals, and traffic from Vancouver and all parts of Western Canada comes over the Soo Line. By-passing the Chicago terminals it is brought to I.C.G.'s Markham Yard to connect with the evening southbound freights. It has been found that up to two days in transit is saved between Canada and the Gulf ports by this run-through service.

Another important link up is between I.C.G. and Conrail. Here the interchange point is at Effingham, Ill., where the former Pennsylvania main line to St Louis intersects the I.C.G. main line from Cairo to Chicago. The result is an excellent series of through services from the cluster of originating centres of traffic in the south — Baton Rouge, Montgomery, and Birmingham, Alabama, in addition to New Orleans and Mobile — fanning out again eastwards from Indianapolis to the main line cities of the former New York Central and of the Pennsylvania. The third new through service is known as the 'Delta-Cannonball', and involves a link up with the Norfolk and Western at Tolono, which like Effingham is a crossing point of a competitive east–west line to St Louis, formerly part of the Wabash. In this case the fanning out eastward begins at Fort Wayne, and ultimately involves former Nickel Plate routes, as well as the Norfolk and Western's original network, to Roanoke and Tidewater on Chesapeake Bay at Norfolk itself.

If one considers these important through services as well as the original basic traffic of the Illinois Central, and studies the map of the system, the vital link between north and south becomes apparent; the bridge over the Ohio River at Cairo. When the Illinois Central was first projected the site of the southern railhead was chosen as close as possible to the point of confluence of the Ohio and Mississippi rivers, so that full advantage could be taken of existing steamboat service downstream to carry traffic to the cities of Mississippi State and Louisiana. When the lines from the south reached East Cairo, on the opposite bank there was at first not an overriding need for a bridge, because they had built to the 5 ft gauge, and transhipment of goods would in any case have been necessary. But even before the Illinois Central had obtained a lease of the lines south of Cairo conversion of the gauge was undertaken, and then the need for a bridge became paramount. The river had already been bridged at Louisville and Cincinnati, and the men of the Illinois Central felt that they were slipping behind. To see the momentous link, first made in October 1889, I was now travelling through the night on the 'Panama Limited'. We reached Cairo in the small hours of the morning, at 3.40 a.m. to be exact, and George McCann had organised a car to meet us and take us to a welcoming motel for what remained of the night.

CHAPTER EIGHT

I.C.G. — Cairo to the north

The bridging of great rivers in the USA posed many problems for railroad engineers. Their length, the number of large tributaries, and the vast catchment areas that they drain — not to mention their normal width — give rise to great variations in their volume of flow, and height; and while they are not normally subject to the devastating torrents that are the usual condition of some Indian rivers in the monsoon season, the areas on both banks are liable to severe flooding. At Cairo the Ohio is no exception, and from 1880 onwards surveys and soundings were being made preparatory to getting firm estimates for construction of the great bridge that would form the final link in the railway line between Chicago and New Orleans. Fortunately the Illinois Central had a general manager who was an outstanding all-round railroad man, Edward T. Jeffery. Born in England in 1843 he entered the service of the Illinois Central as an office boy at the age of thirteen, and he progressed to draughtsman, mechanical engineer, general superintendent and finally to general manager, all in the space of twenty-nine years. In 1886 he estimated that the Cairo bridge would cost $3m. Its total length would be no less than four miles, including the lengthy approach embankments, while the bridge itself was to be 4644 ft long. By midsummer of 1887 work was well under way.

The bridge had a total of twelve spans. Two of these were over the main channel of the river, each with a span of 518 ft, providing a clearance of 104 ft above low water level. The maximum recorded variation in river level had then been 58 ft. Then there were seven additional spans of 400 ft, and three of 249 ft. The massive masonry piers that supported these trussed girders were built to accommodate the marked rises and falls in the river level, rather than to withstand violent torrents, and the construction went through without any untoward incidents. Unhappily Jeffery, the master-architect of the project, did not remain with the Illinois Central to participate in the ceremonies attendant upon its completion, because no more than a few weeks previously a severe disagreement with the President of the railroad had led to his resignation. It was nevertheless remarkable that against his original estimate of $3 million the actual cost came out at $2,952,286. Although there were to be no formal speeches, or tape-cutting, the opening of the bridge was signalised in a very practical way by steaming nine 75-ton 2−6−0 locomotives, coupled in tandem, slowly across. These were the largest then in service on the railroad, and together represented a load of 700 tons. The date was 29 October 1889. A great crowd, assembled on both banks of the river, watched well-nigh breathless while this cavalcade proceeded from one bank to the other, and once they were safely across a wild and joyous fanfare of steamboat whistles, cheers, and engine whistles broke out from the vast throng of onlookers. The 'last spike' in the railroad chain from Chicago to New Orleans had been driven.

It was a serene morning of cloudless sunshine when my friends of I.C.G. took me to see Cairo bridge. It was nearly eighty-eight years since the completion of the original structure, and although looking superficially much the same, the bridge I saw was a replacement of the old one that had been completed in 1952. It was somewhat significant that estimates for the work, obtained in 1949, showed that the work of modernisation was going to cost more than double that of the original bridge. Except at one end, where three of the 400 ft spans were each to be replaced by two 197 ft spans, thus necessitating the building of three new masonry piers, it was to be a straight replacement job, girder for girder, though putting in heavier members the better to withstand the greater loads of modern traffic. The plan of reconstruction, which I was told had never previously been attempted on a bridge of this size and height, and carrying so relatively heavy a traffic, was to deal with one span at a time. Obviously such work could not be carried through without some interference with regular traffic, and the plan adopted was calculated to cause the minimum derangement.

94

Each new span was erected on a falsework of long steel piles, in its correct location abreast of the existing span that was to be replaced. Falsework was also built up on the opposite side, so that when the new span was ready the old one could be rolled out of place, and into the clear. During this operation traffic was, of course, suspended. Once the old span had been run clear and was resting on its temporary supports, the new span was rolled in. In the case of the two 518 ft spans, the time during which railroad traffic was suspended was 20 hours, in one case, and 22¾ hours in the other. After traffic was resumed the old span was stripped of as much material as practicable, and the remainder, consisting of the main girders and some of the cross-bracing, was pushed off its temporary supports, and dumped, with a mighty splash, into the river. There it was cut up by divers and the material recovered as scrap. Then when all was finished on one span, the temporary supports were moved to come alongside the next old span to be replaced.

By this procedure interruption of railroad traffic was reduced to a minimum. During the period of suspension passengers were conveyed from one side of the river to the other by ferry, and such freight traffic as could not be held for the maximum period of interruption was re-routed via another river-crossing at Metropolis, Illinois. The time of interruption during the replacement of the shorter spans was as little as nine hours in one case. The work was planned and seen through by the distinguished chief civil engineer of the Illinois Central, C. H. Mottier, born a farm boy, and eventually rising to the post of vice-president engineering, a position which he held for seventeen years.

From Cairo bridge we went some forty miles upstream beside the Ohio River to Paducah, to the splendid locomotive shops of I.C.G., where I was welcomed by Mr J. T. Jones, the General Manager. This was one of the visits in my tour of American railroads to which I had looked forward with the keenest anticipation, because I had learned previously that activities there did not consist merely in the repair and maintenance of locomotives, but in what they term re-manufacturing them 'better than when new', to quote their own words. This interested me particularly, because some forty years earlier, these self-same shops had earned great distinction in carrying out a major

95

modernisation programme with steam locomotives. A reference to this will set the stage for a description of what they are doing now. In the 1930s the Illinois Central, like most other American railroads, was engaged in a programme of accelerating all its principal train services, both passenger and freight, to try and win back traffic that had declined so seriously during the worst years of the great depression. The passenger 'Pacific' locomotives were no more capable of sustained speeds of 80 m.p.h. on level track than the heavy freighters were of 60 m.p.h. The financial situation was not such as to permit of large-scale investment in new power.

Besides the passenger 'Pacific' engines the railroad had a considerable number of freight locomotives of the 2−8−2, 2−10−2 and 2−8−4 types. They were sturdy reliable units in themselves, but designed for an era in railroad operation that was rapidly disappearing. It had been an era when the freight was there in plenty, just waiting to be carried, and speed of transit was of no great consequence. But in the 1930s long-distance 'trucking' was to prove a serious rival. The trouble with the existing freight locomotives was that because of the heavy running gear, and old-style methods of balancing, quite apart from the small diameter of the driving wheels, they could not be used at speeds much in excess of 40 m.p.h. They became very rough and uncomfortable to ride and had a simply murderous effect on the track. But the boilers were good and had many years of service left in them, and so a process of rebuilding of the 'engine' was undertaken. Much of this was as drastic and costly as that of the Reading 2−8−0s rebuilt as 4−8−4s, as described in connection with the Chessie Steam Special earlier in this book, and at Paducah, before the second world war, they modernised the 2−8−2s, converted the 2−10−2s into 4−8−2s, and completely rebuilt the 2−8−4s as 4−6−4 express passenger engines!

The principal alteration to the 2−8−2s, which were the most numerous class, and had driving wheels 5 ft 3 in. diameter, was to lighten the motion work, and to secure better balancing. New hollow spoked driving wheels were fitted, which enabled more counter balancing metal to be got in without increasing the overall weight, at the same time taking advantage of improved technology in the art of balancing. A relatively simple structural alteration to the boiler enabled the working pressure to be increased from 185 to 225 lb per sq.

in. and to cope with the increased firing rates anticipated from working the locomotives continually at much higher speed, and at high
rates of evaporation, mechanical stokers were fitted. The tenders were
lengthened to permit of longer runs without the need for too many
fuel stops on accelerated schedules, and the outcome of these extensive
alterations was that the engines could be run at speeds up to 65 m.p.h.
on severe demanding duties. All this work was done in the shops at
Paducah, and as a result the Illinois Central had a stud of reconditioned
2−8−2 locomotives that was to prove invaluable for the heavy traffic
of wartime.

The rebuilding of the larger engines was even more extensive, and
in both cases involved the provision of entirely new frames. The aim
in each case was to have a faster, smoother-running engine. The new
frames, in conformity with the practice then becoming general in the
USA, were embodied in one-piece steel cast beds, with the cylinders
and valve chests cast integrally. These were not manufactured at
Paducah. The 2−8−4s were converted into 4−6−4s, with 6 ft 1 ½ in.
diameter coupled wheels particularly for the accelerated services between Chicago and St Louis. They were the first engines of the 4−6−4
type to run on the Illinois Central, and to signalise what was regarded
as the beginning of an entirely new era in passenger motive power on
the railroad the first of the rebuilds outshopped from Paducah was
given the running number '1'. The 4−8−2s, rebuilt from the slow
freight 2−10−2s were extensively used on the fast night freights from
Chicago to the south.

In 1940, when this modernisation programme was getting fully into
its stride the Illinois Central had scarcely begun its transition from
steam to diesel traction. It was operating 1406 steam locomotives
against no more than 33 diesels, and this situation changed little during
the years when America was at war. The railroad may not have been
one of the quickest to replace steam, nor on the other hand did it hang
back like the great coal-hauling roads of the eastern states. In 1950 it
was still running 1129 steam locomotives. One does not need to probe
statistically into the subsequent metamorphosis, except to say that by
1965 there were no I.C. steam locomotives left in service, and that 653
diesels had replaced the total of 1439 of both categories that had existed
in 1940. In the meantime of course Paducah shops were re-organised

and re-equipped to deal with the new power. But in 1967 the transition began to move a great deal further. Until then the diesels in use on the line had come directly from the assembly lines of the manufacturers, and the works had been re-arranged for their repair and maintenance. This was a vital enough job in itself, but then there was developed a more dynamic and forward-looking policy. Paducah began to *build* locomotives.

With the 'big three' giants of the steam era in mind, Baldwin, Alco, and Lima, one does not normally associate the American railroads with construction of their own locomotives, though already in this book I have stressed the past achievements of Mount Clare, Huntington, and Roanoke in this respect. Now, at Paducah, I.C.G. are carrying forward their old traditions into the diesel age. With more than twenty years of diesel operation behind them they have found ways in which the power, reliability, and running costs of the commercially produced models can be improved, and they began remanufacturing them, at first purely to meet their own needs. Since the year 1967, however, other railroads have been taking advantage of the facilities and expertise built up at Paducah, and with a big order book for their own, and other railroads' locomotives to be 're-manufactured', as they termed it, the shops were working right round the clock, three shifts a day when I was there. Mr Jones told me that he had the capacity to turn out one completely remade diesel locomotive every day of the year. The up-rating process is even more spectacular. The design work had been completed for a 'remanufactured' 1850 horsepower unit, with what is termed 'solid–state' electrical equipment that would compete in selling-price with existing lower-powered designs.

The term 'solid-state' refers to electrical control gear that has no moving parts. In diesel and straight electric locomotives, as in modern signalling, the switching of the numerous electrical circuits was originally performed by contactors, electro–magnetic relays and such–like. But more recent practice is to replace such equipment with transistors. These latter are a great deal cheaper, take up far less space, and have now been brought to a high degree of reliability. It would be putting too rosy a light upon it to add that transistors have the same virtually unfailing dependability of the older forms of electrical switch gear.

But this is fully realised by the designers, and various safety and 'back-up' features are included in the control circuits. One can in any case be sure that solid-state 'electrics' are coming to stay in diesel-electric locomotive control gear, and Paducah works are certainly to the fore in this development.

Quantity-production methods are used in the building of the electrical equipment. For the control panels complete wire-forms are built up before insertion into the panel assembly, and then the panels are finished and given a complete electrical test before assembly in the locomotive. Before being finally handed over to the operating department remanufactured locomotives are first given a static test, and then a full-load test as one of a team on a multiple-headed freight train, from Paducah to Louisville and back. Then they are taken into the works and thoroughly re-examined before being passed for regular traffic. The I.C.G. modern locomotives are of 1750 and 3000 horsepower. The freight route to the south from Memphis is by the Yazoo River line via Gwin, which is a crew change point. This route is operated on train orders. On the water level route through Vicksburg and Baton Rouge freight trains of up to 200 cars are hauled by no more than two locomotives.

It had originally been intended that George McCann and I should fly from Paducah to St Louis, to pick up the Amtrak train 'The Inter American', which comes up from Laredo, on the Mexican border, and connects there with the 'Aztec Eagle' express from Mexico City. This train left St Louis at 4 p.m. and would have landed us in Chicago at 9.25 p.m. But the connecting time between plane and train in St Louis was too short, and so we continued by air. The distance by rail between the two cities is 294½ miles, and so the 'Inter American' averages a little under 52 m.p.h. overall, including intermediate stops. In years before the second world war, this stretch witnessed the fastest running on the Illinois Central, where the company was in competition with the Chicago and Eastern Illinois, and with the Wabash. While most of the running was made by steam, the Illinois Central had put on a fine diesel train, 'The Green Diamond', in 1936.

In 1940, which represented the climax year in the speed enterprise of many American railroads, the 'Daylight' of the Illinois Central had a run over the 54·1 miles from Kankakee to Gibson City in 46 minutes, at an average of 70·6 m.p.h. When the speeding-up had begun in 1934, this train was booked to run the 47·9 miles from Chicago 63rd Street to Kankakee in 45 minutes, and from there to Clinton, 92·7 miles, in 87 minutes. At that time both the Illinois Central and the C. & E.I. maintained an overall time of 5½ hours between Chicago and St Louis, equal to the present Amtrak time; but the C. & E.I. had a route shorter by about four miles. 'The Inter American' of today passes on to the tracks of the Missouri Pacific south of St Louis and makes its way to the border via Little Rock, Dallas, and Fort Worth. So far as the section between St Louis and Chicago is concerned, it does not stand much chance against airline competition. I was, however, sorry not to see the great Union station in St Louis, the train shed of which has one of the most remarkable arched roofs in the world. Although from outside it looks like a single arch, there are actually several intermediate supports. I had no more than a glimpse of it from the air. It covers no fewer than thirty-two tracks abreast under the one arch, and the track layout in the immediate approach to the station is impressive.

There was perhaps something a little ironical in my first coming to Chicago, claimed as the greatest railway centre in the world, by air, because there was not a convenient train; but once in the city, several more railroads besides the Illinois Central sought to fill me in with many details of their operations. But with the Illinois Central I had special interests in their great mechanised marshalling yard at Markham, about twenty miles to the south of the city, and a concentration and classification point for both northbound and southbound traffic. Markham was one of the first yards anywhere in the world to be fully mechanised, to the extent of having power-operated remotely-controlled rail brakes. This technique, which has become widespread in recent years, had a preliminary airing at the northbound Gibson yard on the Indiana Harbor Belt Railroad in 1924, with a form of rail brake that was of German origin; but the Union Switch and Signal Company secured the contract for the much larger Markham northbound yard with a new wholly-American design of brake, which became known as the Markham type. I remember it well. As a young trainee it was part of my work to study current American practice, and I was fascinated by the whole philosophy and layout of Markham. For

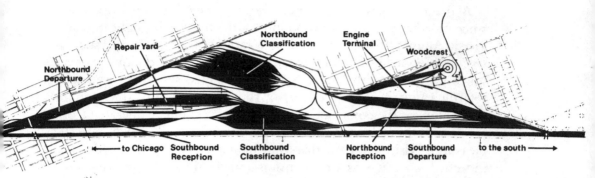

12. Schematic layout of Markham Yard

what was virtually a prototype it was a huge installation, with no fewer than 67 tracks and 121 rail brakes, or car retarders, as they are known in America. The total 'rail-feet' of retarder was 7072, making the average length of each one 58 ft. There were 69 pairs of pneumatically operated points, and the control was divided between 5 towers. The track layout as originally installed is shown in the accompanying diagram. A large yard for southbound traffic was installed at the same time, with electrically-operated retarders.

The full area, all located on the eastern side of the main line, extends for nearly three miles and the capacities of the various sections are at present as follows:

Yard	Number of tracks	Capacity: No. of cars
Southbound receiving	15	945
Southbound classification (beyond hump)	45	1700
Southbound departure	11	958
Northbound receiving	12	1200
Northbound classification (beyond hump)	64	2500
Northbound departure	10	764
Repair Yard	8	760

A great deal has been learned about marshalling yard operation since Northbound and Southbound Markham was brought into service in August 1926. In England, at Westinghouse, we studied successive development of the American retarders. The Markham type was quickly superseded by more powerful designs, so that many fewer retarding units were needed. Also, the introduction of track circuit protection for the points meant that the yards could be operated from fewer towers, with a greater centralisation of control. When I had the pleasure of visiting it I saw that Markham itself had been considerably modified since it was first commissioned. Where there were two parallel tracks over the hump, now there is only one, but the enormous spread out to 67 classification sidings still remains. Before my tour of American railroads was finished, I was to see some of the latest yards to be installed, and to have confirmed the view that in no facet of railroad operation do so many scientific principles have to be integrated: point operation; choice and layout of tracks and gradients; all the factors involved in the rolling of cars; precision locomotive operation, and, today, the computerisation of the various points to be taken into account in applying brake force to car wheels passing the retarders. Except that it was installed long before the days of computers, Markham remains in most respects the father — and the guinea pig! — of all modern marshalling yards. Adjacent to the northbound receiving, and the southbound departure yards there used to be a steam locomotive roundhouse, but this has now been replaced by a new mechanical terminal. It is situated about halfway between the passenger stations of Hazelcrest and Homewood, and has been given the name of 'Woodcrest', from a synthesis of parts of the two names. It is equipped for dealing with light repairs to locomotives, cars and cabooses, and includes a machine for turning wheels without removing them from the unit, of whatever type. There is a servicing bay with accommodation for twelve locomotives, where they are replenished with fuel, water, sand, and given a washdown. No locomotive is in for more than one hour, and with engines running all the time the noise level is high inside the building. The accompanying diagram shows the complete layout now existing at Markham Yard.

The Illinois Central enters Chicago from the south along the lake front, and thereby hangs something of a tale. Under the original charter of the railroad the main line ran from Cairo in the south, due north through the State to La Salle and then veered round to the north-west to end at Dunleith, where Illinois meets both Iowa and Wisconsin. The Chicago 'branch', as it was originally known, forked from the main line at Centralia, and ran through Urbana and Kankakee to the 'Windy City'. The completion of the 'Charter Lines' took place on 27 September 1856, and as will be seen from the map no railroad was more appropriately and accurately named. Branch line or not, however, it was very soon evident that Chicago would soon become the key station on the entire system, and it was a Chicago newspaper that set the seal of approval on the completion of the enterprise, thus:

The completion of this gigantic improvement so that passengers and freight can without change of cars be transported from the south-ernmost point in our state to either the extreme northwestern or northeastern corner of it is an achievement which every citizen must consider with the highest gratification. Probably very few of those who contemplated the enterprise at its inception dreamed of its realization in their day. Only a few years have intervened and it is finished. The transit from a point on the Mississippi to the Lakes is but the ride of a few hours. Twenty years ago the man who would have persisted in prophesying the event would have been confined to an insane asylum!

Certainly the construction of 705 ½ miles of railroad mostly across virgin prairie land in 4 years and 9 months was a tremendous feat of construction.

The choice of a site on the lake-front at Chicago for the terminal station was an imaginative stroke, but one that was to have an unexpected sequel. Before the building of the railroad the foreshore in front of what is now the gracious and impressive Michigan Avenue was just an open seashore, with the waves of the great lake breaking upon it in the manner of an ocean, except for the tides. Over the centuries the Chicago River debouching into the lake had built up a small delta formation, on which the city itself was rapidly growing. By approaching from the south and along the lake front, the Illinois Central secured for themselves an unrestricted 'right of way' by carrying the line on a trestle viaduct *in the lake*, at some little distance offshore, and impinging directly upon the 'delta' to build their terminus adjacent to the very heart of the city. At that point there was space to spread out freight and passenger facilities just where the business was likely to grow. The central passenger station was built alongside, and on the outer side of the trestle two large grain elevators were erected, next to the wharves where so many ships docked. What a prospect it must have been in the 1860s to stroll on the beach below Michigan Avenue, look out across the water to where trains of the Illinois Central hauled by wood-burning 4–4–0 locomotives were constantly passing across the trestle, while the background to the passenger station and the grain elevators was a forest of tall sailing-ship masts.

But even before the line was finished, the Illinois Central Telegraph Company, in what was called at the time 'an alliance akin to wedlock' with the railroad company, was building a telegraph line beside the track, that could be used not only for railroad purposes but also by the public, if so desired. Before the completion of the railroad, workshops for the maintenance and construction of locomotives and rolling stock were set up on the lake front at Weldon. Naturally, the offices there were linked into the telegraph line, and it was there that one of the greatest railwaymen who have ever lived got his first job, at the age of fifteen years. His name was William Cornelius Van Horne, but then he was just Billy the telegraph boy. His stay on the Illinois Central was brief, but characteristic. Fascinated by the power of electricity he was always experimenting, sometimes giving his sense of humour full rein. One day he ran a ground wire from a storage battery to an iron plate outside the office window, so placed that workmen touched it as they passed. Billy charged this plate so that they got a mild shock as they passed, to their bewilderment. Then one day the superintendent came along before Billy had time to switch off the current, and he too got a shock. Unlike the others he realised what had done it, stormed into the office, and in less time than it takes to describe Van Horne was slung out literally, neck and crop, never to return! I wonder if that superintendent lived long enough to see the day when Van Horne was knighted by Queen Victoria for his great work in getting the Canadian Pacific Railway finished?

I now come to one of the greatest disasters to befall any city in comparatively recent years, comparable to the great earthquake, tidal

104

wave and fire that devastated Tokyo and Yokohama in 1924, or to go back in history to the destruction of Pompeii. The holocaust that swept Chicago in October 1871 was all the more stunning in its impact, because it had so trivial a beginning. Here was no violent cataclysm of nature, nor the appalling man-made destruction of an atom bomb — nothing more than a fire in a barn. But at the time the 'Windy City' was living up to its name and a stiff 40 m.p.h. breeze was coming up from the south-west. Before anyone fully realised what was happening, the fire quickly spread, and in the aftermath of a summer of prolonged drought, with everything as dry as tinder, the flames tore through everything like a tornado. Dwellings, offices, public buildings were completely consumed. This fearful conflagration went on for two whole days, by which time hundreds of lives had been lost; over 100,000 people were homeless, and the damage to property was staggering. The fact that the Illinois Central depots were out beyond Michigan Avenue did not save them. The flames leaped across. The passenger station and the goods depots were reduced to ashes. The wooden trestle took fire, and the first of the grain elevators was utterly destroyed. In the meantime every locomotive that could be found had been used to haul away stock, cars, and equipment of all kinds, trains crowded with refugees, until amongst the debris some railroad men found a small fire engine. With this, working at risk to their lives, they managed to save the second grain elevator.

The aftermath of the fire was ultimately beneficial to the Illinois Central. Tens of thousands of wagon-loads of debris were dumped into the once pleasant lagoon between the former shoreline of Michigan Avenue and the railroad trestle until it was gradually filled up completely, and the trestle disappeared. For the first time the Illinois Central tracks in the approach to the Chicago terminal were on dry land. There was, however, a long legal dispute over the ownership of the reclaimed land — a dispute which, believe it or not, went on for upwards of thirty years! But the outcome of it all was that the Illinois Central widened their approach line and built new passenger and freight terminal buildings in a very advantageous site adjacent to the business heart of the city. It was there that one early evening, one of the best known of all American railroad photographs was taken, showing a group of five fast freight trains for the south awaiting the 'right-away', with the impressive backcloth of South Michigan Avenue and its fine buildings behind the locomotives. Illinois Central passenger trains also went from this same area; but now with Amtrak operating the passenger business main line trains for the south leave the Union station, leaving only the commuters on the lake front. For many years now these have been electrically operated. The inception of this fine organisation and the recent development of its equipment is referred to in Chapter Ten of this book, which deals with the commuter services of Chicago in general.

The great headquarters building TWO ILLINOIS CENTER is probably unique in the railways of the world. Looking south along the lake front, over the area that has seen so much Chicago history, it nowadays houses not only the administration headquarters of the railroad, but is also the operational nerve centre of the whole system. By far the greater proportion of the total route mileage is controlled by C.T.C., and nearly all the panels are at TWO ILLINOIS CENTER. Some, that control sections of the former Gulf, Mobile and Ohio Railroad, have not yet been brought in, but it is not expected to be long before they are. The principal freight line to the south between Memphis and Jackson, via Gwin, referred to in the previous chapter, which is throughout a 'dark area', is operated by train orders from a separate dispatcher, also at TWO ILLINOIS CENTER. Traffic over the entire 9600 route miles of the company is regulated entirely from this one building in Chicago. One vital adjunct of such a system of remote control is the need to detect all cases of hot axle-boxes, because trains are running for such long distances without any systematic visual observation. In the control centre in Chicago the tapes registered by the detectors positioned at carefully selected strategic points on the line are checked. There are bound to be some 'false alarms'; but it has been found that about 60 per cent of all cases reported are valid. There were, at the time I visited the centre, about 1500 cases a year.

· As long ago as 1908 the matter of air pollution had been taken up by the Chicago newspapers. Really it was not surprising. There, below Michigan Avenue, along the lake front the steam locomotives of the Illinois Central belched smoke and steam. The entire activity of the railroad was there — commuter, long distance passenger, and freight; the commuters accounted for by far the most, and in the early 1900s there were more than 200 of these trains in and out of Chicago daily. A considerable agitation was worked up for the suburban services at least to be electrified, with the hope that in due course the Illinois Central in Chicago would follow the example of the New York Central and the Pennsylvania in New York by eliminating steam traction entirely in the city area. But in Chicago the financial situation was much the same as in most other commuter areas. This traffic accounted for 46 per cent of all travellers on the Illinois Central, but for only 6 per cent of the total passenger revenue. There had been much dispute as to the rights of various interested parties in the development of the area between Michigan Avenue and the lake, but in 1919 the Lake Front Ordinance was passed, which authorised the city to take over the lakeshore, to pursue its 'City Beautiful' plan, while the Illinois Central, which was a party to the ordinance, was required to electrify its suburban service within the city limits.

The project involved conversion from steam of 132 miles of suburban track, covering more than 50 suburban stations. The system chosen was 1500 volts direct current, with overhead line current collection. The new rolling stock was arranged in 2-car sets, consisting of one powered and one trailer car. Working on the multiple unit principle they could be made up into four, six, or eight car trains according to traffic requirements. The new cars had a capacity to accelerate much more rapidly than steam trains. Their speed from a standing start was 15 m.p.h. in 10 sec.; 28 m.p.h. in 20 sec. and a maximum speed of 57 m.p.h. The new service was brought into operation in August 1926, with a total stock of 130 powered and 130 trailer cars. The electrification as a whole was a good investment, and the commuting public patronised it wholeheartedly. Unfortunately it had little time to get fully into its stride before the coming of the great depression, when the decline in traffic all over the system brought the Illinois Central Railroad perilously near to bankruptcy. The electric train sets of 1926 had a life of more than forty years, and it was only in 1971 that replacement of them began with new 156-seater double-deck cars. More detailed reference to this type of car, generally on commuter services around Chicago, is made in a later chapter.

CHAPTER NINE

Louisville and Nashville

It was my lifelong interest in steam locomotives of all kinds that first drew my attention to the Louisville and Nashville Railroad, and to its notable subsidiary, the Nashville, Chattanooga and St Louis. Although steam traction has long ceased on both these lines, a visit to them became a 'must' in my American itinerary. By the time I travelled to Louisville the L. & N. had become a partner with the Seaboard Coast Line in the Family Lines System and a look at the map of the combined network extending from Chicago to Miami makes one question whether there would be room — and traffic! — for anyone else in the states it covers so comprehensively, until one remembers the presence also of the Southern, certainly in equal strength. When my itinerary began to take shape, however, I found that from Chicago I should be travelling for almost the entire way to Louisville over a line that did not become part of the L. & N. until 1971, the Monon Railroad. Until then it had a somewhat chequered existence, as the Chicago, Indianapolis and Louisville, ending in bankruptcy just after the end of the second world war. The city of Monon was the junction of its four main routes, and after reorganisation, its name was changed to the Monon Railroad. It entered Chicago on trackage rights from Hammond northwards, and reached Louisville over the Southern Railway bridge across the Ohio River.

I travelled down from Chicago on 'The Floridian', an Amtrak train that covers the 1600 miles to Miami in 39 hours. The make-up consisted of three coaches, dining car, sleeper car (for St Petersburg), dormitory car with bar, baggage-dormitory, and box car for stowage and mail. There were two coaches being worked down empty. My most lasting impression of the start out of Chicago was of grade crossings in all directions, much slow running and of taking 75 minutes to cover the first 20 miles. After passing Hammond, and getting on to L. & N. tracks, over two double-track grade crossings in rapid succession, we settled down to a pleasant run at 60–65 m.p.h. through an open country of large but isolated farms. Our first passenger stop was at Lafayette, Indiana, but beside the freight yards north of the city we had stopped for fourteen minutes for a crew change. Then we proceeded slowly to a stop in the main street, outside the Lahr Hotel, where passengers with their luggage were waiting on the pavement. Cars were parked on both sides. Highway traffic was flowing, while our train stood in the middle of the road. I was to see this kind of railroad operation more vividly two days later, when I rode part of the way back to Chicago in the locomotive cab.

We had lost nineteen minutes on schedule from Chicago to Lafayette, but made much better time on the next stage, through more hilly country that reminded me of the Chiltern Hills at home. This is not to say we made any speed records, but by running the 103 miles from Lafayette to Bloomington in 140 minutes, we made up all the lost time. The line is single-tracked throughout, and with electric upper quadrant semaphore signals, working on the absolute permissive block system, we had many intermediate slowings, and some speed orders. I was not riding on the locomotive in this direction but was given copies of the four orders handed to our engineer at Lafayette. As an example of train working arrangements they are worth quoting:

O/No. 578   Siding at Lafayette Jct blocked with cars.
O/No. 577   19 cars on siding at Cement.
O/No. 572   Do not exceed 25 twenty five miles per hour between Milepost 179·5 and Milepost 185.
O/No. 585   Between the hours ....track is clear

I did not see the orders we picked up at Bloomington, but at Milepost 249 we had a lengthy stop to cross the corresponding northbound Amtrak train. It should have been in Bloomington at 3.15 p.m. We had left there on time at 2.20 p.m. and it was an hour later that we

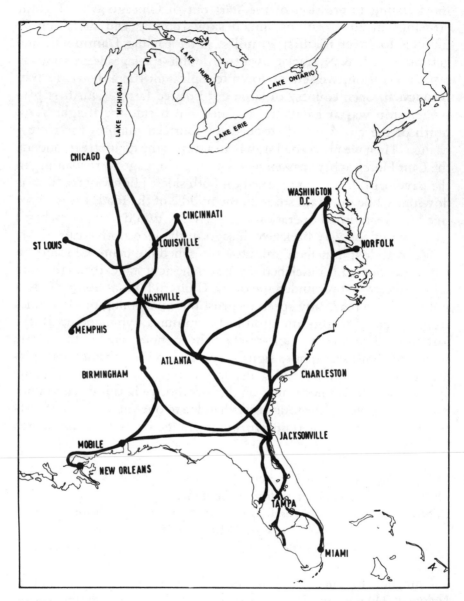

13. The Family Lines system—Louisville and Nashville and Seaboard Coast
Lines

were stopped to make the 'meet', nearly thirty miles farther south, at 3.37 p.m. The station names hereabouts are intriguing: Bedford, Orleans, Leipsic (thus), Campbellsburg — a curious mixture of Scots with the Teutonic — Salem, and Pekin! After passing the last-mentioned station, at 4.37 p.m. we were nearing the railroad complex of Louisville upon which five other companies beside the one-time Monon converge. The accompanying sketch map shows the situation. In riding in for the first time, however, I must admit to being a bit mystified. Having crossed the Ohio River and threaded our way through a series of junctions, we passed to the right of a big city that I thought must be Louisville; but there was no large station — no station at all in fact — and before long we were heading out in the country once more. Only when we were some ten miles south of the Ohio River crossing did we draw up at the new Amtrak station beside the National Turnpike. Charles Castner was there to meet me, and we drove back into Louisville to spend a pleasant evening in that most interesting city.

The Louisville and Nashville Railroad was incorporated in 1850, to build a line 185 miles long connecting the two cities. The original project was just that, and Louisville was a terminus with the exit towards the south. The oldest constituents of the greatly enlarged L. & N. that emerged from 1882 onwards, however, date right back to 1830. Within a week of each other in the January of that year there were chartered the Ponchartrain Railroad, down in Louisiana, to build an east–west line from the north shore of the lake to Mobile, and the Lexington and Ohio. In the latter case the Ohio River was to be reached at Louisville, but the enterprise, which was most curiously conceived, did not get farther west than Frankfort, a matter of twenty-five miles. Perhaps it was just as well! It was originally intended only to carry passengers. It was constructed with longitudinal limestone sills on which were laid iron strips for rails. The coaches were double-decked, with a strange segregation of the passengers: men upstairs, women and children below! The motive power was furnished by mules and stationary engines.

The Louisville and Nashville itself did not get off to a very good start either. A sparsely-settled hilly country between the two cities brought labour troubles, followed by an epidemic of cholera among

111

the navvies, and it was not until 1859 that the first train ran the entire 185 miles of line. Operation had barely had time to settle down when there came the Civil War. Unlike some American railroads, however, the Louisville and Nashville benefited from it. Although so near to the scene of much severe fighting, it was largely undamaged, and was used extensively by the Federal Government for moving troops and ammunition. It had none of the excitement experienced by its neighbour and ultimate subsidiary, the Nashville, Chattanooga and St Louis, which, at that time as the Western and Atlantic, was the scene of the great locomotive chase, in which the 4−4−0s *General* and *Texas* played a part.

Like every other railroad in the USA at that time the Louisville and Nashville relied almost entirely upon 4−4−0 locomotives. In 1865 out of a total stud of 61, only nine were of other wheel arrangements, and of the 4−4−0s, the most powerful had cylinders no larger than 16 in. diameter by 24 in. stroke. The extent to which the traditional American type was suited to the lightly laid, and sharply curved tracks of the period was never more convincingly shown than in the 'great locomotive chase' when speeds up to 60 m.p.h. were reputed to have been attained. The Louisville and Nashville was projected as a 6 ft gauge line, but after 2½ miles had been laid this was changed to 5 ft. It was not altered to standard gauge till 1886. Until that time nothing larger than the 4−4−0 type had been found necessary for passenger traffic, although 'Moguls' and a few 'Consolidations' (2−8−0s) had been introduced for freight.

For nearly forty years, from the 1880s to 1921, the Louisville and Nashville had the distinguished Milton H. Smith as chief executive, and his motto was 'never spend a dime when a nickel will do'. This philosophy was applied as much to motive power as to everything else, with the result that well-proved standard designs were used, of modern size, but superbly maintained in the shops at South Louisville. They were adequate for the years of depression in the 1930s, but when war came in Europe in 1939 and when American involvement seemed more and more inevitable, much larger locomotives were needed for the heaviest duties. A 4−8−4 for passenger runs was proposed, and there was much consultation over the new freight type. The passenger problem was quickly solved by purchase of standard EMD diesel-

112

electrics which, used in pairs, could run through from Louisville to New Orleans as a single working. As to 'freight' the consultations with the Baldwin Locomotive Works went otherwise. There was a limitation in size. A 2−10−4 would have been too big for the round-houses, and too long for the curves, and decision went for a 2−8−4. Roy F. Anderson, chief locomotive draughtsman at South Louisville, put it succinctly:

What L. & N. wanted in this design was an engine that would take any kind of train and run with it. Pull and run — that's what we wanted. And brother, that's what we got!

The first of the new 'M 1' class — 'Big Emmas' — was delivered to the L. & N. at Covington, Kentucky, in July 1942, just across the Ohio River from Cincinnati, and caused some consternation because she was too big for the turntable in the De Coursey roundhouse. L. & N. men came to gaze with astonishment at her, and the consensus of opinion was, 'the biggest damned hunk of engine ever to show up around these parts'. It was the typical reaction of railroad enginemen to the introduction of a new and enlarged class, but in the severe conditions of the war years the 'Big Emmas' proved an absolute godsend to the L. & N. Because of their size they had a limited route availability, but within their orbit they did a mammoth job. There was no question of teething troubles. Within 24 hours of delivery at De Coursey the first engine of the class No. 1950 was away on a fast freight for Corbin, and W. E. Hunter, master mechanic at De Coursey, usually had the 'Emmas' ready for traffic within 24 hours of their delivery from the Baldwin works.

The history of the 2−8−4 type in the USA, the 'Berkshire' as it was known, is interesting. It was first introduced in 1925 by a single unit built experimentally by Lima for the Boston and Albany; but from the success of this engine it was taken up by the Santa Fe, the Erie, and by the Boston and Maine between 1927 and 1928. All these had a splendid record of service, but it was not until 1942 that the Louisville and Nashville could afford to buy new steam power. It is interesting to compare the proportions of the L. & N. 'Berkshires' with those of their predecessors on other railroads (see page 114).

2–8–4 Fast Freight Locomotives

Date introduced	1925	1927	1927	1928	1942
Railroad	B. & A.	Santa Fe	Erie	B. & M.	L. & N.
Cylinders dia. in.	28	27	28½	28	25
stroke in.	30	32	32	30	32
Coupled wheel dia. ft in.	5–3	5–3	5–10	5–3	5–9
Heating surfaces sq. ft	–	–	–	–	–
Tubes and flues	4773	4239	5249	4726	4191
Firebox	284	294	320	284	257
Syphons (etc.)	53	44	128	121	204·3
Superheater	2111	1246	2545	2111	1908
Combined total	7221	5823	8242	7242	6562·1
Grate area sq. ft	100	99	100	100	90·2
Boiler pressure lbs/sq. in.	240	220	250	240	265
Tractive power					
Main cylinders lbs	69,400	69,200	72,000	69,400	65,290
Booster lbs	13,200	13,600	13,000	12,000	14,100

The first regular duty of the L. & N. 'Emmas' was on freight service from De Coursey yard over the South Fork line through Paris and Winchester to Corbin, a run of 180 miles. This was the Kentucky sub-division, and carried the heaviest traffic of any L. & N. main lines. Coal was the principal commodity in solid 100-car trains of 7300 tons. On the faster freights the 'Emmas' were scheduled to run those 180 miles in 5 hours, but their crews soon found that these splendid engines could run a great deal faster than the schedules required, and in the wartime winter of 1942-3 a number of them were equipped for the heaviest passenger duties. There were not nearly enough of the diesels to meet the extra demands of wartime, and the loads were too heavy for the older engines to tackle single-handed. In those anxious days there were not enough crews to permit of regular double heading. What was termed the 'second main line' of the L. & N. from Cincinnati to Atlanta developed a tremendous increase in passenger loadings and four of the new engines were put on to the job to work down to Corbin. On these duties they went into Cincinnati, instead of finishing at the freight yards of De Coursey, and at the passenger engine terminal they shared facilities with such celebrated runners as New York Central 'Hudsons', Pennsylvania 'K 4' Pacifics, Norfolk and Western 'J' class 4−8−4s, and Chessie 4−6−4s. What a spectacle the roundhouse there must have made at times!

About half the distance on the Kentucky sub-division, the ninety miles along the level or slightly falling grades beside the Licking River, was fast-running track, and northbound trains were often made up to 10,000 tons, with one 'M 1' engine from Winchester or Paris. But it was a very different matter south of Winchester. A single 'M 1' could take no more than 4000 tons northbound from Corbin, and even then had to take a pusher from Ford up to Patio. Charles Castner has described when northbound 'main trackers' were loaded to 8800 tons out of Corbin:

The Big Emmas got their stiffest workout on the 9-mile pull up Winchester Hill. And to make the pull in one try a third 'M 1' (in addition to the pair out of Corbin), coupling on behind the caboose during the water stop at Ford, was necessary. Leaving Ford, hoggers on all three Emmas cut in the boosters, covered their faces for protection in a tunnel just ahead, then widened out throttles to get their train up to 15 m.p.h. — if the weather was good and the rails were dry. Between mileposts 105 and 103 a pair of 10-degree reverse curves and the 0·97 per cent incline cut speed to 5 or 7 m.p.h. At Elkin the grade steepened to 1·07 per cent but when the track straightened out the 'M 1s' usually got back to about 15 m.p.h.

The Louisville and Nashville eventually had forty-two of these mighty engines, the last being built by Lima in 1949, but the life of those last additions to the stud was regrettably short. By then the trends of traffic from Cincinnati and Louisville to the south were changing. There was no longer such a dependence on coal, and just when the major challenge to steam from diesel traction was beginning in earnest there came the disastrous coal strike of 1949 which lasted from September till December, and even then only to the extent of restoring a three-day week. The severe slump in traffic was an unhappy prelude to the centennial year of the Louisville and Nashville, 1950; and although the railroad still considered itself a steam line, the challenge was growing. The economic advantage of diesels in heavy freight haulage could not be ignored, not only in avoiding the use of that increasingly expensive fuel, coal, but in permitting the mutliple heading of heavy trains without multiplication of the number of crews. The life of the 'M 1' class was shorter than it might otherwise have been. Their size and weight precluded their use south of Corbin and west of Louisville, and ironically it was in the massive freight hauls in their own particular area that the diesels showed up to the best advantage! As early as 1953 work on steam power ended at South Louisville shops. The last 'M 1' to receive heavy repairs had been complete in November 1952, and such work as was needed on them was henceforth done at De Coursey. The entire remaining L. & N. steam stud was retired in 1957.

The history of the fine locomotive shops at South Louisville is most interesting. They were built in 1905, providing the L. & N. with a large central establishment for repair of locomotives and wherein not a few classes were built new. The so-called SHOP ONE, a long 40-bay building, was where heavy repairs to steam locomotives were done, while in a 24-stall roundhouse routine servicing and such light repairs as might be needed between runs were carried out. With the first

116

| FORM 19 | 495-1-74 LOUISVILLE & NASHVILLE RAILROAD COMPANY TRAIN ORDER NO. 5 8 5 | FORM 19 |

JUNE 8 ____ 19 77

TO C. AND E. _____
TO C. AND E. __SOUTHWARD TRAINS_____
TO C. AND E. _____
TO C. AND E. _____ AT LAFAYETTE

BETWEEN THE HOURS OF 7 30 SEVEN THIRTY AM
AND 4 01 FOUR NAUGHT ONE PM JUNE 8, 1977
NORTHWARD TRAINS MUST APPROACH CONDITIONAL STOP TRACK
SIGN LOCATED AT MILE POST 187 AND SOUTHWARD TRAINS
MUST APPROACH CONDITIONAL STOP TRACK SIGN LOCATED AT
MILE POST 179 PREPARED TO STOP AND MUST NOT PASS DESIGNATED
POINT UNTIL NOTIFIED BY MAINTENENCE FOREMAN J L SCOTT
BY RADIO COMMUNICATION BY TELEPHONE OR IN PERSON THAT
TRACK IS CLEAR

JL

EACH EMPLOYEE ADDRESSED MUST HAVE A COPY OF THIS ORDER

MADE____Com_____ TIME 12 13 A M Ritchie _____ OPR.

14. An original Train Order—Louisville and Nashville

introduction of diesels the roundhouse was switched over to diesel maintenance work, this making possible the vital necessity of keeping steam and diesel work separate, and far from each other. Then, from 1953 onwards SHOP ONE went all diesel, and provided yet another example of the skilful transformation of a building and its basic facilities from steam to the new power. But the changes did not end with this first transformation. The rapid increase in the diesel locomotive stud, with greater power, more intensive utilisation, and a most welcome and almost sensational increase in traffic called for a review of the maintenance facilities at South Louisville, with the result that the entire shop layout and methods of working have been modernised, very successfully, to achieve two major objectives: first, by a system of preventive maintenance to spot defects before they become serious enough to cause a failure of the locomotive in traffic, and secondly, by streamlining all the repair operations to ensure that the time locomotives are out of service is reduced to a minimum. As one who has spent much of a lifetime in engineering production I was most impressed by South Louisville.

But not even the modernisation of the works prevented South Louisville from carrying out one more job on a steam locomotive as recently as 1962 — not a 'M 1' or a 'Mikado', but none other than the *General* — which was to run once again in steam, on the hundredth anniversary of the 'great locomotive chase'. What with film scenarios and other elaborations, it is to be feared that the story of what really *did* happen on 12 April 1862 has been rather improved in the telling, as the saying goes. The Confederate forces were using the main line between Atlanta and Chattanooga to such good effect that the Federals determined upon a daring and systematic act of destruction. Captain James Andrews of the Federal Army and twenty-one picked men disguised as civilians in the best 'fifth column' style, made their way south to Big Shanty, now Kennesaw, a station about thirty miles north of Atlanta, where the 6 a.m. train for Chattanooga stopped for the breakfast interval. The train, hauled by the *General*, was in charge of Captain Fuller of the Confederate Army, and while he, his crew, and his passengers were enjoying their meal they were surprised to see twenty-two more supposed passengers arrive. Instead of joining the train, however, they smartly uncoupled between three empty box

118

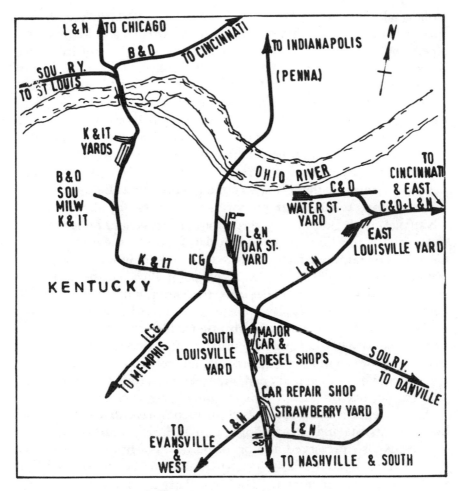

15. Lines round Louisville

cars that were next to the engine and the rest of the cars, boarded the engine and drove off to the north. Capt. Fuller with the driver and a locomotive shop foreman dashed out, and the 'great locomotive chase' had begun — with the pursuers running behind!

After sprinting about two miles the trio came across a gang of surface men who said that those on the *General* had held them up at gun point, taken their tools and cut the telegraph wires. The intrepid Fuller and his companions then plodded on with the surface men's

119

trolley, taking turns at pushing it — some chase! — until they came to Etowa. There at least they were able to commandeer a locomotive, albeit nothing better than a wheezy old contractor's unit called the *Yonah*. What was more important, Fuller collected a detachment of Confederate soldiers who had been completely bluffed by Andrews. He had told them that the *General* and its three box cars was a special carrying munitions to Chattanooga, and they had believed him. Still managing to coax the old *Yonah* along they eventually came to a southbound freight train hauled by the 4−4−0 engine *Texas*. Fuller took this at once, detached it from its train, and now the chase had begun in earnest, with the *Texas* running tender first. Because of their frequent stops to cut telegraph wires, the raiders, for all their initial advantage, were not making very rapid progress, and Fuller and his men, driving the *Texas* as fast as they dared, soon came in sight of the *General*. The raiders detached one box car and left it in the way of the pursuers, who coolly proceeded to propel it ahead of them. Then a second was detached, but Fuller came to a siding where the two could be pushed out of the way. By this time the raiders had knocked a hole in the end of the remaining car, through which they threw obstructions in the path of the *Texas*. Eventually, after an escapade extending over eighty-seven miles, the *General* ground to a stop, denuded of fuel and water. The raiding party fled, but were soon rounded up and they paid the penalty of crack troops masquerading as civilians.

A representative of another type of locomotive that ran the road between Atlanta and Chattanooga, though in less dramatic circumstances, is also preserved and on display in Nashville's Centennial Park. This is one of the big 4−8−4 express locomotives of Class 'J 3' of the Nashville, Chattanooga and St Louis Railway. These fine engines, built by Alco in 1943, were a modernised version of a class of four introduced in 1930, and one of the earliest designs of the 4−8−4 type in the USA. They were needed primarily for the difficult 152-mile section through the Cumberland Mountains between Nashville and Chattanooga. They were very powerful engines, with cylinders 25 in. diameter by 30 in. stroke, 5 ft 10 in. diameter coupled wheels, and carrying a boiler pressure of 250 lbs per sq. in. The railway itself was known familiarly as the 'Dixie Line', and its principal expresses were the 'Dixie Limited', the 'Dixie Flyer', and the 'Dixie Flagler'. Because of the difficulties of the route, however, the booked average speeds were not high. The fastest run was that of the 'Dixie Flagler' from Nashville to Tullahoma, 70·5 miles in 75 minutes. The 'J 3' class 4−8−4s were very handsome engines, adorned with copper-capped chimneys and the running plate valences painted yellow. They earned the nickname of the 'Yellow Jackets'.

When I was in Louisville in June 1977 the huge new Strawberry Yard had just been brought into full commission. Its homely nickname is derived from the previous use of the 357-acre site, known as the 'Strawberry Patch'. Now it contains the most modern mechanised marshalling yard in the USA. British readers familiar with the closing of several relatively modern yards in Great Britain may question whether the installation of plants like 'Strawberry' is fully justified — and I shall have several more to mention before this journey round America is finished. But as I watched the almost continuous procession of cars going up and over the hump, and saw the different ownership, I appreciated perhaps as never before the need for these great modern yards. Through Strawberry Yard come cars from literally a thousand different places, destined to journey to as many more. As an L. & N. man put it to me, for just a few seconds each of them has the stage to itself, because they come over the hump singly. Every day from sunrise to sunset around 2000 cars go 'up and over' — gondolas, box cars, hoppers, flats and tankers — and are separated out from one train and made up into others. And all through the night, under brilliant floodlighting, the process continues. Very little in the way of 'block load' traffic comes through Strawberry — 'solid trains' as they are known in the USA; but I did see two dealt with when I was there. One was a 125-car load from Cincinnati to New Orleans, which arrived at 10 a.m. and was away again at 10.52. The second was from Birmingham (Alabama) to Cincinnati, which put off only one car; it arrived at 11.05 a.m. and left at 11.55. In addition to Strawberry there are big yards on the L. & N. at Atlanta, Birmingham, Cincinnati and Nashville, and on the Seaboard Coast Line at Hamlet (North Carolina), Rice, and Waycross (Georgia).

When the time came for me to leave this absorbing manifestation of modern railway engineering, and take the Amtrak 'Floridian' back to Chicago, I felt for a moment that I was stepping down from a colossus

121

to something very small in the total operating scene, though certainly designated a 'first class' train. But I had the privilege of a cab pass, and there is nothing to equal such a viewing point for getting the 'feel' of a busy railroad. The first hour out of Louisville was in many ways a classic example of American operation. In English railway literature the case used often to be quoted of fast express trains in America running down the main streets of large cities, at walking pace, after a long spell at 70 m.p.h. or more in open country. Leaving Louisville we had much running at no more than 5 m.p.h., stops at unprotected level crossings, and a signal stop to collect orders. We crossed an enormous southbound freight powered by six locomotives, and at times we also were making our way cautiously down the middle of a highway. We crossed the large single-tracked bridge over the Ohio River, getting a glimpse of one of those marvellously picturesque river steamers with the paddle wheels at the stern, and then we headed down no more than a narrow lane between country dwellings, where the locomotive and the cars behind us almost brushed the hedges on either side. Imagine having six-engined freights pulling 150 cars passing along the road at the bottom of one's garden! A board near the lineside said 'Doghouses for Sale'. So we took 43½ minutes to cover the first 14½ miles, to Vernia, and just beyond we were stopped again briefly because of a signal failure; but then we were really passing out into the country, and on good track we soon began to cover the miles.

Before Borden we reached 64 m.p.h. but we were slowed through the passing track there to cross the second section of the southbound freight we had passed earlier, and then had a stiff climb to follow, past Pekin. Our diesel could have made quite fast time here with a load of only seven cars, but for the most part we were doing around 40 m.p.h. Our engineer told me we were closing up on a northbound freight. The line is signalled on the 'absolute-permissive block' system; the 'permissive' semaphore signals have pointed ends, as distinct from the fishtail ends of 'distant' signals leading to an absolute block signal, and we were getting a succession of them in the horizontal or warning position. At one crossing loop we passed another lengthy southbound freight, but then ahead we sighted what our engineer had been expecting — the tail of the train we were following under our permissive caution signals. We were then running at about 20 m.p.h.

and its caboose was no more than a quarter of a mile ahead. Then coming on to a straight stretch we saw he was being put into a passing track, the entry to which was protected by a colour light signal. The dispatcher, many, many miles away, must have been watching the movements intently on his illuminated track diagram, because in no more than seconds — or so it seems — after the caboose had cleared the facing points the switches were reset, and the signal reading over them changed from red to green for us to go ahead on the main track. It was a very smart piece of operation.

And now we really began to run. For ten miles we averaged exactly 70 m.p.h. with the fastest mile at 73·5 m.p.h. But we had to slow down to 30 m.p.h. through Mitchell, where there is a grade crossing with the Baltimore and Ohio, and afterwards the track is more curving beside the west fork of White River. The miles here were covered at 50·7, 54·5 and 48 m.p.h. We had an order to meet the southbound Amtrak, and at Sand Pit we headed into a side track to wait for it. We had a long wait, but in pleasant company and in beautiful country the time passed quickly enough, though when we were under way again and passing down the main street of Bedford the last 3¾ miles had taken 28 minutes. The rest of the run to Bloomington included many speed restrictions. The track is very winding; we were crossing and recrossing a narrow creek, and just before entering the town we passed another big northbound freight — 160 cars and 3 locomotives. As we came into Bloomington, and driving down the middle of the main street, automobiles were passing on both sides; pedestrians were crossing in front of us, and two men crossed carrying a heavy piece of domestic furniture. All the animation of a busy country town was there ahead of this very long–distance express train. The 109 miles from Louisville had taken 3 hrs 43 min., an average of only 29·5 m.p.h. Our schedule time was 3 hrs 20 min. and our lateness of 52 minutes leaving Louisville had now become 75 minutes. The loss of time was amply explained by the delays we had experienced. Our locomotive was a General Motors 'E 8' class, of 2250 horsepower.

My spell on the locomotive ended at Bloomington and I enjoyed the next stage of the journey from the train and the dining car. The 103 miles on to Lafayette were allowed 2 hrs 40 min., but there is plenty of margin for recovery there, and we picked up no less than 40 minutes, doing the run in the level two hours. At times we were running at about 75 m.p.h. It was getting dark by the time we left Lafayette. There was a stop for crew change shortly after leaving, and after passing Monon the feature of the journey that left the most lasting impression was the almost incessant whistling for grade crossings. There were numerous checks, but again there seemed to be ample recovery margin in the schedule, because we were still 40 minutes late on leaving Lafayette, but arrived in Chicago exactly on time, 118 miles in 2 hrs 50 min., an average speed, inclusive of all checks and stops, of 41·5 m.p.h. So ended, in this precision, a very interesting visit to the Louisville and Nashville Railroad.

CHAPTER TEN

Chicago — the greatest rail centre

The oft-quoted claim of Chicago to be the greatest railway centre in the world could be substantiated if one did no more than count the number of different companies, the trains of which enter the city. Even after the mergers that have taken place in recent years there are still fourteen, and if one separated out the large and powerful constituents of Conrail, there would be sixteen. This refers only to main line companies, and does not include the several local lines operating around Chicago itself. The fourteen lines are:

Atchison, Topeka and Santa Fe
Baltimore and Ohio
Burlington Northern
Chesapeake and Ohio
Chicago, Milwaukee, St Paul and Pacific
Chicago and Illinois Midland
Chicago and North Western
Chicago, Rock Island and Pacific
Conrail:
    (a) Erie Lackawanna
    (b) New York Central
    (c) Pennsylvania
Families Lines (L. & N. — Monon)
Grand Trunk Western
Illinois Central Gulf
Norfolk and Western (Wabash section)
Soo Line

    I was aware of the great volume of freight traffic moving into and out of the city, but in the time at my disposal I chose to look at the workings around a city where passenger traffic is heavy, and where five of the lines entering the city centre are heavily involved with commuter traffic. These five are the Burlington, the I.C.G., the Milwaukee, the North Western, and the Rock Island. The Chicago and North Western commuter trains, made up of fine double-decker cars, leave from the northern side of the Union Station, where the line is literally overshadowed by a dramatic array of skyscrapers. It is an historic section too — the first railroad built west of Chicago. The Galena and Chicago Union Railroad was indeed chartered as early as 1836, but the first train did not run until twelve years later. The Chicago and North Western itself was formed in 1859, and in 1864 it absorbed the pioneer Galena line. I travelled out to Lombard on a Sunday afternoon, when the traffic was naturally very light; but it gave a good opportunity to see to the best advantage the numerous interesting features of the line.

Unlike most American railroads the C. & N.W. run on the left-hand track. The signals leaving Chicago are of the three position electric upper quadrant semaphore type and the entire main line from Chicago to Omaha, 488 miles, is protected by automatic train control. Before the second world war the C. & N.W. in partnership with the Union Pacific put on the celebrated 'City' streamlined trains. The first, in 1935, was the 'City of Portland', and this was followed by the 'City of San Francisco', the 'City of Los Angeles', and the 'City of Denver'. They used to cover the 138 miles from Chicago to Clinton (Iowa) in 121 minutes, start to stop. In the years of recession after the end of the war these trains were withdrawn, and the only passenger service between Chicago and San Francisco is now worked over the Burlington route as far as Omaha, and there transferred to the Union Pacific. On the way out to Lombard, on this main route to the west, I was interested to see work to eliminate a very busy highway crossing, at Elmhurst. An underpass was under construction, and to enable the necessary excavation to be made on the line of the railroad the tracks had been temporarily slewed. The bridge was being built over the excavation, without the need for any interference with railroad traffic, other than the imposition of a speed restriction over the sharply curved deviation line.

126

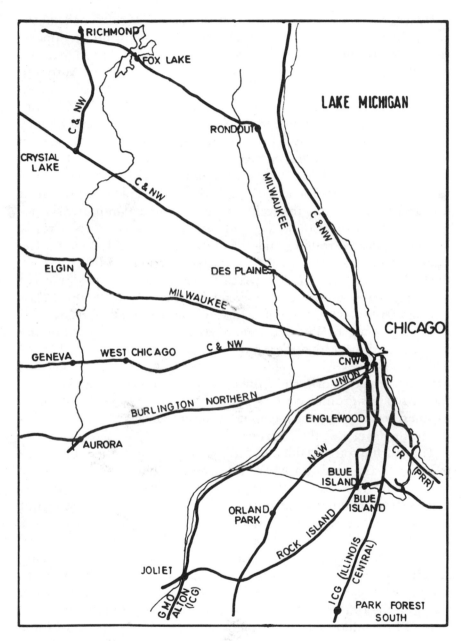

16. Chicago—the commuter routes

My short trip out to Lombard on the C. & N.W. was made in the course of a social visit, but I was able to study the commuter operations of the Burlington Northern in some depth. This line, like the C. & N.W., began in a modest way, with a 12-mile line from Aurora to West Chicago, beyond which this little company, the Aurora Branch Railroad, had trackage rights for 30 miles over the C. & N.W. into Chicago itself. In 1864 however the Chicago, Burlington and Quincy Railroad completed its own line, to establish joint usage of the Union terminal station. Aurora then became the outer terminal of the commuter service that the C.B. & Q. began to develop. The pattern of service began to develop as early as 1869, two years before the great fire, and it is interesting to recall how different that commuter service was, in respect of locomotives and rolling stock, from the already intense operations round London and other large English cities. The British companies used small tank engines, variously of the 2−4−0, 0−4−2, 0−4−4 and 0−6−0 types to haul long close-coupled trains of 4-wheeled cars, all of the compartment type, but in the third class having partitions extending little higher than the 'small of the back' of a seated passenger. With the seats of bare board, and devoid of any internal adornment, they were humorously referred to as 'dog-boxes'! The locomotives were all highly embellished with much polished brass and copper-work, and gaily painted, and the less complacent of the passengers grumbled that some of the artistic work and devoted cleaning bestowed on the locomotives might well have been transferred to the insides of the carriages.

The Burlington certainly had some highly decorative and well-polished locomotives on its commuter runs, but these were of the almost universal 'American' type, 4−4−0 with outside cylinders, cowcatchers and huge headlamps, just as if the train was heading out into some of the darkest and wildest prairie regions. The cars were large bogie vehicles, with handsomely styled clerestory roofs, and entrances only from the end platforms. It would have been an amazing contrast to set one of the South London locals headed by a bright yellow Stroudley 'terrier' 0−6−0 alongside one of these Burlington trains on the run from Aurora into Chicago. One thing they would have had in common; the Westinghouse air brake — a point of some significance on both roads. In the USA George Westinghouse carried

PLATE I

1   Baltimore and Ohio,
one of the 'President' class
4–6–2s as now preserved.

2   Chesapeake and Ohio, 4–6–2
No. 490 as first modernised and
streamlined: now preserved in this
form at Baltimore.

3   Baltimore: Mount Clare
station, preserved, forming
entrance to the Museum in
the roundhouse in rear.

PLATE 2

1 B. & O. in 1949: the 'Cincinnatian' passing through Rowlesburg, West Virginia, hauled by a dark blue streamlined 4–6–2 No. 5301.

2 C. & O.: one of the giant Allegheny-type 2–6–6–6 articulateds, with an eastbound block coal train.

3 The Chessie Steam Special, with ex-Reading 4–8–4 No. 2101.

1   One of the Reading Company's express passenger 4–6–2 locomotives
of 1918 design.

2   Reading Company 2–8–0 heavy freight engine of the type rebuilt into
4–8–4 mixed traffic units, of which the preserved 2101 is one.

PLATE 3

3   The Chessie Steam Special at full speed, near Cumberland.

1 Union station, Los Angeles.

PLATE 4 Contrasts in Station Architecture

2 Pennsylvania station, New York.

1   Streamlined passenger 4–8–4 No. 600; Class 'A' 2–6–6–4 fast freight No. 1203, and 2–8–8–2 Mallet compound mineral engine No. 2123 alongside.

PLATE 5   Norfolk & Western Heavy Steam Power

2   Block load coal train, hauled by Mallet compound 2–8–8–2 No. 2141.

1 Williamson, West Virginia, Norfolk & Western, in steam days.

PLATE 6   Locomotive Servicing Facilities

2 Southern Pacific: West Colton Yard, California, diesel service area.

PLATE 7

1   Bridges at Harpers
Ferry, Baltimore and
Ohio main line.

2   Looking across the
Illinois Central bridge
over the Ohio River,
near Cairo.

1   Coal train for shipment from Norfolk, hauled by 'A' class 2–6–6–4 No. 1226.

2   Mixed freight crossing bridge at Narrows, Virginia, hauled by two diesels.

PLATE 9

1 Grade crossing of the Illinois Central Gulf and Louisiana & Arkansas near New Orleans.

2 I.C.G. bridge over the Ohio River, near Cairo.

3 Hells Gate bridge, former Pennsylvania RR, across the East River, New York.

PLATE 10

1 Illinois Central
six-axle diesel-electric
locomotive.

2 Leading unit of the
Milwaukee six-unit
helper, described in
Chapter 20.

3 Leading unit of the
Amtrak 'Southwest
Limited', Santa Fe route,
at Albuquerque.

PLATE 11

1 Illinois Central Gulf
'Piggyback' units on
trailer at New Orleans.

2 A rake of triple-deck
auto-carrying trailers
being humped at
Strawberry Yard, near
Louisville, Kentucky.

3 Triple-engined coal train on the Norfolk & Western near Martin's
County, Kentucky.

PLATE 12 Famous
Locos of the South

1   The *General*, hero of
the 'Great Locomotive
Chase'.

2   Nashville,
Chattanooga & St Louis,
one of the 'Yellow
Jacket' 4–8–4s of 1943.

3   Louisville &
Nashville, heavy freight
2–8–4 No. 1954.

PLATE 13   Spacious Modern
Yards

I   Strawberry, near Louisville,
Family Lines System.

2   Northtown Yard, near St
Paul, Burlington Northern.

1 Train of 1890 hauled by 'American' type 4–4–0 No. 25.

PLATE 14 Chicago: commuting on the Burlington

2 Modern diesel-hauled double-deck train.

PLATE 15 Chicago: modern
commuter travel

1 Out in the suburbs.

2 Leaving Union station, by
night.

PLATE 16
Rehabilitation on the
Rock Island

1 The rail lifter in
operation.

2 Inserting new ties
(sleepers).

3 The inspection car
(right).

out some of his more important later tests on the grade at West Burlington, while in England the London Brighton and South Coast Railway was one of the first to standardise the air brake.

The epoch-marking trials that were conducted on the Chicago, Burlington and Quincy Railroad in 1886-7 had nothing to do with commuter traffic, or indeed with passenger trains at all. The problem was with lengthy freight trains, and it was so fundamental, and the future of railroad operation in the USA so bound up with its outcome, that the invention of the quick-action triple-valve by George Westinghouse, provided a solution — if not for all time, but good for many years thereafter — which has rightly been described as an epoch, not only in the history of the brake, but in the history of land transportation. And this event, or chain of events, belongs very much to the Burlington, because the trials were conducted on the steep gradient leading westwards from the crossing of the Mississippi River on the main line to Omaha and Denver.

Westinghouse had developed his original air brake into the automatic version incorporating his first triple-valve following his first visit to England, in 1871, and the effectiveness of this had been demonstrated beyond any doubt in trials against a host of competitors at Newark, in England, in 1875. It had become well-established in the USA before that, in passenger train service; but even after another ten years there was no kind of continuous automatic brake in use on freight trains in the USA. It is true that certain roads that had mountain grades, including the Rio Grande, the Northern Pacific, the Santa Fe, and the Union Pacific, were so equipped but the trains were then not very long, and the wide interchange of freight cars between companies that I referred to in the previous chapter when writing of Strawberry Yard had barely commenced. Even so, the casualty list from freight train brakemen running along the top of box cars to apply hand-brakes was sufficiently high to lead to a great and fast-growing agitation to obviate the dangers involved. In the first series of Burlington trials the automatic air brake, with the original form of triple-valve, was up against several competitors; and while it had been adequate on relatively short passenger trains, and proved satisfactory to a point in ordinary service applications on lengthy freight trains of fifty cars or more, any emergency application produced violent shocks towards the rear end of the train. Recorders were shot the length of the observation car and at least one man had his leg broken. The Committee, reporting to the Master Car Builders Association, was not amused!

Westinghouse had to try again. The trouble lay in the sequential action of the brake down the train, with the reduction of air pressure in the main train pipe triggering off the action of the triple valves on each vehicle one after the other. On a 50-car train, even with an emergency application, it would be twenty seconds after the operation of the engineer's valve before the brakes were applied on the rearmost car, and with the amount of slack that existed in the couplings, there would be an almighty crash when the brakes did go on. Rivals of the air brake urged the introduction of electrical equipment, to provide instantaneous application of the brakes on every car. It was prophetic of a development that was to come several decades later, but in the 1880s Westinghouse had no faith in its practicability. He used to say: 'a freight car has no father or mother'. In other words it wandered about in common usage all over the continent, lying idle for days on end, used anywhere. It was not so much the system as the maintenance that worried him. When during the Burlington trials his rivals using an electrically controlled brake had a complete failure because of a broken wire, it encouraged him to persist, and the quick-action triple valve eventually provided the triumphant answer. The time of propagation of the brake action from front to rear of a 50-car train was reduced to six seconds, making stops with no jar in the 50th car great enough to upset a glass of water.

While this vital development was being consummated on the Burlington road, 200 miles out to the west, the Chicago commuter services were rapidly developing, and did much to stimulate the growth of population in the suburbs to west and south-west of the city. As the development progressed and the requirements for rolling stock, traffic control, and safety equipment grew more intense, so the C.B. & Q. began to experience the economic situation common to all intensely worked commuter activities, namely that a great amount of expensive, highly sophisticated equipment had to be provided for usage during relatively brief periods during the morning and evening peak periods. For the rest of the day and night much of the rolling stock lay idle, and the track facilities were much under-utilised. Against the general growth of the railroad, however, and its operations over nearly 10,000 miles of route, from the Great Lakes to the Rocky Mountains, and from Montana to the Gulf of Mexico, the operational deficit on the Chicago commuter services passed virtually unnoticed. It was when the depression came in the 1930s, and still worse when the general recession in passenger business began in years after the second world war that the situation became high-lighted. Chicago suburban was not a traffic that could be cast away to the highways or the air. It had to continue.

The Burlington worked hard to attract more business. In August 1950 it introduced the first double-deck, air-conditioned cars. Traction was still by steam at that time, and no one could accuse Burlington of being over-lavish with its allocation of power. No more than twenty-four steam locomotives were used for the service over a 38-mile line with twenty-six suburban stations, and in 1952 the C.B. & Q. became the first railroad in the USA to dieselise its commuter operation completely, replacing the twenty-four steam locomotives by nineteen diesels. There are now 119 of the huge double-deck stainless-steel cars; they each seat a total of 148 passengers, and are entered only by sliding doors in the centre of the lower level. Motive power is provided by diesel-electric locomotives of 'first generation' nose-cab type that have been modified for 'push-pull' operation. On the outward-bound runs the locomotive pulls the train in the ordinary way, but it is not uncoupled at the terminal. On the inward-bound run it propels the train, and is remotely controlled from an engineer's cab on the leading car. The fastest of the commuter trains cover the 38 miles between Chicago and Aurora in 51 minutes, inclusive of two intermediate stops.

Between Chicago and Aurora the main line is triple-tracked. It is extensively used by freight trains, as well as by the commuter services, and the signalling and control arrangements have recently been completely modernised. The entire 38-mile section has been brought under the surveillance and control of a centralised traffic control plant, at Aurora. The signalling is such that any one of the three tracks can be used for trains running in either direction. There are frequent facilities for crossing trains from one track to either of the other two, and the

131

control console is built in the form of a 'U', so that the dispatcher seated at the centre always has an up to the minute picture of the train working position on this critical section of line. The locomotives are fitted with automatic cab-signalling equipment, so that the engineers are informed of track conditions ahead, while two-way radios enable train crews to communicate instantly with dispatchers, and with the crews of other trains.

The growth of the western suburbs of Chicago brought some increase in traffic on the railroad, but any advantage was at first counteracted by the completion of fast new expressways, which attracted traffic onto the highways. And all the time Burlington was confronted in ever more acute form with the universal handicap of commuter services; the low utilisation of the elaborate facilities for the heavy working during the peaks. An increase in traffic, creating demands for more cars, more locomotives, new stations and larger car-parking areas at the outer terminals, did not supply the money to pay for large capital expenditure, and it was realised that to make large increases in fares would be to discourage travel. For the services to be continued at high efficiency nothing short of a substantial subsidy would be required. The passing by Congress of the Urban Mass Transportation Act, however, made possible the granting of federal funds to officially formed Mass Transit Districts, which were organisations formed with representatives of suburban communities and the railroads concerned, and in August 1970 the West Suburban Mass Transit District was formed, representing ten communities and the former Chicago, Burlington and Quincy Railroad.

The effect was striking. In 1972 Federal and State Department of Transportation grants of $35·8 million were approved to purchase another twenty-five double-deck cars, and to modernise completely the existing rolling stock. It was one of the conditions of the grant that ownership of the existing cars and locomotives should be transferred to the West Suburban Mass Transit District. This provided the local share of the project cost. It enabled further modernisation to take place; more cars to be purchased; more locomotives to be rebuilt. Between 1970 and 1974 the number of passengers per annum, what in the USA is called the ridership, went up from 9,671,312 to 12,098,943. But it was still a case of deficit budgeting. The net loss in

1975 was nearly five times what it was in 1970, and amounted to more than $3·5 million. The mass transport of commuters however had just got to go on, and in 1974 a Regional Transportation Authority was set up. The R.T.A. has imposed service, maintenance and operating standards and has jurisdiction over fares, train schedules and the co-ordination of Burlington Northern service with that of other operators. In exchange it provides annual operating subsidies, and assumes certain capital responsibilities. This is certainly one way of dealing with the festering sore of commuter railroading finance!

When one looks at a map of Lake Michigan, and particularly the coastline of its south-west corner, and sees the number of different railroads swarming in to converge in Chicago, it can well be appreciated why the city was called the greatest railroad centre in the world. In labelling this map I have used the older names before the recent mergers, to show, for example, where the New York Central and the Pennsylvania came in; to show the track of the Erie, of the

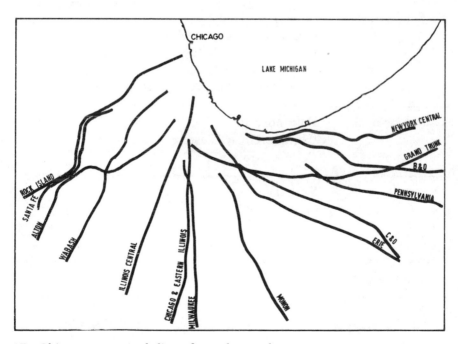

17. Chicago—approach lines from the south

Gulf, Mobile and Ohio which in its turn was the Chicago and Alton before absorption, and also of the Monon and the Wabash. Under the auspices of Amtrak all main line services are now concentrated at Union station, but the commuter services of the Illinois Central still arrive at and depart from the historic site on the Lake Front. When he visited the city in 1912, J. P. Pearson, that great traveller and indefatigable notetaker, considered the Chicago and North Western station to be one of the finest in the world. How he would regard the Chicago stations shown on the map on page 127 is a matter of conjecture. The usage of the others was then as follows:

Union:	Pennsylvania
	Chicago and Alton
	Chicago, Burlington & Quincy
	Chicago, Milwaukee, St Paul & Pacific
La Salle Street:	New York Central
	Chicago and Eastern Illinois
	Lake Shore & Michigan Southern
	Chicago, Rock Island & Pacific
	New York, Chicago and St Louis
Grand Central:	Baltimore and Ohio
	Chicago Great Western
	Pere Marquette
Dearborn:	Santa Fe
	Grand Trunk
	Erie
	Wabash
Illinois Central:	Illinois Central

Pearson fairly let himself go in describing the C. & N.W. station.

The chief glory of Chicago in the way of railway depots, at the time of my visit, was the terminus of the Chicago and North Western line. I write 'line' advisedly, as this railway refers to itself in advertisements as 'The North Western Line'. Built in 1911, it clearly ranks with the Pennsylvania depot in New York and the Union depot in Washington and is undoubtedly one of the finest stations in the world. I fortunately saw it when almost new and it looked wonderfully spick and span. The frontage slightly recalls that of the Pennsylvania New York depot, but is shorter and rather higher. One enters a small arcade from the street and at the end of it is a stairway to the upper concourse or main waiting room. Before ascending to this, we examine the lower concourse, which, on the same level as the arcade, is most roomy and is surrounded by — on the short sides, a lunch room and druggist's shop to left and another entrance to the concourse on the right, and on the long sides, telegraph and ticket offices on one and baggage and parcels on the other.

The roof of this lower course is rather low, but the whole effect is very fine, with the many supporting pillars and the curious flattened circular roof. We now go higher to the main waiting room — a most magnificent and lofty space with walls of whitish-brown stone and an arched roof in white stone and enamelled bricks, supported by superb green polished granite pillars, very massive in appearance. The base of these pillars is gilded, harmonizing well with the green. To the left of this spacious and splendid concourse we find the dining room, while to the right, in the corners only, and opposite one another (thus narrowing the width of the concourse) are a bookstall and a barber's shop. More than 30 long benches of polished brown wood give ample seating accommodation here for waiting passengers.

From this main waiting room, or upper concourse, a series of large folding doors, green in colour (but darker than the great pillars and with metal decorative work) give access to a rather narrow but lofty space — very neat in appearance, finished in green enamelled bricks and with cream white pillars — off which the train platforms open directly. This narrow concourse, which has exits to the street in green and white tiles, can also be reached by stairway from the lower one, and each of the 16 platforms opening from it is furnished with a very neat train indicator, and just inside the entrance to these a luggage lift provides accommodation from below. Unfortunately there is no grand single roof span over the platforms, but only a series of what, I think, are called 'Bush' roof screens — very neat it is true — but only such as we might expect at some wayside junction of importance.

The Chicago and North Western Station, later known as Madison Street station, evidently impressed Pearson far more than it did Carroll L. V. Meeks, when he wrote his architectural history of railway stations. While he has a good deal to say about Grand Central, Dearborn, and Illinois Central, he does not even mention it, except in criticism, and only a passing reference to the older station it replaced:

From the viewpoint of the traveller, the most regrettable arrangement is one in which the tracks are above street level and the connection from the waiting room is by staircases. This unfortunate arrangement persisted in stations like the North Western in Chicago (1906-1911), and culminated in gigantic flights of stairs at Milan.

As regards great arched roofs Meeks comments:

The great days of the train shed were coming to a close. The railroad companies, finding them very costly to maintain, began to feel toward them as an elderly gentleman feels towards the fading but still extravagant mistress of his youth. This attitude grew up at the moment when the justification for such heavy expense was suddenly eliminated by Lincold Bush's new type of shed. Another contributing factor was the reappearance of electrification, which permitted tracks and platforms to be depressed directly underneath the head-house, thus eliminating the need for any shed whatever.

As a passenger, rather than a student of railway station architecture, I must admit that my recollections of the Union station in Chicago are not of the happiest. There is a central concourse 320 ft by 200 ft on to which butt twenty terminal tracks, supplemented by three through lines. This layout is all below street level and is reached by staircases and cab-drives. Waiting rooms, offices and other facilities are contained in a second block of buildings connected to the concourse by a tunnel. The approach to the platforms is dismal, especially when a crowd of passengers is kept queued up interminably, in a confined, low-roofed area in sweltering heat, waiting for the barriers to be opened. The platform area is like a dark and none-too-clean carriage shed, and were it not for the jostling haste in which one eventually boards the train the European traveller might find himself yearning for the airy spaciousness of the 'train shed' at Paddington, the Gare de Lyon, or Frankfurt-am-Main. It was rather an intimidating start to a journey on a train with the distinguished history of 'The Broadway Limited' — though probably in the opulent days of the Pennsylvania Railroad passengers were not herded like sheep prior to departure. In taking over the long-distance passenger business of nearly all the American railroads at a more than critical point in the financial fortunes — or misfortunes! — of some of them Amtrak had a difficult task, and in the subtler arts of customer relations we can no doubt look forward to great improvements in the future.

The Illinois Central terminus, on the Lake Front, completed in 1893, was the work of Bradford Gilbert, and was in the Romanesque style, and Carroll Meeks considered it his masterpiece. He writes:

The metropolitan site and an ample budget permitted him to surpass his previous efforts. There are four main elements: train shed, tower, office building, and waiting room. The latter, in the form of an arched train shed, is a clear instance of the metamorphosis of the train shed with another element of the station complex. This noble room is placed on the second floor over the tracks, so that passengers are required to climb up to it and then descend again to the tracks. Louis Sullivan made an apt criticism of this type of plan, presumably with reference to this station: 'My son, here is the place — perhaps a unique spot on earth — holy in iniquity, where to go in you go out, and to go out you go in; where to go up you go down, and to go down you go up. All in all it seems to me the choicest fruit yet culled from that broad branch of the tree of knowledge, known as the public-be-damned style'. The waiting room was elaborately decorated, perhaps partially to compensate for this inconvenience. It had a mosaic floor, marble wainscoting, and stuccoed ceiling studded with incandescent lights. At the end towards the lake there was a huge arched window recalling that of the Gare de l'Est (in Paris) but transformed with cathedral glass set in rich and glowing colors.

This fascinating period piece among American railroad terminals was the departure point of the Illinois Central crack express trains for the south for seventy-nine years, and on 5 March 1972 the familiar call of 'All Aboard' was sounded for this last time. On the following day, under the Amtrak banner, Illinois Central trains began running out of the Union station. All that is now left of the one-time I.C. major terminal are the suburban line platforms, now named Randolph Street station. All the old buildings have been torn down, and the site levelled to make a parking area, like some famous British railway landmarks of old. But the present operations of Illinois Central Gulf on the Lake Front are not without distinction. The company operates the only electric double-deck commuter cars in America. As with the Burlington Northern the I.C.G. is connected with a Mass Transit District, in this case the Chicago South, and in 1968 the Department of Transportation approved a grant of $25·2 million to provide for two-thirds of the purchase price of 130 new double-decker air-conditioned suburban cars. Each of them is self-propelled, with each of the four axles being powered by a 160 horsepower motor. These huge cars are 85 ft long and have a maximum speed of 75 m.p.h. The seating capacity is 156 per car, and although each car is self-powered, they are coupled to make a maximum train length of six cars in the peak periods. They are maintained at the Woodcrest shops, adjacent to Markham North and South marshalling yard.

CHAPTER ELEVEN

The Rock and farther west

In the late 1930s the land between Chicago and the crossing of the Missouri River at Omaha was one of the greatest railroad racing grounds in the whole of America. Four companies operated fast express trains over this stretch, and one of them, the 'Burlington Zephyr' was one of the fastest trains in the world. Then there was the Chicago and North Western, in partnership with the Union Pacific in running the celebrated 'City' streamliners, and also the Milwaukee. The fourth competitor, and second only to the Burlington in speed was the Chicago, Rock Island and Pacific, with its diesel-powered 'Rockets', one of which had a run over the 44·3 miles from Joliet to Ottawa (Illinois) in 36 minutes, an average speed of 73·8 m.p.h. start to stop. But in the years of recession that set in so severely after the end of the second world war, the Rock Island was afflicted more heavily than most railroads west of Chicago.

It is important to appreciate what it was in the first place that drove the Rock Island into bankruptcy and near-collapse. Essentially this railroad had many miles of light density lines through country given up entirely to farming. Its service was very important to states like Iowa, Kansas, and Oklahoma, in which Rock Island routes form some of the principal lines of communication. On the other hand, it was not only between Chicago and the Missouri River that the railroad faced severe competition on its busiest routes. Between Chicago and Kansas City there was stiff competition from the Santa Fe, and the north to south run from Kansas City to Houston was similarly involved. In most competitive cases the Rock Island had the disadvantage of not being the shortest route, though it certainly enjoyed the easiest gradients. Faced with postwar inflation and road haulage competition, its

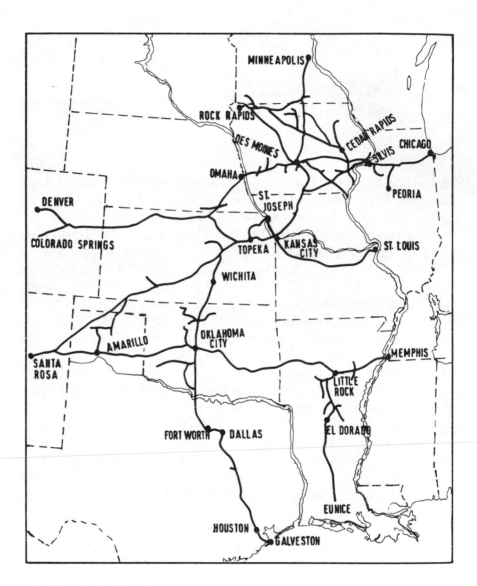

18. The Rock Island system

net income declined steadily from 1953, and from 1966 onwards it dropped deeper and deeper into default.

In 1964 an amalgamation between Rock Island and the Union Pacific was proposed, and according to American business law, application for permission to merge was made to the Interstate Commerce Commission. Such a proposal was interesting, and rather cut across the existing alignment of the Union Pacific with the Chicago and North Western. If the U.P.-R.I. merger had gone forward there is little doubt that the Union Pacific transcontinental trains would have been transferred to Rock Island tracks east of Omaha. The proposal did indeed spark off a whole series of inter-industry disputes, and counter-proposals; while as usual the wheels of bureaucratic progress ground very slowly. In the meantime the Rock Island was being slowly beaten down to its knees. Funds were scarce; little was available for maintenance of rolling stock or track, and running speeds fell far below old-time standards. Business concerns transferred their traffic elsewhere, and with further rapid deterioration it seemed that the Rock would not survive. When eventually I.C.C. approved the merger, late in 1974, it was too late. The situation on the Rock Island had deteriorated to such an extent that the Union Pacific no longer wanted it!

Early in 1975 it seemed that the railroad was on the brink of dissolution. Investigations showed that it would soon run out of cash to pay wages and buy the diesel fuel. But a determined trustee, vigorous management, and a staff loyal to the extent of accepting desperate, even brutal measures to stop the cash drain, stopped the financial bleeding, and by July of 1975 the cash flow had turned positive. The management could then turn to plans for reorganising and rebuilding the railroad. A loan of $17·5 million secured by Trustee Certificates guaranteed by the United States Department of Transportation was obtained, for rehabilitation on what has been called the 'spine of the Rock Island' — the main line from Chicago, through Kansas City to Fort Worth, Texas. When the programme for my tour of American railroads was being schemed out the Rock Island gave me a special invitation to see some of the work in progress on the main line across the state of Illinois, and I spent a remarkable day out on the line. I must admit, however, that when Ted Zirbes, Manager of

141

public relations, asked me to call early at his office in South Michigan Avenue, Chicago, I had little idea of what was in store for me. I met J. F. Scheumack, Director of Engineering Programs, who was to be my guide and philosopher for the day — and what a day!

Outside that most elegant of business addresses in Chicago, looking out across Grant Park to the Lake Shore Drive, was a little rail-car, similar to the one in which I had travelled from New Orleans to Hammond, and in this Mr Scheumack and I set off for Joliet. The Santa Fe, and the Gulf, Mobile and Ohio section of I.C.G. also pass through Joliet and from Chicago their lines follow the course of the Des Plaines River, which we did approximately on the highway; but the Rock Island itself, as will be seen from the maps in the previous chapter, left Chicago in a due-southerly direction, then passing through Blue Island, and turning west after Tinley Park. At Joliet itself the Rock Island crosses the other two railroads to reach the left bank of the river, and it was there that we changed from the highway to the railroad, just forty-seven miles out of Chicago. It had been explained to me that the rehabilitation programme across the state of Illinois was being worked by two separate engineering forces, one working west from Joliet and the other east from Silvis, near Rock Island. Between them they had 134 miles of double-track main line to deal with. Even today, with the work barely started, there are twenty-eight freight trains a day over this section of line.

The first sight of it, from the incomparable viewpoint of the rail-car, was certainly rather daunting. For a main line railroad over which very fast running was once performed, it looked terrible. Weeds were growing in the ballast and between the sleepers; one had only to look along the rails to see how uneven the 'top' was in places, and many of the sleepers themselves were rotted, split, and in some cases broken. To anyone who has railroads at heart it was dreadful to see how lack of funds and diminishing traffic had led to this deterioration. And once such a situation gets its grip the effect snowballs. While Scheumack was showing me a particularly bad piece of track an eastbound freight train approached, a very long one hauled by three diesel-electric locomotives. It was running at no more than 25 m.p.h. — the maximum permitted over lengthy stretches of the line — and to see those huge box cars rocking about as the train trundled along was an

142

eloquent expression of the state the track was in. Scheumack made no bones about it: 'lousy' was the word! Apart from everything else, there was the awful dross that was passing for ballast.

But I saw also the tremendously vigorous work in hand to get the road back to 60 m.p.h. standard. A work force of 200 men formed the tie, surfacing and rehabilitation gangs concentrated on the 134 miles from Joliet to Rock Island, and $5 million out of the $17·5 million made available in Trustee Certificates has been allocated to track renewal on this one section alone. As we made our way westward even our little rail-car did not like the rough track, and at one point we became derailed. Then we came to a section where the sleepers were being renewed. This was a mechanised operation carried out in two stages. First of all a 'rail lifter' is brought along and positioned over a sleeper to be replaced. The spikes had previously been pulled out, and then the rail lifter, strutted against the sleepers, lifts the rail sufficiently for the tie plates to be slid out sideways.

The rail lifter is followed by a remarkable special purpose machine, a kind of travelling crane. The control cabin has attached to it an extending jib, and cabin and jib can be rotated to a position at right-angles to the line. On the jib is a travelling grab which first of all attaches itself to the old sleeper, draws it out from under the rails and throws it aside. Then the end of a new sleeper is grappled, and this is propelled into place beneath the rails. It was a fascinating operation to watch, in the speed and efficiency with which the job was done. At another place we came to one of the large tamping machines, specially designed for packing and consolidating the ballast. The whole job was being undertaken with speed and skill. For the most part the line was in open country running on no more than slight gradients, and I could well imagine that on good track there would have been little difficulty in maintaining the fast passenger train schedules of former days.

Scheumack gave me a plan of the line showing the curves, gradients, and layout of sidings at the intermediate stations. On this section of 134 miles there are grade crossings at Ottawa, just west of La Salle, near Sheffield, and at Rock Island itself. At the western end, over prairie-like country, there is a stretch of forty miles with scarcely a curve. I was interested in the signalling arrangements. Automatic block signals are used for protecting train movements made under timetable and train order system of operation, but on some of the busier sections C.T.C. is installed. Speed signal aspects, using the searchlight type of signal, are used at some stations, as shown in the photograph of the eastbound signals at Bureau, 114 miles from Chicago. So far as the track rehabilitation programme is concerned, when I visited the work they had a gang of 65 men working from Joliet and 135 from Rock Island.

Absorbing as was the nature and extent of the work on this busiest section of the entire railroad, a section which by reason of its importance one would have expected to receive some form of preferential treatment in times of financial stringency, I could not help wondering what some of the remoter parts of the line were like. After all, Rock Island is only 180 miles from Chicago, and the railroad has a total route mileage of 7920. Funds from the $17·5 million loan are being used for attending to the main line through Kansas City to Fort Worth, the latter city being more than 800 miles beyond Rock Island. Another section that was receiving attention was the so-called 'Sunbelt Line', 750 miles between Memphis and Amarillo, Texas. Money

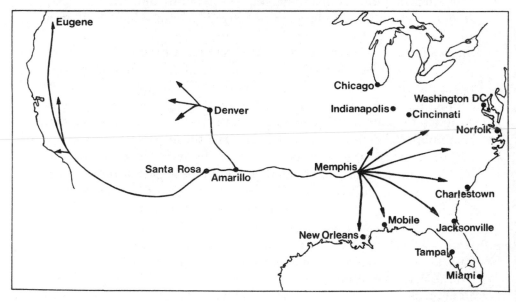

19. The Sunbelt Line, and its strategic connections

for this latter programme was taken from earnings, not borrowings. The accompanying sketch map of the railroad provides some sobering thoughts on the rehabilitation of the railroad as a whole, with its great extent, when the state of its busiest section between Rock Island and Chicago is borne in mind.

But from what I saw on the line, and from what I was told during the short time I was in the head office in Chicago, the whole operation is being tackled with wisdom, skill, and immense enthusiasm. To appreciate how light the traffic is on the remoter parts of the line, I should explain that in the mid-1950s, before the decline set in seriously, the Rock Island had only 429 locomotives, all diesel-electric, to operate its 7920 miles of route; and at that time it was running no fewer than eight 'Rocket' high-speed passenger trains. In a nostalgic look back, in conjunction with the sketch map of the line, these may be recalled, thus:

Name of train	Route
Peoria Rocket	Chicago–Peoria
Des Moines Rocket	Chicago–Des Moines
Corn Belt Rocket	Chicago–Omaha
Rocky Mountain Rocket	Chicago–Denver–Colorado Springs
Twin Star Rocket	Minneapolis–Kansas City–Houston
Texas Rocket	Kansas City–Oklahoma City–Fort Worth–Dallas
Zephyr Rocket	Minneapolis–St Paul–St Louis
Choctaw Rocket	Memphis–Oklahoma City

It is interesting to see that not all these fast trains were based on Chicago. The Rock Island did not enter all its principal passenger destinations on its own track. The approaches to St Paul and Minneapolis, to Memphis, and to Houston were by virtue of trackage rights over short distances, and while the Rock Island reached Colorado Springs on its own road, to Denver it ran for nearly a hundred miles over the Union Pacific, from Limon.

By 1956 the Rock Island had no steam locomotives left; but looking

at a photograph of one of their big, sleek, 4−8−4s of the '5020' class —
surely one of the smoothest, neatest exteriors of all American 4−8−4s
— one could well imagine them thundering along that 40-mile
straight out in the west of Illinois. The road maximum speed for all
steam locomotives on the Rock Island used to be 70 m.p.h. but at one
time the diesels were allowed to run up to 90 m.p.h.

Four Mid-west 4−8−4s

Railroad Date built	Rio Grande 1929	Santa Fe 1929	Burlington 1930	Rock Island 1930
Cylinders dia. in.	27	30	28	26
stroke in.	30	30	30	32
Coupled wheel				
dia. ft in.	5−10	6−1	6−2	5−9
Boiler pressure lbs/sq. in.	240	210	250	250
Total evaporative				
heating sq. ft	4917	5672	5317	5443
Superheater sq. ft	2229	2426	2403	2243
Grate area sq. ft	88	108	106·5	88·3
Tractive force				
main engine lbs	63,700	66,000	67,500	66,000
booster lbs	–	–	–	13,100

Dimensionally it would seem there was not a great deal to choose
between the four, except that the Rock Island class had boosters, no
doubt to permit of rapid acceleration with heavy trains. All were
designated equally for passenger and fast freight service.

Proceeding west, sometimes on the railroad, sometimes on adjacent
highways, I saw the work of renovation in progress: where the
alignment was being adjusted, where crossings and turnouts were
being repaired, and all on a serene day of early summer sunshine. I
enjoyed the talk and mid-west railroad jargon of many Rock Island
men and not least that of my genial host. We had still some way to go
to journey's end — for me that was — when a bit of bad track sent the
rail-car off the road for the second time. We decided to 'call it a day', as
the English expression goes, and once righted, to get on to the
highway for the last stage into Rock Island itself. At one point in the

planning of my trip it had been hoped that I might transfer to the Burlington and continue westward on the 'San Francisco Zephyr'; but to make the interchange would have curtailed my visit to the track works of the Rock Island and so I decided to stay the night at Rock Island itself.

My destination by the next evening was Salt Lake City, and I was sorry to miss the opportunity of travelling over the Union Pacific, though much of it would have been in darkness. But for many years I had studied the locomotive prowess of this great railroad, and if denied the pleasure of riding over its tracks on the mountain section between Cheyenne and Ogden, I was able to see in Salt Lake City and in Denver preserved examples of two of its greatest steam locomotives. The 'FEFI'-class express passenger 4−8−4, of which a magnificent example, the '833', stands on a pedestal outside the station at Salt Lake City, featured in a strenuous series of road tests carried out in 1938 by the Mechanical Division of the Association of American Railroads, to determine the drawbar horsepower required to haul a train of 1000 US tons (907 tons Imperial) at 100 m.p.h. on straight level track. Three types of locomotive were tested on suitable stretches of their own line, namely a Pennsylvania 'K 4' Pacific, of which I have much to say in Chapter Twenty of this book, a Chicago and North Western streamlined 'E 4' class 4−6−4, and the Union Pacific 4−8−4. This last-mentioned engine was the only one of the three to get anywhere near the target speed, and this was attained only down a gradient of 1 in 770. But it was an exceptional assignment, and with lighter loads these fine engines frequently attained speeds of 100 m.p.h. They differed from the Mid-west 4−8−4s mentioned earlier in having smaller cylinders, but used the high boiler pressure of 300 lbs per sq. in. The tractive force was much the same as that of the Burlington and Rock Island 4−8−4s.

It was, however, the fast freight locomotives of the Union Pacific that fairly captured my imagination, and walking around the 'Big Boy' outside the museum in Denver — one of the giant 4−8−8−4s of the '4000' class — the largest steam locomotives ever built, thoughts went back to the days when they ran the road through the Rockies, from Ogden to Green River. That great locomotive artist Terence Cuneo has painted a magnificent picture called simply 'The Gradient', and it shows one of these engines fighting its way up Echo Canyon, Utah, with a heavy freight train. That picture conveys more in the way of all-out railroading than could many pages of description. I have ridden on many large locomotives in different parts of the world but never on one the size of a 'Big Boy'. In cylinder volume alone, whereas the Union Pacific 4−8−4s had two cylinders 24½ in. diameter by 32 in. stroke, the 'Big Boys' had *four*, of the same stroke and only a little less in diameter, 23½·in. Engine and tender together weighed 535 tons — Imperial tons too! — and from his cab the driver had to look ahead past 70 ft of boiler and firebox!! When they were working the 'block' fruit trains eastward from Ogden, Utah — 70 cars, weighing about 3000 tons — one can only guess at the crashing orchestration, on and off the locomotive. Echo Canyon indeed!

It was an extraordinary experience to walk round and climb aboard this vast locomotive. Although designed for heavy grade working, they were essentially *fast* freight units, and were designed with 5 ft 8 in. coupled wheels. The problem of securing stable riding of the large articulated types of locomotive had been solved in the design of the 4−6−6−4s built in 1936 for the Union Pacific which could be safely operated at speeds up to 70 m.p.h.; but with the 4−8−8−4s the provision of a boiler and firebox large enough to make the *nominal* tractive force represented by the cylinders a practical reality presented no small problem with coupled wheels beneath that boiler as large as 5 ft 8 in. It was successfully done, even though the firebox located over the rearmost coupled wheels and the trailing four-wheeled truck was relatively shallow. One thought of the 50 sq. ft grates on some British locomotives as large, but the 'Big Boys' had 150 sq. ft! They steamed well, on thin fires mechanically stoked, and provided ample tractive power. The power rating was 7000 horsepower at 40 m.p.h., but in maximum working conditions their output was sometimes over 7500 horsepower. They ran steadily up to 60 m.p.h. and more on favourable stretches of line.

The mountain section between Ogden (Utah) and Cheyenne (Wyoming) was divided into two for locomotive operating. The total distance is 485 miles and the 'Big Boys', of which there were 25, worked on the western 'half', although this was actually only 160 miles. East of Green River the 4−6−6−4s were used on the faster

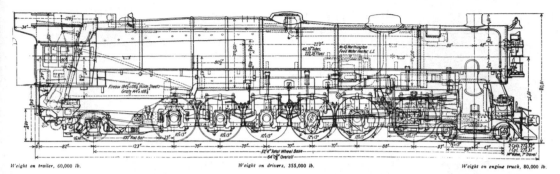

Weight on trailer, 60,000 lb.   *Weight on drivers, 355,000 lb.*   *Weight on engine truck, 80,000 lb.*

20. The Union Pacific 3-cylinder 4–12–2 locomotive of 1926

freight trains. These were also magnificent locomotives, though of smaller capacity than the 'Big Boys'. The Union Pacific had altogether a notable record in freight locomotive development, because in 1926 they had introduced a class of 4−12−2s — twelve coupled! — but unusual in American practice in having three cylinders arranged with the well-known Gresley conjugated valve gear standard on so many classes on the London and North Eastern Railway. The respective dimensions of these three classes of fast freight locomotive make an interesting comparison.

In his book *Railroads at War*, S. Kip Farrington Jr. describes a journey on a block-load fruit train eastbound from Ogden, on which the locomotives were successively of the three types featured in the table:

UNION PACIFIC Fast Freight Types

	1926	1936	1941
Year introduced			
Types	4−12−2	4−6−6−4	4−8−8−4
Cylinders no.	3	4	4
dia. in.	27	22	23¾
stroke in.	32	32	32
Coupled wheel dia. ft in.	5−7	5−9	5−8
Boiler pressure lbs/sq. in.	220	255	300
Total evaporation heating surface sq. ft	5817	5381	5755
Grate area sq. ft	108·3	108·2	150·3

149

UNION PACIFIC Fast Freight Types

	Year introduced	1926	1936	1941
	Types	4−12−2	4−6−6−4	4−8−8−4
Superheater sq. ft		2550	1650	2043
Tractive force lbs		96,600	97,400	135,400
Weight:				
engine tons		221	252	345
tender tons		128	138	194

4−8−8−4 No. 4015 to Green River; 4−6−6−4 No. 3961 to Cheyenne, and then 4−12−2 No. 9056 to North Platte (Nebraska). The author gives little detail of the actual running — not one mention of the speeds attained by the two articulated engines, but the engines were watered and *re-coaled* seven times on the journey. Seeing that the 4−8−8−4, 4−6−6−4 and 4−12−2 carry very large tenders, this suggests a healthy appetite for coal. The only speeds that Farrington quotes are those with the 4−12−2, which on several stretches sustained 50 m.p.h. But while he refers to the 4−6−6−4 as 'a honey of an engine', the 4−12−2 is a 'big mauling freight engine'. Strangely

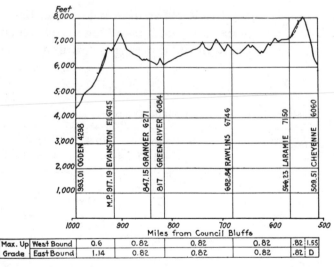

21. Profile of the Union Pacific line between Ogden and Cheyenne

150

enough he gives no impression whatever of what the 'Big Boy' was like to ride, and how she did the job. This is all the more curious because at the time his book was written those engines were featured extensively in the world's railway press.

In climbing out of Ogden (Utah) the line rises 2447 ft in the seventy-six miles to Evanston, an average inclination of 1 in 165; but in Echo Canyon the gradient is 1 in 87 for sixteen miles. Farrington recorded that engine No. 4015 hauling 3200 tons, reached Evanston in 3 hrs 35 min. inclusive of a stop at Echo for twenty-three minutes to take on coal and water. The running time to Evanston therefore was 3 hrs 12 min., an average speed of 24 m.p.h. But the hardest gradient on this mountain section is westbound out of Cheyenne, up the formidable Sherman Hill. Here the line climbs from an altitude of 6060 ft at Cheyenne to 8000 ft in 31 miles, an average inclination of 1 in 84, and including a ruling maximum of 1 in 64. The 'Big Boys' in their later years took freight trains up to about 50 cars, 2000 tons, up Sherman Hill without assistance, but on passenger trains even the latest 4−8−4s used to have a helper when the load was more than 14 cars. The diesel-hauled streamliners of the post-war years like the 'City of Portland', run in conjunction with the Chicago and North Western, required a steam 4−8−4 as helper up the grade from Cheyenne.

Under Amtrak management the one through express train between Chicago and San Francisco, the 'San Francisco Zephyr', takes the Burlington route to Denver, then turns due north to join the Union Pacific main line at Cheyenne. It takes 12½ hours to cover the full 590 miles, and 9¾ hours from Cheyenne. In flying from Denver to Salt Lake City we made a course midway between the Union Pacific and the Rio Grande routes through the mountains, arriving in Salt Lake City in late afternoon. Being then so relatively near to one of the most historic sites on the American railways — Promontory, Utah, where the last spike in the first transcontinental line was driven in 1869 — I had wondered if a quick visit would be possible, a sentimental pilgrimage. After all, what would another hundred miles mean during such an itinerary as that on which I was embarked. But it was scorching hot when we landed in Salt Lake City, and with the prospect of a solid fourteen hours of sightseeing and note-taking on the following

151

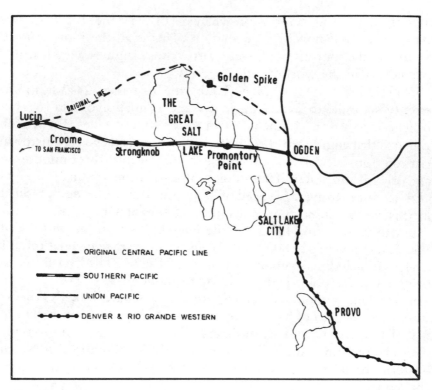

22. Site of the Golden Spike ceremony

day, I decided for a quiet evening, strolling round this interesting city. I had with me a copy of the beautiful photograph my friend Victor Goldberg took of the famous site at Promontory, which at the Centenary of the event in 1969 was created a National Memorial.

Two vintage 4−4−0 locomotives were restored and repainted to represent the actual engines that stood, cowcatcher to cowcatcher, at the 'last spike' ceremony. Now they stand out in the near-desert country, in the blistering sun, and from all accounts their condition is not improving. Perhaps it is as well I did not make the pilgrimage. Because the photograph of the actual 'golden spike' ceremony in 1869 is so familiar, and appears in nearly every book one sees about world railways — not excepting two of my own! — the astonishing technical quality of that photograph is usually overlooked. It is breathtaking! It

152

would be graceless to bemoan the fact that it is not in colour; but had it been so, we might have been saved the widely divergent opinions as to how No. 119 of the Union Pacific, and the *Jupiter* of the Central Pacific were actually painted at the time. I have two 'book-match' covers issued by Alco, showing both locomotives in colour, and while the fabricated-restored *Jupiter* at Promontory corresponds fairly closely to the Alco print, the engine representing No. 119 of the Union Pacific definitely does not. It is finished in an altogether more garish style. In looking at Victor Goldberg's photograph, I was reminded of the world traveller who went to see the Giant's Causeway in Northern Ireland, and remarked: 'It's just like its photograph!' Instead, I walked down to the Rio Grande Station after dinner to look at U.P. No. 833.

I had always regarded these engines, and their counterparts, the '3771' class of the Santa Fe, as among the most efficient, as well as the *puissant* of all express passenger locomotives. There was no doubt about it; they were intended to *run*. The eight-coupled express locomotive of the Union Pacific was developed from as early as 1922, with the '7000' class 4−8−2 designed specially for working between Cheyenne and Ogden, 484 miles. These locomotives, of which fifty-five were built, did excellent work. They had a rated cylinder horse-power of 3000, and at speeds of 40 to 50 m.p.h. this expectation was handsomely exceeded, with actual outputs of 3400 to 3500 horse-power in the cylinders. They took trains of twelve and thirteen cars of the type then operating over the Cheyenne-Ogden section without assistance, and on favourable sections of the line ran up to 75 m.p.h. The fine engines, and the experience gained with them over many years, formed the basis of the splendid 4−8−4 design, of which No. 833, standing on its pedestal near Salt Lake City station is so worthy an example.

When the 4−8−4s were introduced, in 1937, maximum speeds of 75 m.p.h. would have been regarded as quite pedestrian. The fast trains had to be run at 100 m.p.h., or something near it, on straight level track. During the A.A.R. tests in 1938 the Union Pacific 4−8−4 No. 815 developed 4000 horsepower at the drawbar at 70 m.p.h. This would have required about 5000 horsepower in the cylinders. The advance in locomotive design technique in the intervening years is vividly shown by a comparison of the basic proportions and weights of the 4−8−2 of 1922 and the 4−8−4 of 1937, thus:

UNION PACIFIC Passenger Types

Date introduced Type	1922 4−8−2	1937 4−8−4
Cylinders dia. in.	29	24½
stroke in.	28	32
Coupled wheel dia. ft in.	6−1	6−5
Total evaporative heating surface sq. ft.	4974	4597
Superheater sq. ft	1242	1473
Grate area sq. ft	84	100·2
Boiler pressure lbs/sq. in.	200	300
Tractive force lbs	54,838	61,750
Total engine weight tons (Imperial)	154	211·4

As a result of the A.A.R. tests the cylinder diameter of the 4−8−4s was increased to 25 in., and to permit of still freer running at high speed later engines of the class were fitted with twin-orifice blast pipes and double chimneys, while the coupled wheel diameter was increased to 6 ft 8 in. It is a locomotive of this latter variety that is on display at Salt Lake City.

CHAPTER TWELVE

Rio Grande

After a day in the atmosphere of the Union Pacific, up and over its territory, browsing anew over many items of its literature that I had collected in long years of railroad studies, and then having my fill of sentiment in walking round No. 833 in Salt Lake City, I went down to the Rio Grande station to see the thrice-weekly 'Zephyr' arrive from Denver, at 9.30 p.m. The Denver and Rio Grande Western, to give this splendid railroad its full title, has one of the most varied, exciting and successful histories of all American transportation companies; yet its present name, and particularly the popular abbreviation of it, could now perhaps be regarded as a misnomer. Under its original charter, as a 3 ft narrow gauge line, it certainly did strike out from Denver, heading south through Colorado Springs and Pueblo, and then turning westward from Walsenburg to tap the mineral riches in the upper reaches of the Rio Grande River; but visitors to the United States would think more of the 'Great River' where it has gathered immense volume, ultimately to become the national frontier with Mexico. To that part of the Rio Grande the D. & R.G.W. does not go anywhere near. The history of the railroad, in its picturesque and dramatic origins alone, would fill whole volumes; but in this chapter I must be content with riding its stately passenger train, over 570 miles of track through scenery of incomparable variety and grandeur.

At the outset, however, I must dispel any ideas that the Rio Grande of today is a nostalgic survival of narrow gauge mountain railroading, albeit now on standard gauge. It is a mighty artery of heavy east–west freight traffic. I was travelling on a Sunday when business would not be expected to reach a maximum; but in less than 400 miles from Salt Lake City we passed eight westbound freight trains, none of them less than sixty cars, and some requiring five diesel-electric locomotives. This traffic comes from two eastern exchange points, at Denver itself, and at Pueblo. The former dates only from 1934 when the Dotsero cut-off line was opened. Until then in travelling from Denver to the west by the Rio Grande a huge geographical detour via Pueblo was necessary. Today, as can be seen from the map (page 177), traffic from the Missouri Pacific and the Santa Fe feeds in at Pueblo, and from the Union Pacific, the Burlington and the Rock Island at Denver. One can see how the one-time Denver and Salt Lake ground to a halt at Craig, having reached there in 1914.

I spent a delightful day as the guest of the Rio Grande. Outside, in a

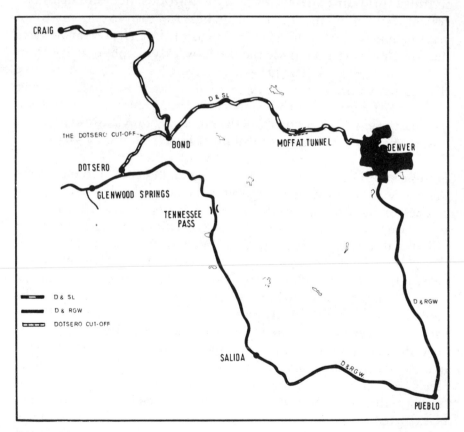

23. Rio Grande—location of the Dotsero cut-off line

terrain that was near-desert in places, the heat was blistering, but the air-conditioning in the dome cars and the diner was working very efficiently, and one could enjoy the passing scene in comfort and delight. The Rio Grande 'Zephyr' is one of the very few crack trains of America that is not under the Amtrak banner and our 8-car formation was hauled by two 1750 horsepower diesels in the attractive Rio Grande passenger colours of silver-grey and orange. There was a baggage car next to the locomotives, and then in order came cars named *Silver Aspen, Silver Mustang, Silver Colt, Silver Bronco, Silver Pony,* the dining car *Silver Banquet*, and the *Silver Sky*, a trailing load of about 545 tons. Leaving Salt Lake City at 7 a.m. we were soon called to breakfast, and I sat opposite to a young man not quite out of his 'teens who had never been in a train before. As we worked up to a good brisk pace on the opening run to Provo, though not quite touching 60 m.p.h., he became rather concerned at the riding of the car. Actually it was extremely good, as everywhere on the Rio Grande, but it evidently did not come up to his expectations. I suggested one or two places where he might go to experience what a really rough train ride was like — without even venturing outside the USA.

Leaving Provo we began our climb over the Wasatch Range. For many years previous to making the trip, I had been aware that this was something out of the ordinary. In building up my collection of the famous 'F. Moore' coloured postcards issued by the Locomotive Publishing Company between 1904 and 1914 I was fortunate enough to acquire one entitled 'The Fast Denver Limited climbing Soldier Summit'. It shows a train of eleven cars hauled by four 4−6−0 locomotives and a banker in rear, and by the look of the exhausts, shooting vertically skywards, the speed was very slow. Actually, in 48¾ miles, the line climbs from an altitude of 4517 ft above sea level at Provo to 7440 ft at Soldier Summit; but the really steep part of the ascent does not begin until we pass Thistle and enter Soldier Creek. Then, for twenty-seven miles the inclination averages 1 in 66, with long stretches at 1 in 50, and near the very outset of this fascinating day of travelling there came a remarkable manifestation of American railroad operating. The line here is double-tracked and controlled from a C.T.C. panel at Denver, more than 500 miles away. It is

157

signalled for running in both directions on both tracks — what the French call *banalisation* — and I was soon to see this facility most spectacularly used. Before this, however, there was an incident of a different kind.

The weather was gloriously fine, and for some distance up Soldier Creek the river and the railroad are paralleled in this narrow glen by a main highway. Along this, in a small automobile, an enthusiast was chasing us. On the heavy gradient our speed was varying between 32 and 42 m.p.h., and from one vantage point after another he would photograph the train, leap into his car, dash ahead and be ready for us a mile or so farther on. I lost count of the number of times he fired off at us, because by then things were happening on the line. I had noticed we were running on the left-hand track, and five miles above Narrows, in a glen with nothing but scrub on the bleak hillsides, we began to overtake an enormously long freight train. It had two pusher locomotives in rear, and the operation became still more exciting because we were approaching a horseshoe curve location. We were doing about 30 m.p.h. and as the freight itself was making quite good speed, it took us eight minutes to overtake its full length, 130 cars, and when we came to the head end it had a *posse* of five locomotives — seven in all, on the one train.

But there was yet another thrill to come. In another eight minutes after we had drawn ahead of the ascending train we met another, going down, on the same track that the eastbound was using to come up! I thought of the C.T.C. dispatcher in far-away Denver, who would be watching the movement of these three trains by the lights on his control panel. There was a crossover road behind us, and he put the 'westbound' over on to what had been our track and a few minutes later, looking down from a great height to the horseshoe curve, I saw the two freights passing each other. It was a superb demonstration of the way in which C.T.C. can expedite train movement in complete safety. In the meantime, our two passenger diesels were taking the 'Zephyr' up the last miles to Soldier Summit at a steady 30 m.p.h. — easy work by comparison. The freight we had overtaken had a load at least ten times greater than ours. The 48¾ miles uphill from Provo had taken 78½ minutes, and the train was then eased down the 26 miles of steep descent into Helper.

158

From this point the nature of both the landscape and the railroad undergoes a complete change. We were soon running out into a sandy, near-desert country, on much easier gradients, but in passing through Helper I could not avoid wondering about the name. It looked a purely railroad colony, with many locomotives on hand. Now in the USA when the train or 'road' locomotive needs assistance, either because of unusual loading, or on a heavy grade, the additional locomotives are known as 'helpers'. In Great Britain, in steam days, some distinction was usually made, particularly on the Northern lines, as to whether assistance was provided by a second engine coupled on in front, or whether there was a pusher in rear. The former was called a pilot, and the latter a bank engine. The station of Helper, Utah, is in much the same category as Tebay and Beattock used to be in steam days, and when the Rio Grande line was built it is probable that there was nothing more than an Indian pueblo in the neighbourhood, if that; the station that was established to provide helper locomotives up to Soldier Summit naturally became 'Helper'.

It was significant of the changed physical conditions beyond Helper that the line was now single-tracked, and on a first class road we were soon running at well over 70 m.p.h. The crossing places were twelve to fifteen miles apart, and if the C.T.C. dispatcher could not exactly synchronise a 'meet' at one of these between opposing trains, the one that was stopped would not have to wait long, and could get under way readily enough afterwards. On such a heavily-graded section as that between Provo and Helper, stopping a 130-car freight with locomotives front and rear, could be a time-consuming business. The doubling of the line between Provo and Helper was completed by 1914. As we now swept along with the dome cars riding luxuriously up to 79 m.p.h. I looked northward to what the local map calls 'roan or brown cliffs', consisting of fluted or columnar vertical formation, ranged along the skyline for mile after mile. At the foot of these cliff ranges there are slopes of loose scree, and between these ranges and the railroad, miles of level desert-like ground. Our maximum speed was 79 m.p.h., the most that is now permitted on lines not equipped with automatic cab signalling on the locomotives. The line is equipped with C.T.C. throughout, so that we were continuing under the watchful eye of the dispatcher at Denver. We had passed another westbound freight starting up the hill from Helper, and at Grassy loop we passed another. The last-named station seemed oddly inappropriate in absolute desert country. For miles hereabouts the sand came right up to the line of the railroad.

We were making good time, and despite one 10 m.p.h. 'slow order' passed Green River 71¼ miles from Helper in 82½ minutes. This passing station on the Rio Grande, which we went through at 58 m.p.h., takes its name from the same Green River after which the locomotive divisional point on the Union Pacific Railroad takes its name. The two stations are nearly 200 miles apart as the crow flies, and between the two the river itself has flowed through the Flaming Gorge National Recreational Area, past the Dinosaur National Monument, through Desolation Canyon, and past the large Uintah and Ouray Indian reservations. Even in this distance the river itself had not gathered a great volume of water, though in the valley, where the line dipped briefly to an altitude of no more than 4066 ft the countryside was green, if no more than briefly.

From Green River the line rises, on gradients not exceeding 1 in 100, for twenty-seven miles to the watershed between the Green and the Colorado rivers, and the speed averaged 60 m.p.h. At Thompson, the summit of this part of the line, we made a brief stop. Just outside the station was the Desert Moon Hotel, in a small oasis, but we were soon out into desert country again. Descending towards the Colorado River the line includes much curvature and there were numerous slowings. It is a harsh primaeval country, with some quite fantastic rock formations, and although we had a brief spell at 70 m.p.h. after passing Cisco, we were pulled up at a red signal beside the Colorado River, and had a long slow run under permissive signals afterwards just as we were coming to the State border between Utah and Colorado. Eventually we were stopped again at Mack to await the coming of a westbound coal train. We were held for seventeen minutes and when it came, hauled by four locomotives, I counted sixty gondola cars, fully loaded. Over the concluding run to Grand Junction we had a fine sprint, covering fourteen miles at an average of 70 m.p.h.; but because of the delays we were fifty-five minutes late in arriving, although we had left Thompson practically on time. The 78 miles had taken 133 minutes, instead of the sharp 80 minutes timetabled.

Grand Junction fully justified its name in the heyday of the narrow gauge. From it there spread out a group of lines through wild mountain country the stories of which are cherished in the exciting history of Colorado railroading in the last century. Gunnison, the Black Canyon, Marshall Pass, are names to fire the imagination of those who have read the racy literature of the narrow gauge, and of the youthful engineers who sometimes dared all in keeping open the lines of communication. Some of the most dramatic sections of line have now been closed, and there are no regular passenger trains running south from Grand Junction. The branches were converted to standard in 1906. Grand Junction itself, in near-desert country, is hardly a tourist resort. The scheduled stop of fifteen minutes is for servicing the locomotives and train, and for refuelling. In the blazing noonday heat I went forward to photograph our locomotives, but was glad enough to get back to the air–conditioned comfort of the train. At the east end of the yard we were held briefly for an arriving westbound freight to clear. It had 5 locomotives and 130 cars.

Our next spell of running, entirely beside the Colorado River, took us for sixty-three miles, to a brief stop at Rifle. At first the valley was very wide, with stark hills on both sides, but at Palisade we came into a stretch of quite stupendous rock scenery, that continued for very many miles. The speed hereabouts was around 45 m.p.h., and at both Akin and De Begue we crossed 5-engined freight trains. Beyond this last station, coming into more open country, we made faster time, and the twenty-four miles leading towards the stop at Rifle took only twenty minutes — 72 m.p.h. No time was wasted at Rifle, where the stop lasted a mere 28 seconds. Then, at speeds of around 60 m.p.h. we went on into a greener stretch of the great river valley. There was pleasant farm land, and though it was still Canyon country, the scenery was less awesome, and on the fast-flowing river I saw some canoeists. So we came to Glenwood Springs, a favoured resort, and by far the busiest passenger station on the line. A big crowd of week-enders was waiting to join the train. The outward service at 7.30 a.m. from Denver on Saturday mornings, and the return leaving Glenwood Springs late on the Sunday afternoon, is a very popular weekend outing. We left, at 4.15 p.m. with practically every seat in the train taken.

161

The first eighteen miles eastward from Glenwood Springs leads through one of the most spectacular pieces of railway I have ever seen. Deep in a great canyon of the Colorado River, winding in and out of tunnels cut in the solid rock, we ran slowly. On the opposite bank of the river was a highway cut just as dramatically from the vertical rock walls. The gradients were not severe; it was the curves that governed our moderate speed. Then, as we began to emerge from the canyon we came to Dotsero Junction, and so entered upon the important 'cut-off' line, constructed as recently as 1934. It is from this junction that the original main line of the Rio Grande turns south towards Salida over the tremendous gradients of the Tennessee Pass, while we were continuing beside the Colorado River over the cut-off line to Bond, built by the Denver and Salt Lake Railroad. Before operation over this line began it was leased to the Rio Grande, and it became fully merged from 1947. There was also a considerable change in the scenery. The hills looked grey and shaley, and there were patches of snow on the higher peaks occasionally glimpsed in the distance. The valley itself had become sandy and desert-like once more, and then we came to the Red Canyon — another spectacular piece. About this time after such a long day of intense and varied sightseeing, I felt that I must relax for a while, to save up my interest, as it were, for the great climax of the journey — the approach to, and passage through the Moffat Tunnel; so after coming to Bond, and the end of the Dotsero 'cut-off' line, it is a good time to write something of the great steam locomotives of the Rio Grande, that ran the rails in pre-diesel days.

The passenger locomotives were mostly of the 4−8−4 type, though an interesting earlier class, the '1600' with the 4−8−2 wheel arrangement, had three cylinders. The most powerful of the 4−8−4s, the '1800' class, had coupled wheels 6 ft 1 in. diameter, making them suitable for fast running on the easier gradients west of Glenwood Springs, as well as capable of hard climbing on the many severe sections. They were handsome engines distinguished by having the smokebox painted silver colour. These huge machines, which had a nominal tractive effort of 67,200 lbs, took passenger trains of up to eighteen cars on the easier gradients, though with such loads they needed a helper on the most severe sections. We have still to come to the tremendous ascent from Denver to the Moffat Tunnel, but even this looks relatively easy compared to the 1 in 33 gradient of the Tennessee Pass, on the line between Dotsero and Salida. On such gradients the 4−8−2 or 4−8−4 road locomotives usually had as helper one of the giant articulated engines, either of the 2−8−8−2, or of the 4−6−6−4 type. Both these were designed to haul maximum tonnage fast freight trains at speeds approaching those now run by the multiple-engined diesel trains, and the 2−8−8−2 built in 1930 with coupled wheels 5 ft 3 in. diameter, was one of the largest of the type ever constructed. They had a nominal tractive effort of 131,000 lbs.

The 4−6−6−4, introduced in 1938, was one of the truly outstanding steam locomotive designs in the United States. They were the outcome of the successful introduction and excellent balancing of the 4−6−6−4s on the Union Pacific, referred to in the previous chapter, which enabled huge articulated locomotives to ride so smoothly and such stability as to permit of speeds up to 60 m.p.h. and more. While the Rio Grande has some backbreaking inclines, it has many stretches of relatively straight, favourable road over which I had travelled at speeds up to 79 m.p.h. on the 'Zephyr', and the 4−6−6−4 was intended to make fast time with freights of fifty, sixty or even seventy cars. Consequently they were given coupled wheels of 5 ft 10 in. diameter. At the same time there was the Tennessee Pass, not to mention Soldier Summit, and the ascent from Denver to the Moffat Tunnel. By the late 1930s no American railroad would have thought of using anything but a valve gear that was entirely outside, and accessible without the need to get a locomotive over a pit. The Walschaerts was admirable, except in one respect, when it came to such duties as the Rio Grande 4−6−6−4s were designed for.

Lead steam, giving some cushioning of the pistons at high speed and providing a smooth action, is essential for fast running but it is not needed when slogging hard up a steep gradient at 20 m.p.h. or less. It was then that the variable lead feature of the Stephenson's link motion was so advantageous, especially if as set on the Great Western 2-cylinder engines in England, in providing a slightly *negative* lead in full gear. It gave considerably extra power in the cylinders at slow speed, to such an extent that at speeds below 30 m.p.h. when going hard, the 2-cylinder 'Saint' class could produce equal or greater power than the 4-cylinder 'Castles' even though the respective nominal tractive powers were 24,300 and 31,625 lbs. The latter engines had Walschaerts valve gear. To secure the same effect the Rio Grande 4−6−6−4s of the '3700' series had a novel and ingenious mechanism that provided variable lead on the Walschaerts gear. Instead of the constant lead normally inherent in this gear, an additional link mechanism automatically varied the effective length of the combination lever, so that the lead was varied from zero when in full gear to ⅜ in. when the gear was linked up to 25 per cent cut-off — an ideal arrangement for locomotives working in such a terrain as that of the Rio Grande.

Apart from this special feature they were tremendously impressive engines to look upon, with their large driving wheels, great boilers, and a firebox with a grate area of 136·5 sq. ft. The engine alone weighed 287 tons (Imperial) and the tenders another 176 tons. It is a pity that an example of so notable a class should not have been preserved, but such a giant, with a total engine and tender wheelbase of 108 ft is not the easiest thing to accommodate. The class certainly provided a fitting conclusion to the saga of steam traction on the Rio Grande, though to be sure the running conditions in such country favoured the diesels. For the record the '3700' class had cylinders 23 in. diameter by 32 in. stroke; coupled wheels 5 ft 10 in. diameter; and a boiler pressure of 255 lbs per sq. in., which combined to provide a tractive force of 105,000 lbs. Fortunately we have Dick Kindig's magnificent photographs to remind us what railroading in Colorado was like in the days of steam.

But I must return to the 'Zephyr'. By this time we had made our last stop, at Granby, and at last, after 5½ hours travelling beside it, we were leaving the Colorado River, and had, to the north of the line, the magnificent prospect of the Rocky Mountain National Park. We were indeed approaching the main range of the Rockies, and in the valley of the Fraser River. There was reminiscence in the name too, because in winding our way through a densely wooded area — so different from the harsh prospects of Utah — the countryside was more like that of the great river valleys of British Columbia. At Tabornash, where the rising gradient steepened to 1 in 57, we passed a four-engined westbound coal train and three miles farther on, at Fraser, entered upon the final stage of the ascent, on 1 in 50. It was then nearly 8 o'clock in the evening, and in contrast to the cloudless skies of this long day, there was piled up cumulus to the north, and the sunset light of the snow-covered mountains and the splendid trees made a delightful picture as we ground our way up the steep approach to the great tunnel.

The line from Denver to Bond, where the Dotsero cut-off begins, was originally that of the Denver and Salt Lake, and from the map it will be seen how the line struck out towards the Green River valley, but eventually got no farther west than Craig. At first it was known as the Denver North Western and Pacific, and made a staggering course over the mountains on gradients of 1 in 25. The present route through the Moffat Tunnel was brought into operation in 1928. The tunnel itself is 6·2 miles long. From the west it is entered on a gradient of 1 in 111, which continues for 3¾ miles to the summit point, at an altitude of 9239 ft. There the gradient changes to 1 in 330 down, to the east portal. We had been sustaining 30 m.p.h. on the steeply graded approach to the tunnel, and it took us just ten minutes to pass through. At the eastern end there is a Y-track, usually spelt 'Wye' in official documents, where the helper engines used to turn, so as to return to Denver chimney first. In the next 37¾ miles the line descends 3543 ft, an average inclination of 1 in 57.

It is an incredible piece of railway. In the first thirteen miles, to Pinecliff, we were rolling gently at about 40 m.p.h. in a tree-clad glen, using the dynamic brake to full advantage, and experiencing none of the sensations of the brakes being constantly applied. But then we came on to a more dramatic piece of line beside a turbulent river, with majestic mountain vistas, and passed through a succession of tunnels cut from the solid rock, with their portals blackened from the exhausts of hard-worked steam locomotives of old. I find a note in my log book: 'What a place with steam!' The track became a bewildering succession of curves and horseshoes. At one time there were *five* tunnels in view at once, and actually there were three more on the same stretch that were then out of sight. On this remarkable stretch speed was being held to about 30 m.p.h. and in the twilight the effect was extraordinary. I lost count of the number of tunnels we passed through in weaving our way down the main escarpment of the Colorado Rockies; actually there are thirty in a distance of sixteen miles! On emerging from the last but one we suddenly came in sight of the plain stretched out below. Pointing to a galaxy of shimmering lights someone said: 'There's Denver'; but actually it was Boulder. We did not see the far greater constellation of Denver itself until some minutes later. When we did see it, it looked so near, and yet another 45 minutes of travelling was to pass before we came to rest in the Union station.

We were still cavorting down the contours on a continuous 1 in 50 gradient, the track twisting and turning to take every advantage of the tumbled foothills of the main mountain range. In the passing tracks at Rocky, still eighteen miles out of Denver, there were two freights, one headed each way, and so finally at 9.36 p.m. we arrived. We had been just one hour late on leaving Glenwood Springs, and this had been reduced to 53 minutes at Granby. But we were favoured with a clear road afterwards, and finally reduced the lateness to 36 minutes. At Denver, Dick Kindig was waiting to meet me. There is a particular delight in meeting face to face someone with whom one has enjoyed a correspondence across the world for nearly forty years, and that meeting late on that Sunday evening was the prelude to a couple of most enjoyable days in and around the 'Mile High City' — for Denver, despite the precipitous descent from the Moffat Tunnel, is still 5200 ft above sea level!

Next morning, in Dick's car, we headed out towards the Moffat Tunnel. Neither of the two highways to the west cross the mountain range near to the tunnel. The one making for the Fraser River climbs over the Berthoud Pass at an altitude of 11,314 ft, while Highway 70 goes through the Eisenhower Memorial Tunnel. We were making for Pinecliff, and from there onwards we followed the line of the railway on what was little more than a dirt track. It was grand country up there in the mountains, though I was warned not to be too energetic in walking and climbing around, because of the high altitude. Pinecliff, a name highly appropriate to the surroundings, is nearly 8000 ft above sea level, and by the time we reached the east portal of the Moffat Tunnel we were 9195 ft up. Seeing the country thus, above and below the line of railway, in such a confused and tumbled array of high ridges and deep clefts, with so much of it densely covered with great forests, I could only stand wrapt in admiration for the surveyors and engineers who had built a railway of such completely uniform grading through such a countryside. Although the instruments for survey, and

166

machinery for construction had advanced a great deal from those of the pioneer days of American railroading, this tremendous piece of line was built fifty years ago.

The eastbound 'Rio Grande Zephyr' is scheduled to cover the 570 miles between Salt Lake City and Denver in 14 hours, an excellent overall average of 40·5 m.p.h. Our actual running time, without allowance for the long slowings that preceded some of the stops at crossing places, was 13¾ hours, nearly 42 m.p.h. My overriding impression of the long Sunday ride — apart of course from the wonderful variety of the scenery — was of a superb railroad. The track maintenance seemed immaculate, eloquently reflected in the smooth riding of the cars, whether we were running up to 79 m.p.h. on the 'desert' stretches, gliding round the curves in the canyons, or coasting smoothly down the amazing descent from the Moffat Tunnel. It was a pleasure and a privilege to make the trip.

Denver Union station, with its impressive facade, is the meeting point of the Rio Grande with the Union Pacific and the Burlington railroads, and in addition to the celebrated streamlined diesel 'Zephyrs' there came great passenger trains from Chicago hauled by the '5629' class of huge steam 4—8—4s. Although there are no standard gauge Rio Grande steam locomotives surviving, one of the Burlington 4—8—4s has been preserved and is in the museum at Golden, Colorado. This is to some extent anticipating the next chapter, because that fascinating collection, to which I went with Dick Kindig, is mostly concerned with the narrow gauge. In the later 1930s, however, the 4—8—4 type was rapidly becoming the standard for heavy passenger and fast freight service in the USA, and in the introduction of giant locomotives like the '5629', preserved at Golden, the Burlington was in keeping with the majority of railroads. Although there were variations in detail design, the basic essentials were a large boiler, and a stoker-fired grate capable of providing unlimited volumes of steam when required. The particular engine on display was built at the railroad's own shops at West Burlington, Iowa, in June 1940, and was originally a coal burner. It was later converted to oil firing.

CHAPTER THIRTEEN

Golden, and Central City

In and around the fine city of Denver the associations with gold mining abound. The Colorado State Capitol, modelled after the Capitol of the United States in Washington, has a magnificent dome that is gold-plated, and standing high and clear of tower blocks it presents a magnificent prospect. I have in some way prepared readers for the delights that await the railway enthusiast at the neighbouring city of Golden, and in going there I could hardly have wished for a better companion than so dedicated and experienced a railroad 'buff' as Dick Kindig. Golden is only ten miles from the centre of Denver. We were soon there, and on entering the museum grounds the first thing that struck me was the skilful and dramatic juxtaposition of the huge Burlington 4–8–4 No. 5629 with the tiny narrow gauge 2–8–0 No. 191, built in 1880 by Baldwin, and now the oldest locomotive in Colorado. The Burlington engine one is inclined to accept as just another of the last and most effective units of the steam era in the USA; but the little '191' fairly sets the imagination racing. Without going into any technical or historical detail the mere sight of it is enough to take one's breath away, for the maximum diameter of its 'balloon' smokestack is greater than the diameter of the boiler barrel!

This little gem of railway archaeology was built originally for the Denver, South Park and Pacific, and is the only surviving locomotive of that 3 ft gauge line. She has cylinders 15 in. diameter, by 18 in. stroke; coupled wheels 3 ft 1 in. diameter, and carried a boiler pressure of 150 lbs per sq. in. Her initial stay in the State of Colorado was for just over twenty years, during which time she worked for three different railroads, transferring from her original owners to the Denver, Leadville and Gunnison, in 1889, and then to the Colorado and Southern ten years later. In 1902 she went east, to work for thirty years on logging railroads in the forest lands of northern Wisconsin. Happily, when she was retired in 1932 she was not scrapped but given an honoured place in the Rhinelander Logging Museum, near to the scene of her labours, and she remained there for another forty-one years. She came to Golden in 1973, and it does not need much study of her wonderfully picturesque outward appearance to conjure up in the imagination, thoughts of what railroading in Colorado was like in the days of the gold rush. It is significant of the tremendous grades engineered in the mining valleys that this little veteran, ninety-seven years old when I saw her, was not of the typical 'American' type of the day, a 4−4−0, but a 2−8−0. There was mighty hard climbing to be done west of Denver.

Only one year younger than No. 191 is another Baldwin 2−8−0 built for the Denver and Rio Grande in July 1881, No. 346. She is considered by some to be the most historic item in the museum, and was in active service on the Rio Grande until 1947. She was on the Gunnison-Montrose narrow gauge passenger service through the spectacular Black Canyon in her later years. She is a rather more powerful engine than No. 191, having 16 in. by 20 in. cylinders, and a boiler pressure of 160 lbs per sq. in. On her tender she carried the initials and insignia of the Golden City and San Juan Railroad. Another delightful piece is a complete narrow gauge train of the Rio Grande Southern. The engine heading this train, No. 20, is a 4−6−0 built in 1899 by Schenectady for the Florence and Cripple Creek Railroad. Then for two years during the first world war she was transferred to the Cripple Creek and Colorado Springs, until becoming property of the Rio Grande Southern in 1916. She worked on that line for thirty-six years, and in 1952 hauled the last train. Then with the help of donations from many individual enthusiasts she was purchased by the Rocky Mountain Railroad club.

The main line of the Denver and Rio Grande was changed from 3 ft to standard gauge in 1890, and the museum is fortunate in having one of the first standard gauge locomotives, again a 2−8−0 built by Baldwin. Although when seen in the flesh this is clearly a considerably larger and wider engine, it still has all the look of the narrow gauge era. In the museum it stands apart from some of the other locomotives, and from its photograph it could easily be mistaken for a narrow gauger. Its basic dimensions are cylinders 20 in. diameter by 24 in. stroke, coupled wheels 3 ft 10 in. diameter, but the boiler pressure is only 140 lbs per sq. in. No fewer than a hundred of this type of locomotive were purchased in 1888–92 for working on the Denver-Pueblo-Ogden line when it was first converted to standard gauge. Engine No. 583, the museum piece, worked on the Denver and Rio Grande Western until 1947 when it was sold to the San Luis Valley Southern. It was retired in 1955, purchased from that railroad in 1962 and moved to the museum in the following year. It is one of only two survivors of Rio Grande standard gauge steam power.

I found the little cog engine of the Manitou and Pikes Peak Railway a most fascinating exhibit. It comes of a breed that is very rare in the USA. In Europe there were at one time quite a number of mountain rack railways, especially in Switzerland, that were operated by steam locomotives. The problem of maintaining a satisfactory water level in the boiler was tackled in several ways, including the vertical boiler of the Rigi, which had a counterpart, yet to be mentioned, in the USA. Another solution was to mount the boiler athwartships so that the water level was maintained irrespective of the gradient. But what proved the most popular form, and was used in Switzerland, Austria, and North Wales was to incline the axis of the boiler in relation to the frames, so that the water level was approximately correct when the locomotive was climbing the steep gradient.

This solution was adopted on the 0–4–2 engines built by Baldwin in 1897 for the Manitou and Pikes Peak Railway. That the arrangement was considered unusual, if not unique in America, is evident from the reference to it in A. W. Bruce's comprehensive work *The Steam Locomotive in America*, thus:

This engine is odd-looking, because the boiler is so set that the center line remains horizontal on the grade as the engine pushes the observation car up the grade and backs down.

To European enthusiasts the M. & P.P. engine is interesting because it is a Vauclain 4–cylinder compound. The cylinder layout differs from the more usual arrangement, in that the low-pressure cylinders are on top and the high-pressure beneath, though both driving on to a common crosshead. The drive to the road wheels is indirect, through rocking levers pivoted on the frames just below the cab. The cylinders are 10 in. diameter (H.P.) and 15 in. with a stroke of 22 in. and the coupled wheel diameter is 22½ in. Naturally, she put me in mind of the pretty little engines in the Swiss railway museum by the lakeside at Lucerne, and of that delightful little thing at Capulago, that used to climb Monte Generoso.

Remarkable to relate, however, the oldest cog railway in the world, opened in 1869, is not only still operating, but it was being worked by steam locomotives. This is in the east of the United States, up Mount Washington, in the State of New Hampshire, which I was able to see some years earlier. It starts away from the base station on a breathtaking 1 in 2·7 gradient, over a timber trestle viaduct; but in reality even this daring construction is secondary in its appeal to the astonishingly little steam locomotives that work on the line. There are two driving axles, one beneath the smokebox and one beneath the cab. They are quite independent, and each is driven by a separate pair of cylinders. There are no other wheels, and the wheel arrangement has been described as $0-2-0 + 0-2-0$! But the cylinders do not drive directly on to the road wheels. They drive on to jack shafts on the outer ends of the locomotive frame, and each of these jack shafts is back geared on to the axle carrying the road wheels and the pinion that engages with the rack. The gear ratio is 5 to 1, so that the piston speed is five times what it would be if driving through a normal crank-connecting rod mechanism. The outward effect is extraordinary, to see these little engines with their inclined boilers, climbing the mountain, with their piston rods whizzing in and out at what seems an amazing speed. The cylinders are 8 in. diameter, by 12 in. stroke. The time has not yet come for these little heroes to become museum pieces, because they are all in regular service.

At Golden, the collection of narrow gauge passenger cars is second only in interest to the locomotives. Of seven vintage specimens none are dated later than 1889, and the oldest is a Denver and Rio Grande coach of 1872. To a European visitor, recalling what passenger cars were like, even on important express trains, down to the turn of the century, it is at first something of a surprise to find that all these vintage specimens are carried on two four-wheeled bogies, and all with high clerestoried roofs and handsome curving at the roof ends. In length they range from 42 ft 6 in. up to 49 ft and provide seating for forty-four passengers. As with the locomotives, anything other than this form of vehicle as freight box-cars, equally as for passengers, would have been useless on the sharply curved, steeply graded routes of the narrow gauge lines, on which changes of grade came just as frequently as changes of alignment. Two of the vehicles, as now preserved, are business cars, but did not start their long lives as such. One was an ordinary coach, but the second was a postal car. The business car has always been a feature of north American railroad travel for executives on inspections, or on other duties away from headquarters on which ordinary sleeping accommodation might be difficult to obtain; and the presence of these two cars at Golden serve to emphasise that the use of business cars was not confined to the greater standard gauge lines. One of these belonged to the Denver and Rio Grande, and the other to the Rio Grande Southern.

I could have spent days, rather than a single morning at the Colorado Railroad Museum; but as usual time was not on my side, and so, with Dick Kindig continuing as guide, we took the road into the mountains. Today it certainly was a highway on which we were driving; but once this winding track beside the river, between stark, barren hills with a strong yellowish colour, had been a line of the narrow gauge Colorado Central Railroad. Except for some tunnels through the rock the present highway is built actually on the former railroad formation. We were heading towards a famous gold rush area, but when I was told that the Colorado and Southern, which absorbed the Colorado Central, ceased operation in 1925 I wondered what we were going to find at what had once been the terminal point in the valley — Central City. Once an epitome of the prosperity of the gold mining era, when the Colorado Central Railroad was built and carried much of the mineral wealth removed from the mountain, it could have become as derelict as the railroad itself when mining ceased. But fortunately the buildings that were typical of that colourful epoch at the end of the nineteenth century remained intact, and today Central City is enjoying a new prosperity, not as a mining town but as a tourist attraction.

In the approaches, the hillsides are marked with golden coloured pyramids from past workings. I thought of similar ones I had seen near to the busiest heart of Johannesburg, but in this rugged mountain valley, now that the workings are dead they add to the strangely picturesque landscape. But Dick Kindig had not brought me to Central City to see no more than an old mining town, the aspect and spirit of which is being preserved; here was a working museum-piece of a narrow gauge railroad. This splendid conception and marvellously successful enterprise was the work of a group led by Lindsey G. Ashby, in early 1968.

The idea of a narrow gauge railroad fitted in completely with the revival of interest in Central City as a tourist attraction. The one-time track of the Colorado Central could not be used, because over it, on the highway, came all the tourists who were contributing to the town's new-found prosperity; but the track of the old 'high line' was untouched. This was certainly a challenge, because from a station site high above the roof tops the line went zig-zagging down the hillside on gradients up to 1 in 33 in severity, and on 40° curves. Construction on the track began; locomotives and stock were brought in, and on 20 August 1968 Central City heard the whistle of a steam locomotive for the first time in forty-three years. We went up to the 'station', a newly-built platform for dealing with passenger traffic, and on the tracks alongside I saw 2–8–0 No. 40, a Baldwin job of 1920, with 16 in. by 20 in. cylinders, coupled wheels 3 ft 2 in. diameter and a boiler pressure of 180 lbs per sq. in.

While I was enthralled by the whole atmosphere of Central City, the star attraction for me on the Colorado Central Narrow Gauge Railroad was the Shay geared locomotive which I saw working a passenger train. This unusual type of locomotive was invented by Ephraim Shay and patented by him in 1881. It has all its cylinders mounted vertically on one side of the boiler, and connection to all the wheels on that side is made through bevel gears. The Shay now working at Central City is carried on three 4-wheeled trucks. All the axles are powered, and the bevels are mounted on a horizontal jack shaft running the entire length of the locomotive. To accommodate the movement of the individual trucks between themselves and the main frames, on which the cylinders are mounted, the various sections of the driving jack shaft are connected by couplings having universal joints. It may seem a complicated mechanical arrangement, but it provided a locomotive that could operate on poor track, round sharp curves, and mount steep gradients. They proved ideal for logging railroads and between 1881 and 1945 no fewer than 2770 Shays were built, all by the Lima Locomotive Works, which held the manufacturing rights to Shay's patents.

The particular Shay at Central City is an engine with a history in itself. It was built in 1916 for the Sierra Nevada Wood and Lumber Company, operating at Hobart Mills, California, and 6½ miles north of Truckee. It had three 11 in. by 12 in. cylinders, and carried a boiler pressure of 200 lbs per sq. in. One can appreciate how popular this type of locomotive was at one time on logging railroads when I add that although its total weight was only 56½ tons (Imperial), spread over six axles, it had a tractive effort of 25,830 lbs. After twenty years service the Hobart operation closed down, and the engine eventually came into the hands of the West Side Lumber Company in 1939, another narrow gauge line built to transport logs from lumber camps in the mountains to the mill in Tuolumne. The railroad, sponsored by the lumber company, had actually been built as a common-carrier corporation, working under the picturesque name of the Hetch Hetchy and Yosemite Valley Railway. At one time it had 70 miles of main line, and some 250 miles of branches, though much of this mileage was of a temporary nature. A line would be laid to support a particular logging activity, and then dismantled afterwards.

As might be imagined, at the height of its activity the railroad needed quite a number of locomotives, and the stud included several more Shays. The logging operations, however, ceased in 1961, and the equipment went into store. Fortunately the locomotives were kept in a reasonably good condition, and in 1968 part of the West Side line was re-opened, to carry passengers, instead of logs; and then finally, after a spell working passenger excursion trains on the Michigan-California Lumber Company's narrow gauge logging road at Camino, California, this much travelled Shay, No. 14, came to Central City, and I was able to see her at work. She was being used on the passenger run down the 'high line', propelling three open cars on the outward run, and then hauling them back up the 1 in 33 gradient. To a locomotive of such tractive power such a task was simplicity itself.

While waiting for her to come back into Central City, with my camera at the ready, Dick Kindig warned me not to be misled as to the speed of her approach by the rapidity of the exhaust beats, because the geared drive, like that of the Mount Washington cog locomotives, gives the impression of far higher speed than is actually the case.

When No. 14 did arrive I was intensely interested to walk round her, and to note the curious effect, from the front, of seeing the boiler set to one side of the engine centre line. The cylinders, as on most Shays, are on the right-hand side looking forward. I referred earlier to the high tractive power in relation to their weight. There was a far more powerful example than No. 14 at one time working for the West Side Lumber Company. This was No. 10, which had cylinders 12 in. diameter by 15 in. stroke. Like No. 14 it was carried on three 4-wheeled trucks but with a larger boiler to supply its larger cylinders the weight was 72½ tons. The tractive effort, however, was no less than 36,150 lbs — the equivalent of a British 2−8−0 standard gauge freighter, and all on the 3 ft 0 in. gauge! This powerful engine also is still at work, and like No. 14 engaged on passenger tourist business in California.

Driving back into Denver from this secluded treasure house of railroad archaeology I could not help feeling how fortunate we are that in America, as in Europe and elsewhere, there are enthusiasts with the scholarship, the business acumen, and the organising ability to turn their love of railroads and all their equipment into channels that are not only the delight of their fellows, and of countless visitors, but are bringing into the well-nigh limitless field of archaeology the very important era of steam railroads, in so vivid and attractive a form. In visiting railroad preservation activities, particularly where operational steam locomotives are involved, one feels that the word 'preservation' cannot be over-emphasised. It is one thing to save an old locomotive, a passenger car, or other item of historic interest from the scrap heap; it is another to ensure its relative permanence for the benefit of posterity. It was evident to me that the folks at Central City have got away to a magnificent start.

CHAPTER FOURTEEN

Freight over the joint line — Santa Fe

From Denver I travelled south over one of the busiest and most interesting lines in the mid-west of America. In studying the railroad map many instances can be found of strongly competitive routes running roughly parallel to each other between the same cities, profiting at first from booming traffic, but then falling under the influence of trade depression, changing flow of business, and a decline towards insolvency. The routes of the Rio Grande and of the Santa Fe between Denver and Pueblo, in sight of each other for most of the way, certainly followed the familiar pattern for years before the second world war; but after the war, with the generally sound position of the Santa Fe and the strong revival of the Rio Grande following a financial reorganisation in 1947, there emerged a remarkably healthy situation — not in cut-throat competition, but in partnership. An arrangement was made for rational use of the two single-track railroads to the best advantage of the traffic flowing on both.

The sketch map adjoining shows clearly the vital nature of the north-to-south connection that this line provides. No fewer than five main routes feed into it at Denver. Of these, the Colorado and Southern is a subsidiary of the Burlington, while the Rock Island comes in on trackage rights over the Union Pacific from Limon. Until the year 1974 there were separate Rio Grande and Santa Fe tracks throughout, previously crossing each other three times on the way south, at Sedalia, Palmer Lake and North Fountain; but the Santa Fe track through the streets of Colorado Springs began to cause considerable trouble after the introduction of diesel traction. A city ordinance

24. Lines feeding towards Denver from the east

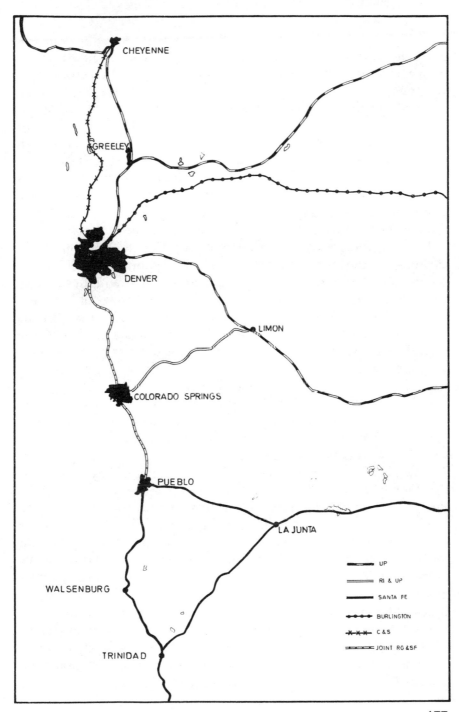

CHEYENNE

GREELEY

DENVER

LIMON

COLORADO SPRINGS

PUEBLO

LA JUNTA

WALSENBURG

TRINIDAD

━━━━	UP
═════	RI & UP
━━━━	SANTA FE
●━●━●	BURLINGTON
✕✕✕	C & S
═╪═╪═	JOINT RG & SF

177

prohibited the use of the air-operated horns, and as an American writer vividly expressed it: 'unheeding motorists were constantly wrapping themselves around diesels'! The Rio Grande line through Colorado Springs avoided the main streets, and even in the conditions of the late 1960s was proving considerably less lethal. So the two companies agreed on a remarkable project of co-ordination. Although freight traffic was heavy and on the increase, it was agreed that both should use the Rio Grande line through Colorado Springs and that its continuation northward to Palmer Lake should be converted into a single line, with passing places, to be used by all traffic. For thirty-three miles the former Santa Fe line was abandoned.

This might seem like a restriction, rather than an improvement in facilities, but the thirty-three mile section was equipped with C.T.C., operated by the Santa Fe dispatcher at La Junta, and with this invaluable aid to traffic movement it was found that the flow could be more readily controlled on the newly equipped single line than on the previous two tracks, streets of Colorado Springs included. More recently hazards of a different kind have come to beset train operation within the city boundaries, of which I was made aware on my own trip. In addition to the owners of the joint line the Colorado and Southern has trackage rights throughout between Denver and Pueblo, and there is pooling of locomotive power between the Burlington as operators of the C. & S., and the Santa Fe. The three users of the line all have heavy freight workings, but nowadays there are no regularly scheduled passenger trains. Occasionally, at times of interruption on the Moffat Tunnel route, the 'Rio Grande Zephyr' is routed via Pueblo, there turning west to take the Royal Gorge route to Salida and over the Tennessee Pass to Dotsero. Although this north-to-south route runs at a considerable distance east of the main range of the Rockies, and in a countryside quite different from the mountain ranges and from the prairie lands to the east, it is a line of severe gradients up to a maximum inclination of 1 in 70. The cross-section between Denver and Pueblo is, however, very simple, consisting of nothing more than one gable. From the altitude of 5198 ft at Denver Union station the rise is continuous, without any level, or intermediate fluctuations, for 52 miles, to the summit 7237 ft above sea level at Palmer Lake. Thence the descent is equally continuous over the remaining 67·2 miles of the line to Pueblo, where the altitude is 4672 ft at the west yard, where this particular trip terminated. The Rio Grande line was built on narrow gauge in 1871-2. Mixed gauge was laid in during 1881, and it was converted to standard gauge in 1902. The line westward from Pueblo into the mountains, the celebrated Royal Gorge route, became mixed gauge between 1887 and 1890, but was not finally converted to standard gauge until 1911.

From Denver I was heading out towards California and the Santa Fe arranged for me to ride one of their freight trains to Pueblo — a non-stop run of nearly five hours. Starting from the 38th Avenue yard of the Burlington, we had a load of 64 cars, given as 5052 short tons, (4510 tons Imperial), and hauled by four Burlington diesels, three of 3000 horsepower, and one of 3600. The leader, No. 921 on which I rode, was an SD 40-2 allocated to the Colorado and Southern, though operated by Santa Fe men — Engineer Setser and Fireman Romero. My own very pleasant guide and philosopher was Mr E. J. Mulligan, Road Foreman of engines at Pueblo. On the steady and continuous climb from Denver to the summit at Palmer Lake, we certainly needed our four locomotives. While the Santa Fe and the C. & S. put all their power at the head end the Rio Grande frequently use pushers from Denver up to Palmer Lake — two locomotives at each end of a heavy train. Pulling out of yards, and negotiating the terminal area of American cities can be a slow business, and we took forty-two minutes to clear South Denver Junction, and enter upon the Rio Grande main line to the south, barely six miles from our starting point. Even then we were not really away, because we had to proceed slowly until the tail end was clear of the junction.

At 6.42 p.m., forty-six minutes after we started from 38th Avenue yard, power was on in earnest, and we were soon making good time. With a load of more than 5000 tons however, we were limited to a maximum speed of 45 m.p.h. over this route. We passed Englewood and then Littleton, shortly afterwards noting a northbound Santa Fe freight with forty cars and three locomotives coasting downhill. I must mention one of the hazards of American railroad operation as seen from the head end — teenage children stoning the locomotives: 'throwing rocks', it is called in the USA, and although the 'rocks' are not much larger than a piece of stone track ballast, they can smash a

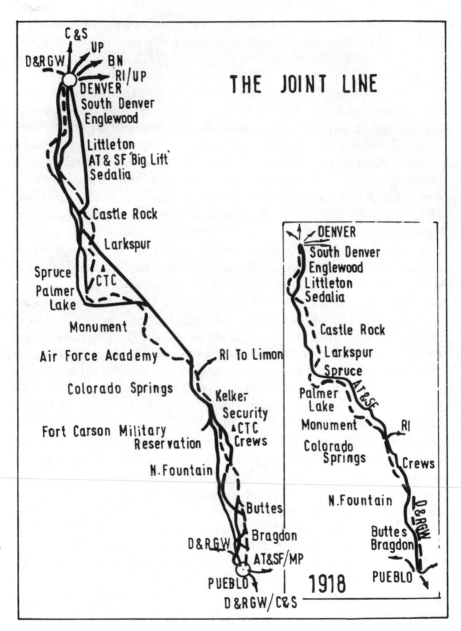

25. The joint line

cab window and injure members of the crew. A group of these little vandals had a go at us just south of Littleton, but they were not very effective shots. The track was excellent, and we were soon bowling along at about 40 m.p.h. — good going with such a load, for the gradient was rising at 1 in 100. The Santa Fe line was closely parallel along this stretch, and when we came to the place when the two original lines crossed, at Sedalia, we transferred to the former Santa Fe line, and the Rio Grande thereafter was the northbound track.

Up to this point the mileposts had been those of the Rio Grande, from zero at Denver. They now became those of the Santa Fe from zero in Chicago. In five minutes we changed from milepost 25 to '710'. What is termed here the 'paired track' operation began in 1919. The gradients on both the Rio Grande and the Santa Fe lines are similar except that on the Santa Fe there is compensation for curvature. To secure such a relatively even rate of ascent in such hilly country, without undue constructional expense when the lines were first built, there is a good deal of curvature. On the Rio Grande, with an alignment planned in the first place for the narrow gauge this was not of any great consequence; but the Santa Fe, standard gauge from the outset, was compensated for curvature. The tractive resistance of a train increases when traversing curved sections of line and by laying out the gradients so that the actual inclination is reduced on curves the tractive resistance of the train remains relatively constant, whether on straight track or on curves. On the southbound run from Denver to Pueblo it was a distinct advantage with a heavy train to have the compensated track of the Santa Fe between Sedalia and Palmer Lake.

It was a delightful evening to see the country, particularly as the scenery was unlike anything I had previously seen in the USA. We were mounting now on a continuous 1 in 70 ascent over open grass lands. The line of the Rockies was still distant, away to the west, with the mountains turning a wonderful shade of blue in the sunset light, and on this route, at our climbing speed of about 30 m.p.h. it was always fascinating to look back and see our seemingly endless train following round the curves. Yet ours, sixty-four cars, was a relatively modest freight train load by American standards. Nevertheless, the full power performance of four locomotives — 12,600 engine horsepower — was necessary to keep it rolling at about 30 m.p.h. For a time we were heading south-eastwards but then we turned south into picturesque Castle Rock, which take its name from an isolated rock tower that looks more like the strange outcrops of the desert country farther west. Despite compensation for curvature of the track, the speed here fell to 22 m.p.h.

Directly ahead of us now, but still nearly forty miles away, was the distinctive profile of Pikes Peak, rising to 14,110 ft, and well known to railway enthusiasts from the rack railway ascending the mountain from Manitou Springs. From Castle Rock the average inclination of the line lessens a little, to 1 in 120, although the maximum steepness remains 1 in 70, and after Tomah speed rose briefly to 35 m.p.h. But the respite did not last long, and nearing the delightfully named station of Larkspur, speed had dropped back to 22 m.p.h., on a combination of a 1 in 66 gradient and 3° curvature. In the light of a cloudless evening the sunset effects were glorious. The mountains to the west, now much nearer, were the colour of blue grapes, while the track became even more winding. Miles from passing Larkspur were run at 24·5 m.p.h., 21·5, 20, 23 and 25·5, and at one stage our leading unit slipped on a curve. Ahead of us the striking profile of Pikes Peak looked even more dramatic in the sunset light, and so we came to Spruce. At this point, 24·1 miles from Sedalia, we crossed back on to Rio Grande tracks.

During this spell on the Santa Fe line we had climbed 1265 ft, 528 ft per mile, and representing an exact average inclination of 1 in 100, and our time had been 57½ minutes, an average speed of 25 m.p.h. So, on a very curving alignment we climbed the last two miles up to Palmer Lake, topping the summit at no more than 20 m.p.h. The 48 miles from South Denver Junction had taken us 111 minutes, and then we began the long descent towards Pueblo. We had now entered upon the section of single line, with passing places, controlled by C.T.C. from La Junta. Although my own signalling work has made me familiar with modern practice in many parts of the world, this seemed a remarkable example of remote control; for here was a section of 33 miles operated from a panel 83 miles away from the nearest end of the line controlled. The rest of the joint line between Denver and Pueblo is worked under automatic block signalling rules.

The Santa Fe dispatcher at La Junta often has quite a lot of traffic on his panel between Palmer Lake and Crews — just south of Colorado Springs — and consideration is now being given to putting in a second track throughout, also under C.T.C. control. It is curious, however, that the railroad holding trackage rights, namely the Colorado and Southern subsidiary of the Burlington, has considerably more traffic than the joint owners. Actual numbers vary, but when I was on the line the Santa Fe was running four regular trains a day, and the Rio Grande between four and six. Beside these the Colorado and Southern runs two fast freights in each direction, and three loaded unit coal trains from the newly-commissioned open-cast mines at Gillette, Wyoming, to Pueblo. The C. & S. also operates a number of semi-local freights, known in the USA as 'drags'. The loaded coal trains are very heavy, usually made up to 110 cars, and require seven locomotives on the climb from Denver to Palmer Lake. There is a *posse* of four at the head end, 'on the point' as it is sometimes expressed in the USA, and a remotely controlled 'slave' group of three usually about 75 cars from the head end. Another very heavy 'block-load' freight operated by the C. & S. is one carrying iron ore from Minnesota to Pueblo. Originally, because of the heavy gradient up to Palmer Lake, its 110-car formation was divided over the Joint Line; but with the successful introduction of radio remote control by the Burlington Northern over this route the ore train is now worked as a single movement, with three locomotives at the head end and two radio units, 74 cars back.

Reference to these heavy trains, and the steep gradients of the line, naturally brings into prominence the operation of the brakes. From Palmer Lake down to Husted the maximum gradient is 1 in 70, and this is no place for hurrying. These locomotives are equipped with the dynamic brake. The traction motors, being geared to the axles, are rotating whenever the train is moving. When using the dynamic brake electrical circuits are set up which change the traction motors into generators when the locomotive is running. Since it takes power to rotate a generator this action retards the speed of the train. The dynamic brake produces a braking effect similar to an independent locomotive brake, but without any wear of brake shoes, or heating of tyres. In normal working, as on this run of mine descending from Palmer Lake, the automatic air brake on the train is used, but allowing the locomotives to roll freely, without use of the dynamic brake. This keeps the couplings between the locomotives and the train taut, and it avoids snatches. Our engineer eased the train down the grade at about 30 m.p.h., giving a very smooth run. In the twilight we were coming into a rocky country, and then ahead of us the lights of Colorado Springs were twinkling. It is sad to know that the run through this city, seen so beautifully at night, should also be notorious for rock-throwing attacks on trains.

At Kelker, 4¾ miles south of Colorado Springs, we passed back on to Santa Fe tracks, and on a good road we began to make some of the fastest running of the journey. The gradients, although continuously downhill, were easier, and for twenty miles we made an average of 40 m.p.h. We were of course precluded from travelling very much faster than this because of the speed limit for trains of more than 5000 tons, and I noted no more than a few miles at exactly the maximum permitted, of 45 m.p.h. Although by that time it was quite dark, I could pick out the mileposts clearly in the beam from the locomotive headlight. The markers indicate only full miles. The quarter miles of Great Britain, and the tenths of kilometres on the continent of Europe are not used. At Pinon, 105·2 miles from Denver, we got a yellow signal and this was the prelude to our first stop. We were put into the loop at Bragdon to clear the road for Santa Fe's No. 194, a priority piggyback freight through from Chicago to Denver. We came to rest at 10.31 p.m. having taken 4 hrs 24 min. for the 108½ miles from Denver Union — passed at dead slow speed. Our average speed over this stretch had thus been 24·7 m.p.h. Although not exactly spectacular it was evidence of a very sound performance over a difficult road.

Santa Fe '194' was not long in coming, and at 10.44 p.m. we were away again, but not for long. At 11.10 p.m. we came to rest in the Pueblo freight yard jointly operated by the Santa Fe, and the Colorado and Southern. We brought the train into the reception sidings, coupled off, and then drew slowly through the middle of the yard, and over the hump. During the many years that I have been associated professionally with marshalling yards and their equipment, this was the first time I had been over the hump on the leading unit of four road locomotives. Although the hour was late, my travelling for the day was not yet ended. I had to get to La Junta, to pick up the Amtrak

'Southwest Limited' at 9.40 a.m. next morning; but Mulligan had everything well organised. His own car was waiting just outside the yard office, and although it was a run of some sixty-five miles by road, closely beside the connecting line of the Santa Fe over which the piggyback freight from Chicago had travelled an hour or so earlier, there was time for a call in to his home, where Mrs Mulligan had coffee ready for us, before he drove me to La Junta.

This out-and-out railway colony, a locomotive station of supreme importance in the days of steam, lies at the point where the old Santa Fe trail turned away south-west from the valley of the Arkansas River. It is interesting to recall something of the history of the Santa Fe trail. All over the USA one finds towns and cities that owe their origin and their very names to the building of the railways, but Santa Fe, the capital city of the state of New Mexico, is much older. But curiously enough the great railroad to which the city has given its name, bypasses Santa Fe altogether. It is reached by a branch line eighteen miles long from Lamy, over which the maximum authorised speed is 10 m.p.h. Yet Santa Fe was unquestionably the goal of the railroad originally pioneered by Cyrus K. Holliday. It was the trade centre of the vast south-west of America, to and from which there was a profitable caravan traffic along the old trail to the Missouri River, and points east. But first Holliday had to establish his bases at the eastern end, and in 1859 he obtained the charter for building the Atchison and Topeka Railroad, a line no more than fifty miles long from the western bank of the Missouri River to the new establishment of Topeka, that through his drive and perception was named as the Capital City of Kansas, in 1859.

As with so many far-sighted projects of the time, however, its fulfilment was much delayed by the Civil War, and it was not until 1868 that construction of the railroad started. But even then Holliday predicted that it would not only extend to Santa Fe, but would in time reach the Pacific Coast. So the Atchison, Topeka and Santa Fe Railroad was launched, and it was with something of a thrill that I went to bed late that night, realising I was now actually on the old Santa Fe trail. It was a short night. I was to meet J. K. Hastings, Superintendent of the A.T. & S.F. at La Junta first thing next morning, to see the various C.T.C. panels in the Colorado Division headquarters — all before I went aboard the 'Southwest Limited' Train No. 3 at 9.30 a.m. On the face of it La Junta looked to me an unlikely place to find a divisional headquarters of a great railway. The Santa Fe is a rail*way* and not a rail*road*. Here was no teeming city, with its tower blocks projected against the skyline; no streets already crowded with traffic at seven in the morning. I had slept at the 'Heart of Town Motel', and the place seemed like a country township mostly of single-storied dwellings out on the plains of southern Colorado. Across the broad street from the motel was the Santa Fe station, standing alone in spacious isolation. I could hardly believe that this was the divisional point where the one engine change between Chicago and Los Angeles took place in steam days.

But in the Santa Fe offices things were busy enough. The Colorado division extends eastwards for 202½ miles to Dodge City, Kansas; this is known as the First District. We were to travel west through the second, third and fourth districts, the boundary points of which are marked by the stations Raton, Las Vegas, and Albuquerque — all in the State of New Mexico. The second of the three must not be confused with Las Vegas, Nevada, the well known holiday resort. I saw the dispatchers at work covering 547 miles of the Chicago to Los Angeles main line; but there was also the line to Pueblo, and the panel covering the joint line with the Rio Grande between Crews and Palmer Lake over which I had so recently travelled. The Amtrak 'Southwest Limited', No. 3 westbound, and No. 4 eastbound, are certainly the only regular passenger trains on the line, but I was handed details of fifteen eastbound freights passing between 7.40 a.m. and 9.20 p.m. All of these were loaded to more than 5000 tons, and as such subject to the general speed limit of 45 m.p.h. For freight trains of less than 5000 tons the limit is 60 m.p.h.

Before leaving La Junta I must refer to the magnificent steam locomotives that ran the road in pre-diesel days, because by many the 4−8−4s in particular were considered the finest passenger engines ever to operate in the USA. There will be many references to their past achievements in the next chapter, so it is good to look over their dimensional details and traffic assignments in advance. There is no better place to do this than at La Junta, because it was from here that they set out west on their remarkable 1234-mile through workings to

186

Los Angeles. Between Chicago and La Junta over relatively level track the Santa Fe used mainly their splendid 4—6—4s of the '3460' class, which were remarkable in having coupled wheels as large as 7 ft in diameter. They had cylinders 23½ in. diameter by 29½ in. stroke, and like the 4—8—4s had the high boiler pressure of 300 lbs per sq. in. One of their toughest assignments was the westbound 'Fast Mail' leaving Chicago at 10.35 p.m. and reaching La Junta, 991·6 miles, at 5.30 p.m. on the following day, an overall average speed of around 50 m.p.h. With La Junta standing 4059 ft above sea level there is a vertical rise of 3278 ft in the 540 miles west from Kansas City.

The 4—8—4s of the earlier batches had 6 ft 1 in. coupled wheels, having regard to the great variations of gradient and service conditions experienced on the run through from La Junta to Los Angeles, but the later ones, numbered from 3765 upwards and introduced in 1938, had coupled wheels of 6 ft 8 in. diameter, and were intended to run as fast as the 4—6—4s where track conditions permitted it. And there were some stretches where the limit was then 100 m.p.h.! They had cylinders 28 in. diameter by 32 in. stroke, and a boiler pressure of 300 lbs per sq. in. They were oil burners, and the grate area was 108 sq. ft. But it was above all their stamina, if one can use a human analogy, that so distinguished these great engines, and their reliability. On the run through from La Junta to Los Angeles they would be handled by nine different crews, and if necessary could be turned round and sent east again no more than six hours after arrival. S. Kip Farrington has written of them:

Often it seems, they are doing the impossible, as they smash at long sustained grades at high speed, tip over high mountain passes, drift down to attack a gleaming tangent at one hundred miles an hour.

So with the statistics of these engines in mind, and a wallet-full of Dick Kindig's photographs, I went over to the station to begin the long ride to California.

CHAPTER FIFTEEN

Santa Fe — across four states

At the west end of La Junta station a solitary Amtrak 'SDP 40 F'-class diesel-electric locomotive was standing, ready to couple on ahead of the two similar units that were bringing the 'Southwest Limited' from Chicago. Over the First district of the Colorado Division, 202·4 miles from Dodge City, the train is allowed 162 minutes and its average speed of 74·9 m.p.h. must make this one of the fastest start-to-stop runs in the USA at the present time. The speed limit for passenger trains over the entire 202 miles is 90 m.p.h. and the scheduled pass-to-pass average over the 166 miles between Howell and Hilton is 79 m.p.h. The two 3000 horsepower units brought in fourteen cars, on time. The make-up of the train from the leading end was baggage car, dormitory car, six of the tall coaches, dining car, dome car, three sleeping cars and a baggage car; an estimated load of about 1000 tons. The third locomotive unit was necessary for climbing the heavy gradients to come. Saying farewell to Mulligan I climbed aboard for a ride that was to take nearly 24 hours. The tall coaches, of former Santa Fe design, are splendid for sightseeing, but not ideal for detailed milepost logging when on single track, and the posts are closely alongside the line. Still, one cannot have it all ways!

The opening run over the 81·8 miles to Trinidad is a fast one, especially considering that the line is rising, with a ruling gradient of 1 in 88 for most of the way. Over a wide parched grassland, interspersed with rocky, near-desert country we ran the 23½ miles between Delhi and Model in 19¼ minutes (average 73·25 m.p.h.), but the next 11¼ miles on to Hoehines took 14 minutes because of some slowing down for curves. The riding was very good, and looking out on the very hot landscape outside, I was glad of the very effective air-conditioning in

the coach. Nearing Trinidad we passed over the Colorado and Southern crossing, a continuation of the line on which I had travelled over
the previous evening, and leading eventually down to the Gulf at
Galveston. The 81 miles from La Junta to this crossing had taken 72½
minutes, and we drew into Trinidad on time, in 75 minutes to the stop
— a good beginning.

We were now faced with the hardest piece of climbing on the
westbound run, the ascent to the Raton Pass, which marks the State
boundary between Colorado and New Mexico, where the maximum
gradient is 1 in 28½. Even the '3765' class 4—8—4s needed assistance
here with heavy trains, and during the second world war the Santa Fe
purchased six of the Norfolk and Western 2—8—8—2 compounds of
Class 'Y 3' for use as helpers on this very difficult section. We got
away to a good start out of Trinidad, passing Starkville, 5·3 miles in
9½ minutes, on no more than moderately severe gradients; but then,
on the tremendous 1 in 28½, with constant and severe curvature,
successive miles from Starkville averaged 31·8 m.p.h., 25·4, 25·7,
25, 22·9, 24·5, 24·3, 20·6, and 21·5 m.p.h. — all this with 9000
horsepower going all-out at the head end. I was so intent upon
securing a detailed record of the locomotive work on this exceptional
stretch that I paid less attention than usual to the scenery; but it was a
rather restricted outlook in any case, with rough crags and tree-clad
slopes blocking out any more distant views of the beautiful Sangre de
Cristo Range — the Spanish peaks of the New Mexico border country. Speed is limited to 20 m.p.h. through the tunnel at the head of the
pass at an altitude of 7622 ft above sea level, and we ran gently down
the 1 in 30 to Raton, in a country that looked to me like the High Veldt
in South Africa, but with Mexican buildings. The 22·8 very difficult
miles from Trinidad had taken just 52 minutes, and we arrived slightly
ahead of time.

We now passed from the Second to the Third District of the
Colorado Division, and made a rapid start on favourable gradients.
This section of line is not equipped with cab signalling equipment and
so there is a general maximum speed of 79 m.p.h.; but we covered the
first forty miles, to Springer, in 36¼ minutes, in a countryside that
continued to remind me of the High Veldt. About this time we were
called for lunch, only to find, to our consternation, that the air-

conditioning in the dining car had failed. With the thermometer standing at 100°F *plus*, outside, it was a decidedly hot meal! In the meantime the locomotive crew of the Third District had recovered the five minutes of lateness with which we had left Raton, because of a station stop nine minutes longer than the scheduled six, and by running the 109·8 miles to Las Vegas in 105¾ minutes, our arrival time was 1.54 p.m., just a minute early. We got back to the coach to find the air-conditioning had failed in that also, but any personal discomfort was forgotten in drinking in the astonishing beauty of the countryside we were now entering. It is not the sylvan beauty of a southern English shire, or the mountain grandeur of the Alps or the Canadian Rockies. It is a raw, wild world, of the most vivid colouring beneath an intense blue sky. The hillsides are dotted, rather than clothed with trees; they are seared with dried up water-ways, and the soil is pink.

Meanwhile, from Las Vegas, the line is climbing again, to the Glorieta ridge, at the southern end of the Sangre de Cristo Range: another summit, 7437 ft up, to be surmounted. The gradient is mostly 1 in 60 for nearly fifty miles, and the going is often spectacular. At Blanchard there was a tremendous zig-zag. Higher still, the track is carried on a steep mountain slope, where the hillsides are still pocked-marked with stunted trees. Near Blanchard we passed an arid truncated cone of a mountain, known as Starvation Peak. Up this long climb we were making speeds of 40 to 45 m.p.h., with the 41·9 miles from Ojita to Fox covered in 64¾ minutes. At Rowe, 4·4 miles before Fox, we had crossed the eastbound Amtrak train No. 4, which was in the crossing loop waiting for us. The passage of these two very long distance trains at the scheduled place, both almost exactly on time, was an impressive example of Santa Fe operating. We passed Glorieta, 55·1 miles from Las Vegas, in 80¾ minutes at about 25 m.p.h., and now we continued at around that speed down the 1 in 33 gradient through Apache Canyon. This is another very spectacular place, reminiscent of some of the wilder Scottish glens, but with the soil as red as that of South Devon. The 'river' was completely dry. We were now directly on the old Santa Fe trail, and at 3.46 p.m. we drew in to stop at Lamy, the junction for Santa Fe City. The 65·1 miles from Las Vegas had taken 105 minutes, with more than 24 minutes for the 10-mile run down the canyon.

From Lamy we started away on one of the fastest stretches of line west of La Junta, where the line maximum speed is 90 m.p.h., and where there are only two curves, close together, that require an appreciable reduction of speed. The countryside was utterly barren, with the red rocky escarpments shimmering in the blazing heat. We were running mostly at around 70 m.p.h., and then at Bernatillo, a modern bungalow town, we came into the valley of the Rio Grande, nearly a hundred miles south of the point, in Colorado, where it leaves the Denver and Rio Grande Western Railroad. On our own line the mountains were now beginning to give way to a more level and greener countryside, and we worked up into a fine concluding sprint over the last miles of the Colorado Division. Speed rose to 82 m.p.h. before Alameda, and so we drew into Albuquerque, 67·2 miles from Lamy, in 66½ minutes. Here the locomotives and the train were serviced, including a welcome repair of the fault in the air-conditioning apparatus! Despite the heat it was good to climb down for a few minutes. I walked up to the front end to photograph the locomotives. The new engineer saw me, and said: 'Gee, you're a rail fan. I guess you'd like these', and handed me a sheaf of train orders, some of which, curiously enough, related to the far-off Southern Railway system.

The Albuquerque Division of te Santa Fe covers the next 429 miles of the main line, in three districts: first to Gallup, New Mexico, then to Winslow, Arizona, and finally to Seligman, still in Arizona. The respective distances are 145, 127·7, and 143 miles, and the total of 115·7 is made up by the distance of the actual divisional changeover point between the Colorado and Albuquerque Division at Isleta, fifteen miles west of Albuquerque itself. The divisional headquarters, and dispatchers' offices are at Winslow, Arizona. Before leaving Albuquerque, however, I must add that in steam days it was the site of the principal locomotive works, and that although the modern power was purchased from the private locomotive builders, it was a rebuilding and modernisation job done at Albuquerque on the original 4—8—4 locomotives of the '3751' class that paved the way for the magnificent '3765' built by Baldwins in 1938. As previously mentioned, the '3751' class had 6 ft 1 in. coupled wheels. In the rebuilding of 1935 they were converted to oil burning, had the coupled wheels replaced by new ones of 6 ft 8 in. diameter, and the boiler pressure was raised from 210 to 230 lbs per sq. in. The success of this rebuilding led to the design of the '3765' class.

The 2−10−2 type of freight locomotive originated on the Santa Fe in 1903, when an experimental 4-cylinder tandem compound was built by the Baldwin Locomotive Works. The wheel arrangement received the class name of 'Santa Fe' from this time onwards. The final development of freight locomotive power on the railway came in 1938 when, also from Baldwins, came the enormous '5000' class 2−10−4s. They epitomised the traffic operating policy of the Santa Fe in running their freight trains in somewhat lighter formations, and at much higher speed. These locomotives had coupled wheels of no less than 6 ft 2 in. diameter; the cylinders were 30 in. diameter by 34 in. stroke, and the boiler pressure no less than 310 lbs per sq. in. They had the exceptional tractive effort, for a non-articulated engine, of 93,000 lbs. They took loads of up to ninety cars without assistance on the level and more easily graded sections of line, though the new diesels took over the freight workings on the severe section west of Winslow, Arizona, early in 1940. It is interesting, however, to set down alongside the principal dimensions of the two greatest of Santa Fe steam locomotives, both built by Baldwins, but conceived out of the long and varied experience of the men of the Albuquerque Works.

SANTA FE Giants

Type	4−8−4	2−10−4
Cylinders dia. in.	28	30
stroke in.	32	34
Coupled wheel dia. ft in.	6−8	6−2
Heating surfaces		
Evaporative sq. ft	5313	5937
Superheater sq. ft	2366	2589
Grate area sq. ft	108	121·7
Boiler pressure lbs/sq. in.	300	310
Tractive force lbs	66,000	93,000
Total engine weight tons	227·5	240
tender weight tons	201·5	202

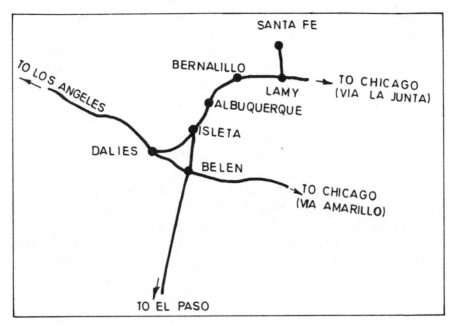

SANTA FE

BERNALILLO

TO LOS ANGELES

TO CHICAGO
(VIA LA JUNTA)

LAMY

ALBUQUERQUE

ISLETA

DALIES

BELEN

TO CHICAGO
(VIA AMARILLO)

TO EL PASO

26. Connections around Albuquerque

Because of the servicing work necessary on the train we were sixteen minutes late leaving Albuquerque. We got away very smartly, passing Isleta in no more than 15¾ minutes; but our running was subjected to several speed orders, and although the 160 miles from Albuquerque to Gallup are scheduled in 145 minutes we actually took 167 minutes and arrived in Gallup 38 minutes late. We were meanwhile passing over a very interesting section of the line, and the sketch map shows the track configuration between Albuquerque, Isleta, and Dalies. Southward from Isleta goes the line to El Paso, on the Mexican border, and at Belen it crosses the alternative Santa Fe route to the east, that runs via Clovis, Amarillo (Texas) and Wellington (Kansas). Some of the freights are run that way, and at one time the 4—8—4s of the '3765' class were running through from Kansas City to Los Angeles on this route — a somewhat staggering mileage of 1788 on a single run. Dalies, where this alternative route joins the main line, is twenty-seven miles from Albuquerque, and from there on to Gallup used to be one of the favourite racing stretches with steam. It was quite normal for the '3765' class to cover that 133 miles in the level two hours, and on a recent run with the 'Southwest Limited' it took only 131½ minutes to do the complete 160 miles from Albuquerque.

By the time we left Gallup at 8.10 p.m. the light was failing, but the sunset colours in this stark barren country were matchless. It is a much favoured tourist region, between the Chuska and the Zuni mountains, in which latter is one of the largest Indian pueblos in the south-west. Between Gallup and the divisional centre at Winslow the line is practically level, though at high altitude, and except for a street crossing in Holbrook, where speed is limited to 60 m.p.h. they can really run. The line is double-tracked all the way, and by that time in the evening the freights were coming up from the west in rapid succession. We passed the first one soon after leaving Gallup, and the second just before we slowed through Holbrook. It was then 8.56 p.m. and we passed three more within the next forty minutes — all heavy trains and obviously making fast time. Our own Second District engineer was clearly out to make up time, and although it was getting too dark for me to get intermediate detail from the coach, we ran the 127·2 miles from Gallup to Winslow in 96 minutes, start to stop, a bracing average speed of 79 m.p.h. For much of the distance we were doing 90 m.p.h. or a little over, and in this way we had recovered eleven minutes of the lost time.

I would very much like to have had details of how we ran through the night and made up the rest of the lost time; but it was nearly 10 o'clock when we left Winslow, and I was getting drowsy. I had just finished nearly twelve hours of note-taking, following a very short night in the motel at La Junta, and when I awoke soon after daylight next morning and found we were running into Barstow, I made a half promise to myself that one day I would return and run the fascinating road across Arizona and Eastern California in daylight. The distance between Winslow and Barstow is 459 miles, and we covered it in just eight hours, including stops at Flagstaff, Seligman, Kingman, and Needles. Those at Flagstaff and Kingman would probably have been brief; but Seligman and Needles being crew-change points would have taken ten minutes each at least, leaving a running time of 7¾ hours at a guess — an average of all but 60 m.p.h. It is interesting to look at the terrain we traversed in the dark hours, because once we were away from Winslow the physical character of the line changes completely from the fast-running levels that have prevailed from Gallup.

Railroad friends in different parts of the USA have told me what it is like crossing the Arizona Divide. The line is important because it was the first section on which the Santa Fe made a complete change from steam to diesel traction for its freight working, and set up extensive diesel maintenance and repair facilities at Winslow. It is interesting that this project was treated geographically rather than by operating divisions, because the section dieselised included districts of both the Albuquerque and Los Angeles Divisions. Previously, lengthy hauls of water in tank cars had been necessary to supply steam locomotives working in the mountain and desert districts of Arizona. The succession of elevations along the line give a good idea of the intermediate gradients:

Winslow	4856 ft
Canon Diablo	5421 ,,
Cosnino	6464 ,,
Flagstaff	6894 ,,
Bellemont	7130 ,,
Arizona Divide	7335 ,,
Ash Fork	5126 ,,

Between the Arizona Divide and Ash Fork there is a descent of 1 in 33, and in steam days even the prestige passenger trains had to stop at the summit to make a brake test before negotiating this precipitous incline.

The next section, from Seligman to Needles, is generally downhill, in fact in this distance of 148·7 miles the altitude lessens from 5242 to no more than 483 ft above sea level, an average inclination of 1 in 165. West of Kingman there is one stretch of twenty-two miles where the alignment was good enough, on a 1 in 91 descent, for the '3765' class 4−8−4s to be allowed to run up to 100 m.p.h. without any restriction. One of my American friends has remarked: 'Wonder what chance the Santa Fe would have had to beat 126 m.p.h. if they had made an official attempt?' Twenty-two miles of 1 in 91 descent, with a speed limit of 100 m.p.h., seem to offer Heaven-sent opportunities, and there must have been many railroad men who were a little envious of *Mallard*'s exploit remaining unchallenged. If the Santa Fe had tried, and one of the '3765' class had not made it, there would always have been one of the 7 ft 'Hudsons' of the '3460' class that could have been brought west from La Junta to 'have a go'. It would have been interesting to know what was the actual maximum speed attained down this very favourable stretch; but 'The Chief' in its steam-hauled days ran this section of line in the middle of the night, as we were doing on the Amtrak 'Southwest Limited'.

Mallards mean something very different to railroad men in the western states of America. A certain dispatcher on the McCook Division of the Burlington, between Akron and Denver, happened to be an ardent duck shooter, and in regulating train working on his C.T.C. machine he endeavoured to regulate 'meets' at the various crossing loops so that both trains passed each other without stopping. If one train looked as though it would reach the loop before the one coming in the opposite direction, he would check it by signal, so that its approach was slowed up. If he succeeded, and neither train was stopped, he called it 'making a mallard'. The Union Switch and Signal Company, makers of the C.T.C. equipment, heard of this and produced a special brochure entitled 'Mallard hunting in Colorado', showing how their panels could expedite traffic, and gradually the name Mallard became a semi-official term for a non-stop meet. It would not apply on this section of the Santa Fe, which is double-tracked right through from Dalies to Los Angeles.

It was daylight again when we rode into Barstow at 4.55 a.m. (Pacific time) on time, and I saw the Spanish-style station buildings, dark cypress trees, and a semi-desert surround; but here all other interests on the railways are inevitably subordinated to the magnificent new marshalling yard just beyond the passenger station. The cynic might say 'just another yard', but Barstow is a yard with an immense difference. Why build a yard with every sophistication of modern control and operating methods out in the desert? It is true that Barstow has been a divisional point, a locomotive centre almost from the very beginnings of the Santa Fe. Trains stopped there for the locomotives to be refuelled, serviced, and for crews to change and little else. That was just the point. The freights, which represent an overwhelming proportion of Santa Fe business, were made up in block loads in Los Angeles, Richmond, and other points in California, for points east of Kansas City. Traffic was held at its points of origin until enough was assembled to make up a full load. It was the same coming west. Now Barstow, out in the desert, is a four-way junction, and the main line from the east divides into three branches in California — to San Francisco, to Los Angeles, and to San Diego.

The new concept was to move all traffic out of its Californian originating points as soon as possible after its receipt, work it to Barstow in mixed loads, and there to classify it make up block trains for the east. Because traffic was coming from a dozen or more originating stations it seemed clear that enough cars to make a block train would be assembled much more quickly and transit times substantially reduced. Similarly, in the reverse direction all California-bound traffic originating west or south of Kansas City moves to Barstow in random order as fast as it becomes available. Then it is classified into station order for delivery. Such was the operational strategy behind the location and equipment of the great new yard. But when it came to detail the civil engineering was in some respects more important than the many-sided electronic disciplines involved for the actual handling of the traffic. For the site was virtually a desert, and a desert of the most treacherous and unpredictable nature. On the north side of the site is the Mojave River — for most of the year a dried up river bed, but in storms transformed to a raging torrent. Moreover, in such storms water poured down the open hillside to the south of the line, just where it was most advantageous to site the yard!

The engineers had therefore to make the most careful provision for checking the effects of sand blowing, for the control of flood water, and for providing a solid foundation for the very extensive yard facilities. After the grading had been completed, but before any track had been laid, the entire area was covered with crushed rock — which in itself was a useful check against sand blowing. I was fortunate to have a seat on the left-hand side of the train, and as we started away I had a splendid panoramic view of the whole yard area. With the crushed rock covering of the ground, it looked superb in the early morning sunshine. I was told that no less than 20,000 trees and

197

countless shrubs had been planted to provide a 10 ft-high wind-break to check sand blowing from outside railway property. Everywhere one could sense a keen feeling of pride in the job, in the way the gardens around the yard headquarters had been tended, and while the high control tower was some distance away from the main line, its striking design made it a prominent landmark. My sight-seeing had certainly started early on this third day with the Santa Fe.

After the well-nigh stunning spectacle of Barstow Yard in its desert atmosphere, I relaxed a little and just let the passing scene roll by for a while. I thought again of the opening chapters of a lovely book on California published as long ago as 1914 by my present publishers, in which the author tells how the great city to which we were now heading got its name. It is closely linked with the geographical conditions that gave rise to the last great operational feature of the Santa Fe route to the west, the Cajon Pass. The mountain range that divides the Mohave Desert from the lush coastal plain is sometimes known as the Sierra Madre, or Mothering Mountains — today more usually referred to as the San Gabriel and San Bernardino groups. To the early settlers these mountains provided the protecting shield for the wondrous fertility of the coastal plain, from the harsh desert beyond, and in gratitude for that protection they named their first abiding settlement *Nuestro Senora, Riena de Los Angeles*, Our Lady the Queen of the Angels. And it was towards the one marked gap in the mountain range, between the San Gabriel and San Bernardine groups that we were now heading.

Cajon Pass — pronounced Ka-hoon — is one of the most photographed spots in the Santa Fe. All the most dramatic qualities of mountain railroading are here in abundance. The descending gradient is 1 in 33, and we wind slowly down into a rocky wilderness. The eastbound and westbound tracks separate for a while. I saw freight trains toiling uphill. The stream in the gorge was almost dried up. By 6.45 a.m., however, we were down to a greener and more level valley scenery, with mountains on both sides. To the south San Gorgonio was vague in the early morning heat haze, and by that time the speed had picked up considerably and we were running at 60 m.p.h. So, at 7.05 a.m., into San Bernardino, on time. We left again at 7.12 and over level ground were soon making some fast running; but then all my thoughts were becoming directed towards journey's end — not that I was anxious to get my 24–hour stint over and done with, but in sheer curiosity.

I do not think that in my travels I have ever come to a great city — not even Hiroshima — with a greater feeling of curiosity than I did to Los Angeles. To a visitor from afar one thinks of Hollywood and the film industry; of magnates of the 'movies' like Cecil B. de Mille and Sam Goldwyn, perhaps more so than great pioneers like Cyrus K. Holliday and C. P. Huntington who brought in the iron road in the late nineteenth century, and laid the foundations of Los Angeles as a great port, and a centre of western trade and commerce, long before the barons of the silver screen arrived and began to consolidate their own unique empire. It is perhaps understandable that the beginnings of that astonishing development, the influence of which was to spread into every city, town and village of the English-speaking world, are not even mentioned in the beautiful colour-book to which I have already referred; but as a stranger I wondered how the nearness and influence of Hollywood would have permeated the look and life of Los Angeles today.

While breakfasting in the train, running at around 70 m.p.h. I looked out upon the orange groves and at the jacarandas in full bloom, on a morning when there seemed to be not a breath of air. Flags were hanging limp and motionless on their masts. Already the sun was beating down as we approached Pasadena down the middle of a great highway. At one time this approach was little better than some of the older city tracks, a crawl through streets and byways, dead slow, because city ordinance prohibited the use of the whistle; but it is very different now. When nearing Pasadena there is a 5-line freeway on both sides of the double-tracked railway, securely fenced on both sides, and at eight in the morning every lane on both sides of the railway was fully occupied with dashing automobiles. In the middle of all this we were bowling along without let or hindrance at about 40 m.p.h. It was an extraordinary experience. Then the track dipped down, passed under the outbound freeway, and emerged on the left-hand side to enter Pasadena station at 8.27 a.m. We were off again at 8.31, and running very slowly through a fully built-up area of small dwellings and small gardens. It was a riot of flowers: jacaranda, bougainvillea, geranium, palm trees, cypress, oranges, roses, though the houses themselves did not look very attractive architecturally.

Now there were tower blocks ahead. We crossed a high viaduct over a valley with a dried up river, the Los Angeles, and continued down the valley, very slowly all the way till we came to one of those general and complex railway junctions that characterise so many of the approaches to great terminal stations in America — Mission Tower. We wound over its curves and track connections at 8.55 and came to rest in Los Angeles Union station at 8.58 a.m., a little ahead of time. The station itself is interesting. From the operating point of view as a terminal it is conventional, with fifteen tracks and the associated platforms covered, almost to their outer ends, by individual awnings. It dates from no longer ago than 1934-9, when the Santa Fe was rebuilding so many of its old stations in a style that sprang from the indigenous Spanish tradition of the States through which it ran. At Los Angeles the main station building, which is connected to the platforms by a series of subways, is a larger and more pretentious version of the mission-inspired style generally adopted by the Santa Fe in the modernisation of so many of its smaller stations. Quite apart from the architecture, which is attractive, there is a spaciousness about the approach, in the beautifully kept gardens, and the discreet but lavish provision for car-parking that gives this station a character quite of its own among American stations. It even inspired one widely-travelled writer to describe it as the 'most beautiful railway station in the world'. But of the proximity of the film industry there was not the slightest evidence.

CHAPTER SIXTEEN

Los Angeles — meeting the 'Octopus'

When I visited Salt Lake City, as related in Chapter Eleven, I referred no more than briefly to the great historical event of driving the Golden Spike, at Promontory, Utah, in May 1869. The photograph of the ceremony, with Grenville M. Dodge, chief engineer of the Union Pacific, and Samuel S. Montague of the Central Pacific clasping hands in front of the two abutting locomotives, must be one of the best known pictures in the whole history of American railroads. The two supreme dignitaries, Durant of the Union Pacific and Leland Stanford of the C.P., who, despite several bad shots, between them did the actual driving of the Golden Spike, are not noted in the famous photograph. But now I am concerned with an even greater enterprise of Stanford's — greater by far in the ultimate than the completion of the first transcontinental railroad. From 1861 he became associated with three other businessmen of Sacramento, California. Stanford himself was a grocer; Collis P. Huntington and Mark Hopkins were hardware merchants, and Charles Crocker was in the dry goods business. These were unlikely callings for men destined to become some of the greatest railroad entrepreneurs of the age; but not many years were to elapse before they were being called the 'Big Four', and with good reason!

Long before the driving of the golden spike at Promontory, Utah, the Southern Pacific Railroad had been launched, to build a line from San Francisco to San Diego. Soon the Southern Pacific and the Central Pacific were being brought into close association, and following a second golden spike ceremony in 1876, with the completion of the San Joachim line between San Francisco and Los Angeles, it was clear that the Southern Pacific was growing much faster than the Central. By

1881 the main line extending eastward far beyond the original goal of San Diego had reached El Paso, on the Rio Grande River, and by 1884 it had penetrated into Kentucky. In 1885 the Central Pacific was leased to the Southern Pacific and what became known as the Golden Empire was being strongly consolidated. But after the first flush of enthusiasm the status of railroads in popular esteem fell sharply and out in the west the slump in economic conditions in the 1880s, the paucity of new settlers, and the lack of markets for California's farm produce were all blamed upon the 'Big Four', and on the monopoly that they had created for themselves in the virtual merging of the Southern Pacific and Central Pacific into a single operating concern.

Frank Norris, a popular novelist of the day, described the Southern Pacific as:

. . . the symbol of a vast power, huge, terrible, flinging the echo of its thunder over all the reaches of the valley, leaving blood and destruction in its path; the leviathan, with tentacles of steel clutching into the soil, the soulless Force, the iron-hearted Power, the monster, the Colossus, the Octopus.

This, of course, was typical of popular attitude toward railroads in many parts of the world, once they had emerged from their exciting pioneer days and from the novelty of steam traction — especially where it could be seen that they were becoming prosperous. When I was in Los Angeles I had the pleasure of reading a paper by Richard J. Orsi, associate professor of history at California State University, delivered in 1975, entitled 'The Octopus Reconsidered', dealing in an appropriately scholarly fashion with the influence the Southern Pacific had upon agricultural modernisation in California during the fifty years from 1865 to 1915, when the railroad was being subjected to the fiercest criticism. Professor Orsi does not deny that there were times when the 'Big Four' rode rough-shod. But he says:

In response to expansion and change within itself and the national industry, the corporation evolved an extensive, specialized organization whose middle-level executives — generally overlooked by historians who have emphasized the more spectacular careers of the Big Four — acquired considerable expertise and responsibility for fostering development. As a result, the company often used its organizational and financial power to strengthen and diversify California's economy, to stabilize her chaotic society, and to further the welfare of her citizens, including farmers.

Southern Pacific diesels are painted dark grey with a red nose in front of the engineer's cab. Those allocated to the Cotton Belt route, and which carry that name on their sides instead of Southern Pacific, are finished in the same style. Today the Southern Pacific Transportation Company operates through no fewer than twelve States, with a main line railroad mileage of 13,600, partnered by a highway truck (or lorry) service over 27,000 route miles. Its main railroad network, as shown on the accompanying sketch map, makes a rough half-circle counter-clockwise from Portland, Oregon, through Los Angeles and El Paso, round to St Louis, with vital eastward prongs to Memphis

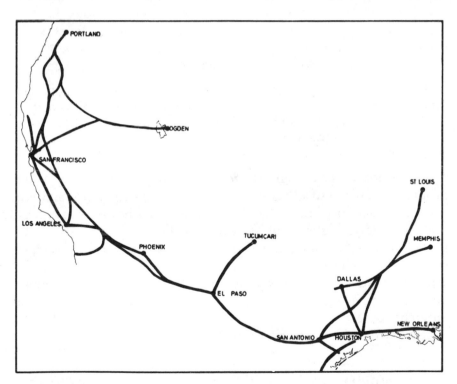

27. Backbone of the Golden Empire—the Southern Pacific system

and New Orleans. Then of course there is the historic west–to–east main line to link up with the Union Pacific at Ogden and the line from El Paso to Tucumcari. So far as the transcontinental route via Ogden is concerned, the original line through the desert country to the north of the Great Salt Lake, past Promontory and the Golden Spike memorial site, was bypassed in 1904 by construction of the Lucin cut–off, whereby the line was carried across the Great Salt Lake, partly on a viaduct and partly on a causeway built across part of the lake.

Around Los Angeles the exposition of Southern Pacific activities arranged for me were centered upon the new West Colton classification yard, the location of which is shown in the map (page 207). Southern Pacific being in the trucking business themselves are well enough aware of its potentialities and of its continuing challenge to railroad freight business, and much of the philosophy of modern operation centres round the one word, speed. In the previous chapter, while referring to the great Santa Fe installation at Barstow, I emphasised the importance now placed upon getting consignments out of city areas quickly. As a Southern Pacific man remarked:

If it takes a day to get a load from Los Angeles to West Colton, and then another day to get it out of the yard, a truck operator picking up a load at the same time would be in El Paso, and speeding eastwards by the time the rail-borne load started on its way on a fast freight from West Colton.

This is not altogether an exaggeration of how slowly freight can progress by rail out of a large city unless there is a strong organisation to ensure it does not linger on the way. But then, one might ask, why build this new, highly sophisticated classification yard fifty miles away from Los Angeles; surely this is asking for delay? The answer, of course, is that a high proportion of the heavy Southern Pacific freight traffic flowing south-eastwards along the arc of the Golden Empire does not originate in Los Angeles. It is Barstow again, but in a different context.

Until 1967 the heavy traffic to and from the Pacific North-West was

28. The Great American Overland all-rail route—the cover of a timetable issued in May 1875

worked mostly over the original main line, via the San Joaquin valley, passing south via Bakersfield and Los Angeles itself. With many through loads this was a slow and uneconomic way of working and dated from the time when the railroad was first built, and Los Angeles was little more than a pioneer settlement. The Southern Pacific fairly grasped this particular nettle, and decided upon the construction of a cut-off line to avoid the highly industrialised area of Los Angeles. It was a cut-off in no half-hearted style — not merely a local bypass! It is nevertheless easy to draw lines on a map and contemplate how much time and distance might be saved; but the cut-off determined upon by Southern Pacific began at Palmdale which, despite its name, lies on the edge of the Mojave Desert in a similar terrain to Barstow. Then it is carried along on the northern slopes of the Sierra Madre till it reaches the Cajon Pass, whence it makes its way, beside the Santa Fe, through this exceptionally difficult country to the coastal plain and a junction with the original main line at West Colton, near to San Bernardino. The merest glance at the map will show the immense advantage to be derived from this cut-off. For through north-south-east traffic the crowded purlieus of Los Angeles itself is avoided, and the local lines are clearer to get city-originating traffic out to West Colton for incorporation in block-load trains.

The Palmdale-Colton cut-off line, seventy-eight miles long, was not unduly expensive to build, in English currency about £140,000 a mile. It was notable as being the longest piece of new main line railroad construction in the USA for more than twenty-five years. It was a highly mechanised operation using the most modern excavating and earth-moving equipment — some of which were described as looking like fanciful monsters out of some science fiction journal. The whole job was completed in the remarkably short time of fifteen months, while the track itself, over seventy-eight miles of main line with twelve miles of siding, was completely laid and surfaced in four months. It was undoubtedly the high degree of organisation and the speed of accomplishment that contributed to the relatively low cost. In England the Settle and Carlisle line, built through the mountain country of the northern Pennines in 1876 cost more than £45,000 a mile, even in those far-off days, for a line seventy-six miles long; having regard to the changed values of money in the meantime

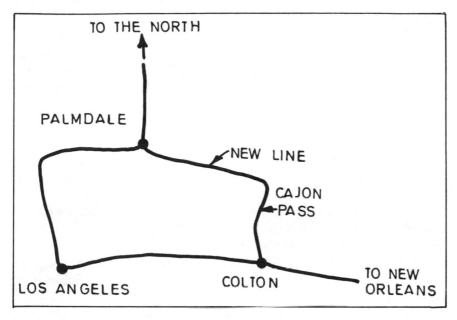

29. Location of the Palmdale line

therefore, the Palmdale–Colton cut-off does not seem to have been an expensive line. The inclusion of the Cajon Pass in its length, with gradients as steep as those of the Santa Fe, presents no problems in these days of multiple diesel-electric haulage. Apart from Cajon Pass much of the new line runs through near–desert country.

West Colton itself is a beautiful example of a modern yard. While all the basic operations are the same as elsewhere there are some interesting refinements. One that interested me was that in the receiving yard the tracks are widely spaced with macadamised roadways between them, so that mobile inspection and repair vehicles can pass readily along. All this work is directed by radio equipment by the Lead Carman, in the Crest Control Tower. In the reception sidings bearings are oiled, safety equipment is checked, minor repairs are made, and empty cars are classified for reloading. At the crest of the hump, in the Crest Conductor's Office, engine foremen monitor the humping of a train. As successive trains are pushed up to the crest they pass over an electronic scale which weighs them while they are in motion, testing them to see if the load is causing any difference in the weight on the left-hand and the right-hand wheels. Any that are out of balance, as it were, or over-weight are automatically switched to special tracks and messages issued giving details of the defects and requests for immediate attention. This is a vital service today, with the huge box-cars now in service, and run at modern freight train speeds. A shifted, or lop-sided load could easily cause a box-car to derail or overturn.

West Colton, like Barstow, has the advantage of not being constrained for space. Consequently the layout of the classification yard with its forty-eight tracks, has space alongside for another twenty-four to be added when required, and has the car-servicing area adjacent. A faulty car detected by the monitoring equipment at the crest of the hump can be switched at once directly into the servicing area. Then also, as West Colton is essentially a staging point in the progress of freight trains, there is a finely equipped locomotive servicing area, with standing room for ninety-eight locomotives. Like all modern diesel depots however the philosophy there is not one of stabling, but of rapid servicing, inspection pits, washing plants, and refuelling. The whole environment of Los Angeles is essentially a 'clean' area, and the diesel servicing area is equipped with anti-pollution industrial waste facilities.

I was taken to see the driving simulator, on which locomotive firemen are trained to be engineers. This was of intense interest to me, because I have the most vivid recollections of the one installed by the London Midland Region of British Railways, at Willesden, for training enginemen in the use of the electric locomotives being introduced on the London-Liverpool-Manchester route. But there is a vast difference between handling a fast passenger train of eleven or twelve cars, running up to 100 m.p.h., and freight trains of anything up to 15,000 tons over mountain grades, on which the control of the brakes is the predominating skill required. Longer, heavier and faster freight trains have imposed new demands, not only upon locomotives and stock, but also on the men at their control, requiring an ability to start and stop the train, control the slack action and speed while running in a variety of track, curve and gradient conditions, without damage to equipment, track, or the goods in transit. When the train is more than a mile long, and the head-end power is supplemented by radio-controlled slave units intermediately, the task of the engineer in negotiating an undulating road is not one for a novice!

Although all American freight trains are equipped with the automatic air brake in its most highly developed forms this does not mean that these very long trains are connected to form a close-coupled assemblage, like a unit passenger train as on the Japanese Shinkansen lines, or a British H.S.T. There is an accumulation of slack in the automatic couplers, and this is an important factor in running a long train. Attempts to start it if the slack is stretched throughout, or bunched at the front end and stretched at the rear, are likely to develop very high drawbar forces. An engineer must know the state of the slack in his train and act accordingly. The same factors apply to increase the difficulty of controlling the slack while running, and with a long heavy train could, if not controlled, result in high longitudinal and lateral forces. A heavy snatch, or a bunch on a curve, could result in damage to the track or the consignments, or at the worst to derailment or a broken coupler. Complete understanding and intelligent use of the brake equipment is vital. This is what the driving simulator can teach the trainee engineer.

The simulator of which a pictorial representation is shown on page 210, simulates all the accompanying locomotive and train motions, and noise, and with visual look-out to the road ahead, its physical features, signals and track facilities, provides a very high degree of reality. The trainee taking the controls in the cab is under the constant surveillance of the instructor, who can vary or impose conditions as the 'journey' progresses. One could imagine, for example, the trainee starting away from New Colton, with four locomotives and a train of 8000 tons to traverse the Palmdale cut-off line. He would have, from the outset, a moving picture of the actual route, and the physical features, gradients, curves and so on have their effects fed, at appropriate speed, into a computer that applies these as traction effects to the simulated traction motor controls. The trainee learns to use the throttle and the brake to meet running conditions and signal aspects, and any mismanagement of the slack, for example, would be reflected in a violent jerk to the cab of the simulator. I was amused to hear that trainees become so absorbed in the experience that they sometimes

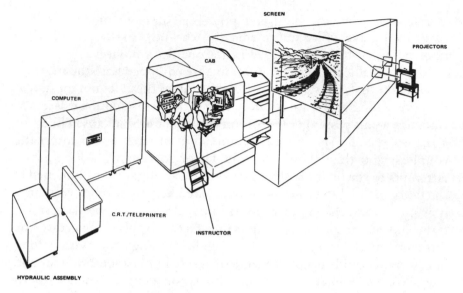

30. Diagram of the locomotive simulator

wave back to people they see at the lineside in the film. I was reminded of an occasion when I was watching the British simulator, and a trainee misjudged his brake application and ran past a red signal. The experience to him was so realistic that he looked out of the simulator cab window to see by how much he had run past! I could have stayed in the Southern Pacific simulator for hours, but as always on this tour, time was not on my side.

There had been no time, so far, to talk about the days of steam on the Southern Pacific, and that evening as it happened steam was very much in my own mind. Next morning I was going north on the 'Coast Starlight', the Amtrak train that runs from Los Angeles to San Francisco and north to Seattle. It is the successor to the celebrated Daylight expresses, for which the very fine 'GS' class 4–8–4s were introduced in 1936. Because of the heavy gradients on parts of the route, and the need for rapid acceleration from the many speed restrictions due to sharp curves, the first six of these engines were fitted with coupled wheels of 6 ft 1½ in. diameter, but experience in running showed that a larger wheel could be accepted to make the faster speeds needed on the more favourable stretches of line. The Daylight expresses, which left both Los Angeles and San Francisco at 8.15 a.m., were allowed 9¾ hours for the run of 471 miles, with intermediate stops at Glendale, Santa Barbara, San Luis Obispo, Salinas and San Jose. The trains were made up of a standard, limited 12-car set, weighing 510 tons tare — Imperial tons. Although this was not a heavy load by American standards the road was very severe in places, with gradients of 1 in 46, and the 4−8−4 locomotives, fitted with boosters, took no assistance on any part of the run. Engines were changed at San Luis Obispo, almost exactly the halfway point on the journey.

The locomotives and their trains had a very striking finish. The deep valences were orange yellow and this band of colour was extended backwards across the tender and throughout the length of the train. Above and below on the tender were cherry-coloured bands, also continued along the coaches, while the smokebox front was in aluminium paint. Technically the locomotives were of advanced design. The four varieties, all built by the Lima Locomotive Works between 1936 and 1942 were as follows:

Class	GS	GS-3	GS-4	GS-6
Cylinders dia. in	27	26	25½	27
stroke in.	30	32	32	30
Coupled wheel dia. ft in.	6−1½	6−8	6−8	6−1½
Boiler pressure lbs/sq. in.	250	280	300	260
Tractive force				
main engine lbs	62,200	62,800	64,760	64,200
booster lbs	12,510	12,200	13,000	11,300

Eventually there were sixty of these fine engines, and those with the smaller coupled wheels were used in fast freight service. Although the load of the Daylights was originally limited to twelve cars, as time went on they were often made up to fifteen cars, or more. These engines were among the last American steam to remain in service; No. 4449 which was not retired until 1958 has been preserved. It was donated to the City of Portland, but in 1976 it was taken out of retirement, given a thorough overhaul, and in the red, white and blue painting style of Amtrak it was used to power the American Freedom Train over part of its travels in Bicentennial Year. In their later years in ordinary service the 'Daylight' 4–8–4s were painted all black, though retaining their aluminium–painted smokebox front and solid pilots (cowcatchers).

I had looked forward to the ride up the coast to San Francisco with the keenest of anticipation. The Amtrak train now leaves Los Angeles at 10 a.m. but because it continues through the night north of San Francisco, its name has been changed to the 'Coast Starlight'. As my taxi took me down to the Union station, I was reminded that what with Southern California Rapid Transit, West Colton Yard, Driving Simulators, and the immense freight activities of the Southern Pacific, I had seen no more of the film industry than a few fifty-year-old photographs of stars of the silent days in my hotel.

The exterior of the Union station of Los Angeles may be very pleasing architecturally but I cannot really commend the present arrangements for handling passengers. The 'Coast Starlight' is an all-reserved train, so that once booked one should be sure of a seat somewhere; but presumably to economise in staffing it seemed that nearly all the passengers for an 18-car train had to pass through a single entrance. I was fortunate in securing a window seat on the western side of the train, from which I would be able to enjoy the prospects along the coast and over the sea; but before long there was great confusion in loading, as more and more very hot and frustrated passengers, many with heavy luggage, struggled through the centre aisle of our coach. The car itself was very hot inside while we waited to start.

Eventually we pulled out at 10.14 a.m. hauled by two General Motors diesels in the Amtrak colours, but almost immediately we were stopped by signal at Mission Tower interlocking and did not get away again until 10.30 a.m. We called at the outer suburban station of Glendale at 10.49 a.m., by then nearly half an hour late, and then at last we were away in earnest. Glendale is 461 miles from Oakland and on a good track, though still running through an area of industrial complexes, we picked up to 60 m.p.h. At a point about twelve miles out of Glendale I noted that we were at last getting out into open country. Our 60 m.p.h. running was soon cut short by the need to slow down for a sharp curve, among a wilderness of arid rocks, and then there was a climb into a long tunnel. Downhill from this point we were soon going much faster, but the scenery was nothing special so far, and there was as yet no sight of the sea. Inside the car there was by this time an absolute babel of conversation. A stretch of thirty-two miles took no more than 29½ minutes, with maximum speeds of 70 to 72 m.p.h. and so we came to our next stop, at Oxnard, 53¼ miles from Glendale in 59½ minutes, start to stop. Soon after restarting we had our first sight of the sea, and then, for nearly two hours, we had a delightful run along the coast.

At first we were running as part of a triple activity inland from the sand dunes. Nearest to the sea were parked, cheek by jowl, hundreds upon hundreds of dormobiles, in perfect line ahead; next came a busy highway and then the railroad, along which we were making an average of about 50 m.p.h. In my notebook I find that I jotted down the 'Dawlish–Teignmouth stretch of the Southern Pacific', but it was really much more than that, because instead of the promenade, there was the very lengthy parking strip next to the sea, plus the highway in between that and the railroad. The sky was cloudless and the scene brilliant. We stopped briefly at Seacliff, and then went on at 55 to 60 m.p.h. gradually climbing until we were high above the sea. By that time we were nearing Santa Barbara. The approach, with palm trees all along the sea front, reminded me of Nice, and resorts on the Italian Riviera. It was all very exotic, and after a very slow run in, we stopped in Santa Barbara station in 48 minutes from Oxnard, inclusive of the brief stop at Seacliff, a run of 37¼ miles. We left again at 12.49 p.m., 28 minutes late, and I took a break from note-taking to have a snack lunch. The air-conditioning in the train was not too effective, but the passing scene made up for any slight discomfort.

Three-quarters of an hour later we had passed on to a stretch of coast that reminded me more of Northumberland than of South Devon. We were running high above the sea, and there was cooler weather coming up. Inland there were rolling moorlands, with the clouds touching down on the higher ridges, quite in the style of northern England. The speed rose to 70 m.p.h. at times, but for the most part our progress was rather slower. It was an interesting coastline with the railroad at times down almost to beach level, amid heathery scrub, then inland for a time into wild upland country, like that of Upper Clydesdale. We ran fast at 70 to 72 m.p.h. down the 'straight' towards the crossing of the Santa Maria River, at Guadaloup, and then there were more slowings. A stretch of thirty-six miles in this terrain took forty-four minutes, and then in moorland country we drew into San Luis Obispo, the halfway house of the journey. The 119 miles from Santa Barbara had taken 137 minutes.

The restart, up a 1 in 46 gradient, is the hardest piece of working on the route, especially as the line is very curving. There is a spectacular double horseshoe, round which we went with screaming wheel-flanges, and as we steadily mounted at 25 to 30 m.p.h. there were some beautiful backward views to San Luis Obispo. Up to this latter station the line from the outskirts of Los Angeles is worked on the automatic block signalling system, but in respect of the critical nature of this heavily graded section, the line from San Luis Obispo is worked C.T.C. as far as Santa Margarita, just beyond the summit. But before reaching this station, while still on the grade, we passed through a succession of tunnels. I did not get the exact mileages here. The milemarkers are fixed on the telegraph posts, and when the range of posts are transferred from one side of the line to the other, it was difficult to pick them up. In this crowded train there was no opportunity for leaving one's seat. After passing Santa Margarita we had a short spell of fast running, up to 75 m.p.h. before slowings for several curves, but by this time we had passed inland, behind the Coast Range, and were travelling amid parched grasslands.

Some day when my total travelling mileage is topping the three million mark, I may be tempted to write a book about fellow-passengers. I have met quite a few. I recall an hilarious hour with six American ladies, fifty years ago, on the 'Shakespeare Express' in England, when their keenness to be in on everything led to some of them taking a hand in the stop-watching of the speed. Then there was the flustered young American, caught in the confusion that seems to surround the departure of many Amtrak trains from their originating station, who, finding himself in the wrong part of the train, wrenched his suitcase from the rack with such violence that it brought one of my cameras with it. The resulting crash on the carriage floor cost my insurance company quite a lot for repairs! Then there was the sprightly Australian girl on the 'North Coast Limited' who tucked in to a steak and chips for breakfast, and was only robbed of having a second

214

helping by the imminence of arrival at her station. Of the insomniac Japanese, who talk loudly and unceasingly all through the night I have suffered several times, but whoever else goes into that book of the future, I shall have several pages for Carol.

She got in at San Luis Obispo, heading homewards after a holiday in California. Our conversation began quite casually, but gradually developed into one of the most delightful I ever recall with a passing acquaintance in a train. She was interested, but not inquisitive. She told me a little about her own life and work as a teacher, a little about the country through which we were passing, and was quietly interested in my own pre-occupation with the railway features of the journey. Usually I am inclined to shun fellow-travellers who take an interest in my own note-taking. They can often be insufferable bores airing their own knowledge — or more usually their lack of it — or weighing in against the shortcomings of the service, and how very much better they could run it themselves. Carol did none of this. We chatted pleasantly about things as they happened; about travels in other parts of the world, and a stage of the journey that would have been relatively featureless passed very quickly. Other passengers in the car who had created the babel of the morning were fortunately mostly asleep by that time in the afternoon!

At Paso Robles we stopped to cross the southbound 'Starlight'. It was very late. We should have passed it before we reached San Luis Obispo. We ourselves called at Salinas at 6.20 p.m. in pleasant agricultural scenery, and were down to the sea again at Watsonville, beside Monterey Bay. The prospect, in the evening light, was very beautiful. We soon turned inland again, however, and had a final spell at 70 m.p.h. before arriving at San Jose. Here the line forks. The accompanying map shows the interesting and distinctive geography of San Francisco, and its environs; the Bay Area as it has become known. In pre-war years the Daylight expresses ran into San Francisco terminus, but the 'Coast Starlight', which is continuing to the north, travels via Oakland, and connection to and from San Francisco East Bay terminal is made by coach. Even having reached San Jose there is another forty-two miles of running before the train comes into the city of Oakland, opposite to San Francisco, and we arrived 25 minutes late, at 9.10 p.m. After the initial delays in the Los Angeles area we had

215

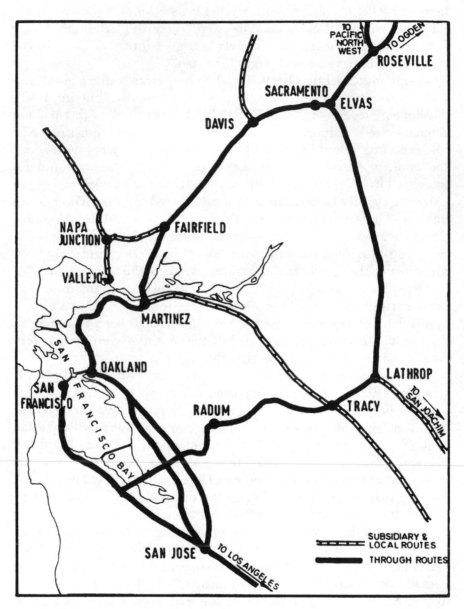

31. Railways in the San Francisco district

therefore held our own, regaining actually a few minutes of time from Glendale. But compared to the pre-war Daylight, we had made eight intermediate station stops, against five, and had conveyed a considerably heavier load.

CHAPTER SEVENTEEN

'Pacific Coast Chapter'

From previous visits I was aware of the particular fascination of the Bay Area, and my friends of the Southern Pacific had given me a delightful welcome on my arrival. But the following day was a Sunday, and then it was the turn of the Railway and Locomotive Historical Society to show me something of the activities of the Pacific Coast Chapter — chapter being used here in the meaning of an organised branch of a society. Brian Thompson, vice-chairman for Northern California, called early for me, and with him I set off for Sacramento, which is 130 miles to the north-east, and, of course, the State Capital of California. If it were for no other reason one would make pilgrimage to Sacramento as the very birthplace of railroads in the west of America, for it is there that the 'ground breaking' and construction of the Central Pacific Railroad began in 1863. This had actually been preceded eight years earlier by the building of a small local line, the Sacramento Valley Railroad; but it was the beginning of what became part of the first transcontinental railroad across the USA that was the catalyst for major development.

Although the Central Pacific eventually became part of the great national enterprise sponsored so vigorously by President Lincoln, the original project at the western end was entirely local. In 1851-2 on 'K' street, Sacramento, between 2nd and 3rd streets there was a block of buildings that carried the sign 'Huntington and Hopkins, Hardware', and in that same block, next door was the Stanford Brothers store. No more than local tradesmen they might have been, but their ideas extended far beyond their home town. Seeing the local success of the Sacramento Valley Railroad they conceived the idea of a line eastwards over the Sierra Nevada Mountains. The bank of the Sacramento River at Front Street and 'K' street was the obvious starting point, because there connection could be made with the steamers that plied on the river between Sacramento and San Francisco, as well as having the advantage of a depot adjacent to the business premises of Huntington, Hopkins and the Stanfords. But although the Central Pacific Railroad was incorporated in California in 1861, such was the general uncertainty prevailing on the outbreak of the Civil War that little was done towards building the line until Congress launched the Union Pacific project in 1862, and the men on 'K' street realised that their own project would form part of a great national achievement. Huntington, Hopkins, and Leland Stanford were joined by Charles Crocker, and such was the zest, tenacity and sheer business acumen that they put into the job that they became known as the 'Big Four'.

How their railroad building enterprise extended far, far beyond the confines of the Central Pacific would fill whole volumes; but I was going to Sacramento to see how the very beginnings of their association is being set on permanent record. On the pleasant road journey out from Oakland, Brian Thompson told me much about the Pacific Coast Chapter of the Railway and Locomotive Historical Society since its formation in 1937; but it is above all the 'Old Sacramento State Historic Park Project' that really fires the imagination. As James Henley has written:

Not since the discovery of gold in 1848 and the great 'Gold Rush' of 1849 has there been so much activity and attention drawn to what is now known as 'Old Sacramento'.

On Front Street, between I and J streets, what is termed the '1849 Scene' is being reconstructed to recreate a portion of Old Sacramento as it appeared to the first immigrants. From the railroad point of view it is remarkable that this reconstruction will include the 'Big Four' building, in which the Central Pacific was born. The original building was demolished to make way for a modern freeway; but with immense foresight, which an Englishman wishes had been shown in some demolition jobs on this side of the Atlantic, all bricks and architectural details were salvaged, and were used in a reconstruction, within the Historic Park, in 1969. One can now look upon the buildings as they were during the building of the Central Pacific Railroad.

219

Historic as this building is, however, it is the reconstruction of the railway depots between Front Street and the banks of the Sacramento River that are providing so utterly fascinating a series of exhibits. It is one thing — and a very great thing — to restore early locomotives and cars to their original conditions, and sometimes to run them in steam; but at Sacramento they are housed in a period depot, in which the greatest care has been taken to render every detail as exact a replica as research can contrive. On arrival at Front Street, and seeing the reconstructed depot, even before going inside and beholding its exhibits, it was not difficult to imagine what the river front had been like in 1869, when the line of the Central Pacific led over the Sierra Nevada, and onwards to its link-up with the Union Pacific at Promontory, Utah. There would still be stage coaches, and horse-drawn cars bringing people to the trains, and above all, the river steamers of the California Steam Navigation Company providing the westward continuation of the transcontinental service to San Francisco. The American river steamer was something completely apart. Earlier in my tour I had seen preserved and working examples, at New Orleans and Louisville, of those amazing stern wheelers; and on the Sacramento-San Francisco run they had gigantic paddlers. What a sight that river front must have presented when the terminus of the transcontinental railroad was alongside.

The preservation of historic locomotives is an activity fraught with many pitfalls, and the critics, who never seem willing to stir far from their favourite armchairs, are always ready to pounce upon details that do not meet with their own self-appointed standards. Having been concerned in a very minor way with certain preservation exercises in England, I could only stand in all humility before the two historic locomotives that are displayed inside the reconstructed passenger depot at Sacramento. They are breathtaking in their perfection of detail. At a second look, however, at the magnificent 4−4−0 No. 60 *Jupiter*, my thoughts strayed to the Golden Spike ceremony at Promontory, and that a locomotive named *Jupiter* stands there today, as part of a national monument. Then, my friends of the Pacific Coast Chapter enlightened me. One could hardly have a reconstruction of the first terminal of the Central Pacific without its most famous locomotive, and the *Jupiter* is also a reconstruction. Recently a famous British locomotive well known in the USA, the *Flying Scotsman*, had its name and number changed twice to feature in a film scenario, and was promptly dubbed 'a preposterous imposter' by an outraged and pedantic correspondent to the railway press. He might have said the same of *Jupiter*, at Sacramento, and had his narrow-minded 'scholarship' laughed to scorn just as thoroughly, because the men of the Pacific Coast Chapter make no secret of the fact their *Jupiter* is no more the *real* one than the disguised *Flying Scotsman* in the film was *Victor Wild*, or *Enterprise*!

The *Jupiter* I saw at Sacramento was originally built by the Baldwin Locomotive Works in 1873, four years after the Golden Spike ceremony, for the Virginia and Truckee Railroad. She was No. 12, and named *Genoa*. She was sold in 1938 to the Eastern Railroads Conference to play the part of *Jupiter* in 'Railroads on Parade', an exhibition staged in New York in 1939-40. After this she was acquired by the Railway and Locomotive Historical Society, and she was splendidly reconditioned in the Southern Pacific workshops at Sacramento in 1969 for the centennial re-enactment ceremony at Promontory in that year. It is in this form that she now adorns the little trainshed of the reconstructed passenger depot. Beside her is No. 13 of the Virginia and Truckee Railroad, the very next engine acquired by that road after the *Genoa*, alias *Jupiter*. No. 13 was also built by Baldwin, but is a Mogul. The enginemen considered the number was unlucky so themselves changed it to 15. It worked on the V. & T. for more than fifty years, and in 1924 was sold to Pacific Portland Cement, of Gerlach, Nevada. After another fourteen years service it was donated to the Pacific Coast Chapter. She was restored, including her original number, 13, by the Bethlehem Shipyard, San Francisco, in 1966. It was an extensive job, and involved provision of a new cab, cowcatcher, smokestack, headlight, boiler jacket, and a new frame for the tender. Replica builders' plates were also added. Today, she is another little gem.

These restoration jobs have involved an immense amount of research and patient work, the unearthing of old drawings, and the exercise of a craftsmanship that only dedicated enthusiasts are nowadays prepared to give. Fred A. Stindt, Chairman of the Pacific Coast Chapter was away in the Pacific North-West at the time of my visit, but from his colleagues at Sacramento I learned something of the work he put in when V. & T. No. 13 was being restored. Hardly a lunch hour passed when he was not at Bethlehem Shipyard discussing some point in the restoration work. It took nearly a year, but it proved that the job could be done, and its completion to the exquisite museum piece now on display was a vital factor in the securing of State assistance towards the inclusion of a railroad exhibit in the now-classic Old Sacramento State Historic Park. And so the two little engines stand side by side, in immaculate splendour.

Then they took me outside to see, by contrast, the largest and most powerful type of steam locomotive operated by the Southern Pacific. By this time in my tour I had seen some pretty large locomotives, treasured as museum pieces, but No. 4294 of the Southern Pacific seemed to occupy a very special place of its own in American motive power development. One of the great problems arising from the growth to gigantic proportions of the traditional steam locomotive was that of giving the engineer an adequate look-out ahead, past boilers of ever-increasing diameter and length. In referring to the largest of them all, the Union Pacific 4−8−8−4 'Big Boy' I mentioned that there was about 70 ft of boiler ahead of the cab window! Such a situation, particularly on single-track routes, could be tolerated only because of the general absence of tunnels; otherwise the exhaust fumes in the confined space, and the obscuring of the look-out would have presented an impossible situation. Now the Southern Pacific has tunnels on its heavily graded single-tracked routes, but fortunately in its general use of oil firing there was a simple and effective solution, to turn the engine round back to front.

The major haulage problem centered upon the 80-mile long section between Roseville Yard, near Sacramento, and Sparks, Nevada, with a ruling gradient of 1 in 37½, frequent curves, many tunnels and some snowsheds. Until 1928 the Southern Pacific had used 3-cylinder 4−10−2s on the heavy freight hauls, and although the engines were oil burners the crews had to wear gas masks for the tunnels. It was in 1928 that the Baldwin Locomotive Works built the first cab-in-front articulated engines of the 2−8−8−4 type for this strenuous duty. Because these were oil-burners there was no disadvantage in having the tender separated from the cab of the locomotive. Articulated engines with a two-wheeled leading truck had a reputation for rough riding at the front end, and on these Southern Pacific cab-in-front versions it was found that the 2-wheeled truck ahead of the chimney rode just as roughly with the locomotive turned back to front, so much so that the crews were forbidden to ride the deck above the two-wheeled radial truck when the speed was more than 25 m.p.h.

Here, at Sacramento, I was able to see and climb aboard No. 4294, the last steam locomotive purchased by the Southern Pacific. Delivery of her was taken from Baldwins in March 1944. There had been several varieties of these great locomotives and the proportions of No. 4294 are generally those of the group first introduced in 1930. In these latter the tenders were of the circular section Vanderbilt type, whereas No. 4294 has the straight-sided tender of the 1942 series. All the Southern Pacific cab-in-front articulateds were non-compounds. They were designated for use on both passenger and freight service, and they were extensively used on troop trains during the second world war. The four cylinders were 24 in. diameter by 32 in. stroke; the coupled wheels were 5 ft 3½ in. diameter and the boiler pressure 250 lbs per sq. in. The tractive force was 123,400 lbs, which compares with 110,200 lbs on the Chessie 2−6−6−6, 105,000 lbs on the Rio Grande 4−6−6−4, and 135,400 lbs on the Union Pacific 'Big Boys' — a mighty engine. They needed to be for working over the former Central Pacific line, with the loads piled on to them in the war years.

Working the fruit trains east from California was a prestige job for the cab-in-front locomotives. Each of them consisted of a hundred cars, a total load of 6000 tons, and to climb the long and severe gradient to Sparks, Nevada, required no fewer than *four* of these huge 4−8−8−2 locomotives. It was found from operating experience that the best results for braking and controlling the slack were obtained if there were two locomotives at the head end. Then came about sixty-five cars, after which locomotive No. 3 was inserted. Then another twenty-five cars, and No. 4 locomotive; ten more cars and lastly the caboose. Thus these trains set off from Roseville, to pound away at 10 to 15 m.p.h. for eighty miles, with nearly 500,000 lbs of tractive force going all out for most of the way! A noted American technical author, Alfred W. Bruce, has written:

223

The movement of these trains over the mountain at night was undoubtedly one of the most impressive train operation sights to be seen on any railroad in the world.

That I can well believe. The '4294' preserved is a noble memory of a mighty job in transportation. To climb into her cab and to experience the extreme height of the foot-plate above ground level is to appreciate something of the scale of steam operation on the Southern Pacific.

To round off the day, and give me yet another vivid contrast, Brian Thompson took me out to Roseville Yard, where trains are marshalled for the runs north, east, and south. A block load train for Chicago was about to leave, and so we motored a few miles farther east to photograph it at speed. It was setting out for the climb over the Sierra Nevada, which needed four 4−8−8−2s for a 6000 ton load. This train had 150 cars, and eventually it came thundering along with three diesels on the head end and a *posse* of four slave diesels, radio controlled from the head end, at mid-train: *seven* diesels, about 23,000 horse-power, under the control of one engine crew. I thought the succession of cars, passing us at about 50 m.p.h., was never going to end.

PLATE 17   The afternoon 'Hiawatha' leaving Milwaukee; 13 cars hauled by a streamlined 4–6–4 No. 101.

PLATE 18   A Quartet of 4–8–4s

1   Wabash class 'o–1' of 1930, for fast freight: T.E. 70,750 lbs.

2   Lackawanna class 'S.447' of 1934 for fast freight: T.E. 72,000 lbs.

3   Great Northern: 'Empire Builder' express passenger of 1930: T.E. 58,300 lbs.

4   Rock Island: mixed traffic, of 1930. T.E. 66,000 lbs main engine; 13,100 lbs booster.

PLATE 19

1   Seattle, passenger
station.

2   Denver, Union
station.

PLATE 20

1   Union Pacific: the 'City of St Louis' leaving Denver in 1948, hauled by 4–8–4 No. 806.

2   One of the Union Pacific 'Big Boys' 4–8–8–4 No. 4023 at Evanston, Wyoming, in 1947.

3   Southern Pacific: 'The Daylight' leaving Glendale, California, for San Francisco in 1939, hauled by 4–8–4 No. 4426.

1   Burlington Northern: C.T.C. control panel for Chicago commuter area at Aurora.

PLATE 21

2   In the control tower, Southern Pacific West Colton Yard, near Los Angeles, California.

PLATE 22
Rio Grande Steam

1   4–8–4 No. 1801 in Denver, 1940.

2   California fast freight crossing the Arkansas River, near Yale, Colorado: 42 cars, hauled by 2–8–8–2 No. 3612.

3   50-car freight emerging from Tennessee Pass Tunnel – 10,240 ft above sea level – hauled by 4–8–2 No. 1517, in 1941.

PLATE 23

1   Moffat Tunnel, east end.

2   In 1940, the 'Exposition Flyer' near Rollinsville, Colorado, hauled by 4–8–4 No. 1702.

3   The 'Rio Grande Zephyr' in Byers Canyon, west of Sulphur Springs in 1970, with 3 diesel locos, Nos. 5761–5762–5763.

PLATE 24   Preserved in Colorado

1   The giant Burlington 4–8–4 No. 5629 and No. 191, 2–8–0 built in 1880 for the Denver South Park & Pacific.

2   Standard gauge 2–8–0 No. 583 of the Denver & Rio Grande, dating from the conversion of the gauge from 3 ft in 1890.

3   The Shay, No. 14, bringing the passenger train into Central City.

PLATE 25   Santa Fe
Steam

1   One of the high speed 4–6–4s that used to work the
transcontinental expresses over the eastern part of the
main line, between La Junta and Chicago: engine No.
3463, at La Junta.

2   'The Chief' in 1941, at the top of Cajon Pass,
California, hauled by 4–8–4 No. 3768.

3   An 83-car westbound freight near Tejon, New
Mexico, hauled by 2–10–4 No. 5017.

PLATE 26   Barstow Yard,
California

1   A striking view of the
elevated control room

2   Configuration of tracks in the
desert–like terrain, that allows
simultaneous arrival and
departure of heavy trains.

PLATE 27
Maximum Steam
Power

1   Santa Fe: the 'California Limited' rounding a curve
near Blanchard, New Mexico, hauled by 4–8–4 No.
3779.

2   Southern Pacific: a heavy freight near Lang,
California; 61 cars with one 4–8–8–2 (cab in front)
articulated pulling, and a second pushing about a mile
in rear.

3   Two of the giant 3-cylinder 4–12–2s of the Union
Pacific on a 68-car westbound freight climbing
Sherman Hill, Wyoming.

1 Eastbound train on Palmdale–Colton cut-off line near Cajon Pass, southern California.

PLATE 28 Southern Pacific Freight

2 Switcher engine pulling containers from Oakland Yard. In the background is the famous Bay Bridge which links San Francisco to Oakland.

1   Inside the reconstructed 1869 station of the Central Pacific Railroad, showing the 4–4–0 No. 60 *Jupiter* in the foreground, and 2–6–0 No. 13 behind.

PLATE 29   Sacramento-Pacific Chapter

2   In the cab of the 4–4–0 locomotive *Jupiter*.

PLATE 30

1 On the Great Northern Line in the Cascade Range: an eastbound freight powered by three 3300 horsepower diesels, crossing the Skykomish River, near Sunset Falls, Washington. The peak to the left of the picture is Mount Index.

2 A Southern Pacific container train in the foothills of the Sierra Nevada Mountains.

PLATE 31

1 Chicago & North Western; the 'San Francisco Overland Limited', 14 cars on, approaching Omaha, Nebraska, hauled by streamlined 4–6–4 locomotive No. 4005 (Class E 4) in 1938.

2 Pennsylvania RR: the LCL–1, fast freight from New York approaching Pittsburgh, hauled by 4–8–2 locomotive No. 6846 (Class M 1a).

3 One of the numerous and celebrated 'K 4' Pacifics of the Pennsylvania, No. 3740.

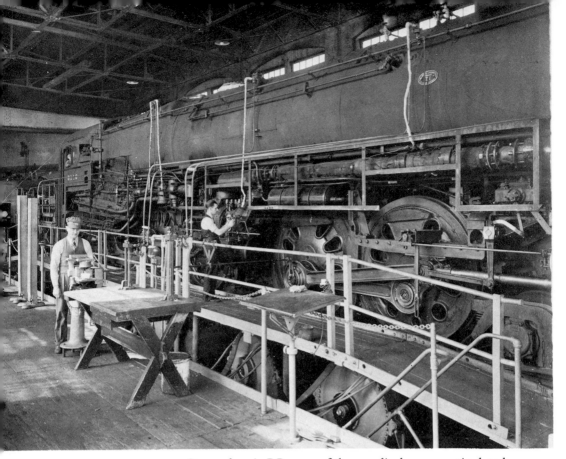

PLATE 32   Pennsylvania RR: one of the 4-cylinder non–articulated 4–4–4–4 locomotives of Class 'T 1', on the stationary test plant in Altoona Works.

CHAPTER EIGHTEEN

Southern Pacific — 'Tops'

The Southern Pacific is one of the most highly organised railways I have ever had the pleasure to study. Its vast geographical extent covering, together with its associated line the St Louis Southwestern, no fewer than twelve States, is reason enough for having a closely-knit centralised control. New Orleans, the most easterly point of its own tracks, is 2480 miles from headquarters in San Francisco, and four days travelling time by passenger train, while St Louis is just 3000 miles away. Then there is the prong running north-eastwards through New Mexico from El Paso to connect with two routes of the Rock Island at Tucumcari; the great transcontinental line across the Sierra Nevada range to join up with the Union Pacific at Ogden, and the north main line through California and across Oregon from south to north to meet the complicated railway purlieus of the Pacific North-West at Portland. In all, the Southern Pacific operates 13,500 miles of line, the great majority of which is single-track. In Chapter Sixteen of this book I described something of the working in the Los Angeles area. It is now time to look at the overall control of the entire system.

Modern aids to efficient working, such as centralised traffic control (C.T.C.) on the critical sections of line; diesel-electric locomotives that can be worked in multiple, and as radio-controlled slaves mid-train on a very heavy consist, and highly automated marshalling yards like West Colton, all have a major part to play; but on Southern Pacific it became evident that these important individual improvements were not enough. What was needed was a greater degree of overall control, and this could not be exercised without information — instant up-to-the-minute information, as to what was happening over every one of those 13,500 miles of line. It is estimated that in the running of this

225

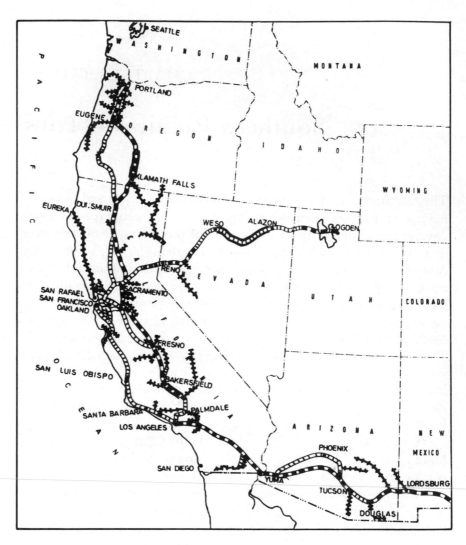

32. The Southern Pacific, and its signalling. A Key is included in the facing extension map.

great railway there are, at any time of the day, about 100,000 items of car and train movement, traffic on hand, locomotives, and of staff, that are in a constant state of change, and the problem was to devise a system whereby a bank of information would be constantly available, constantly updated minute by minute, and in a central 'store' from which those immediately involved could ask the questions they needed answering to run their particular part of the overall job. The outcome was the invention and introduction of the Total Operations Processing System — 'TOPS' — probably the most complete information service ever made available to the departments responsible for the planning, direction, control, and reporting of a great business organisation.

Its prime objective was to gather the many and various pieces of railroad information generated in the daily running of the trains, and to make them available, *as they occur*, throughout the entire Southern

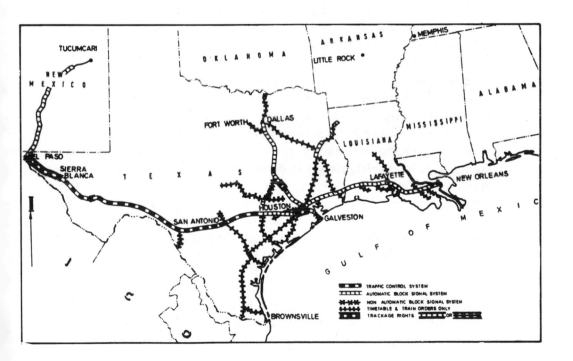

Pacific network. This does not mean that certain key points are constantly flooded with a mass of information, but that the vital information needed to plan or control a certain operation is there, in the 'bank', ready for the asking. In the pleasant headquarters offices of Southern Pacific, in San Francisco, looking out across the Bay, with the teeming road traffic on the great Oakland suspension bridge prominent in view, Mr Jordan L. Glew, senior assistant manager of operating data systems, piloted me gently through the well-nigh incredible processing equipment whereby those 100,000 items of constantly changing information are fed into the central computer, there digested, and quickly made available in the form any operator who needs information requires it. Information was coming in every minute from 109 major yards, 74 teleprinter yards, 75 traffic offices, 16 mechanical engineering offices, 60 administrative offices, and many other activities. The average time for a message from any out-station to be processed and available to those who need it is about three to four seconds.

These are just a few of the things that 'TOPS' does. It maintains a record of *every* car on Southern Pacific lines, using the car initial and number to identify it, whether it is in a yard, in an industrial zone, or while actually moving in a train. It provides those who have responsibility for providing power for the trains reports as to the availability of freight and passenger locomotives, and instant information if there is a likelihood of any shortages developing, anywhere on the system. It promotes better and faster service to traders, through the up-to-the-minute car tracing information and improved yard operation. A consignee awaiting a certain load can be told exactly where it is on the line, and how soon he may expect delivery. Above all, it permits the sharing of information by the operating, traffic and accounting departments, to strengthen controls and avoid costly duplication of effort. Mr Glew suggested that I might like to ask the computer a question, and I thought of the lengthy manifest train I had seen leaving Sacramento for the east on the previous evening. I was interested to know how far it had travelled. The answer came within five seconds, giving its exact location on the paired track section which the Southern Pacific operates with the Western Pacific in Nevada, between Weso and Alazon.

'TOPS' has certainly caught the eye of many other railroads, and in addition to several adaptations of it in the USA and Canada it is being installed on British Railways to cover the entire network in the United Kingdom. In the very week when I was writing this chapter I had a remarkable example of what 'TOPS' can do; and though it was entirely a British case it illustrated most vividly the efficacy of the system initiated on Southern Pacific. It occurred during the production of a television documentary to which I was acting as technical and historical adviser, centred upon the railway races between London and Scotland in the late nineteenth century. The script included a sequence to be filmed *inside* the East Coast express of 19 August 1895, highlighting the hair-raising passage round the S-curve at Portobello, near Edinburgh. To provide authentic sound effects of the running it was necessary to have a six-wheeled coach, and one that could be run at between 75 and 80 m.p.h. In 1978 it was doubtful if any such vehicles still existed on British Railways, but the Public Relations department were co-operating magnificently and in response to the producer's request they asked 'TOPS'. Immediately the answer came back that only four existed, two of which were in no fit state to run at all, let alone at the speed needed to get the sound effects we needed. But one was found at Chester, and after that it was only an operating matter, rather than a search operation, to move it across to York and equip it for what proved to be its last run on British Railways.

Reverting now to Southern Pacific, 'TOPS' has been described as the company's greatest non-human tool for making sure that customers get the kind of service they expect. At any one time there might be 120,000 cars on the line, on every one of which 'TOPS' has up to the minute information, whether a particular car (and its consignment) is in one of the 850 or so trains that will be on the move, in one of the 200 yards, or lying in any one of the 130,000 industry service tracks. A customer in San Jose, or anywhere else, wanting to know how his shipment is progressing telephones his local Southern Pacific traffic office. The question is instantly referred to the central 'TOPS' computer in San Francisco, and in about 3½ seconds — yes, seconds! — a traffic representative would reply, for example, 'Your shipment is just outside of Reno, sir, and the train is right on schedule'.

'TOPS' is used to great advantage to link up consignments at

229

intermediate points with through trains. An interesting, but no more than typical example is that of M.S.E. — Merchandise Special East — that leaves Los Angeles daily for East St Louis. It is a 'hotshot' piggyback freight, making a through run of 2452 miles. According to advice of intermediate traffic that is being offered, via 'TOPS', the normal schedule for picking up cars en route is modified from day to day, so that the M.S.E. gathers up all the available traffic as it proceeds eastwards. At El Paso a number of cars are set down, and at San Antonio the consist is divided to form another train for Houston, Texas; then from San Antonio onwards the M.S.E. has a block load through to East St Louis. But like the daily schedule of the M.S.E. the functioning of 'TOPS' itself, once installed, has not been on a final no-further-change basis. Its users are constantly finding new things for it to do, and Southern Pacific and computer specialists have programmed many thousands of changes into the system since it was first put into service.

From my own long professional association with signalling I was naturally interested in the involvement of 'TOPS' in train movement, and I learned that information on all aspects of *every* train, its crews, cars, locomotives and the waybills, are assembled in the central files. All trains moving across the Southern Pacific system are categorised thus:

(a) Scheduled manifest trains
(b) Overflows
(c) Drags
(d) Bulletin locals

The manifest trains are those regularly scheduled and running to a specific timetable, and the data fed into the master computer will enable the actual train performance to be established in relation to the published schedule, its speed, its consist, and variations in loading as from one station to another. An overflow freight can be regarded as an extra, whereas a 'drag' is the American equivalent of the old-style English slow goods, which picked up and set down traffic at numerous points along the route. It is the existence of 'TOPS' as an information service that facilitates in no small way the running of trains like the 'Blue Streak Merchandise', a 'hotshot' freight leaving East St

Louis each night at 10 p.m. with eighty or ninety cars on, and averaging 49 m.p.h. throughout to Los Angeles, including all stops en route to add extra cars, change crews, refuel and make safety inspections. It is one of America's fastest transcontinental freights, and intermediately runs up to maximum speeds of 70 m.p.h.

It must be emphasised that 'TOPS' is primarily a recording, rather than a control activity. It assembles the information from which traffic control decisions can be taken. On Southern Pacific there are four different systems of regulating the flow of traffic along the lines, namely:

(a) Centralised traffic control (C.T.C)
(b) Automatic block signalling
(c) Non-automatic block signalling
(d) Timetable and train orders only

From Flatonia, about a hundred miles west of Houston, Texas, to Los Angeles the main line is equipped with C.T.C. throughout. So also is the inland Joachim Valley line from Bakersfield to Sacramento. The first part of the Old Central Pacific line from Sacramento eastwards is equipped with automatic block signalling but from Roseville the line to the north, via Dunsmuir, Klamath Falls and Eugene to Portland is C.T.C. throughout. Within this general area there are a number of short critical sections within automatic block signalling territory that are C.T.C. equipped, such as the heavily graded section on the coast line between San Luis Obispo and Santa Margarita, and the general situation so far as signalling is concerned may be appreciated from the system map, with the form of signalling illustrated by coding on the lines. So far as the St Louis Southwestern section is concerned, this line is equipped with C.T.C. throughout from its inter-section with the Dallas–Houston main line of the Southern Pacific itself at Corsicana to Thebes, Illinois, whence the line to East St Louis is jointly owned with the Missouri Pacific. Taken all round the signalling installations on the Southern Pacific make a very impressive set up.

The changeover to diesel traction could be regarded as nothing more than another example of the universal trend on American railroads, until one comes to examine some of the details of operation, then and now. After my sojourn in the San Francisco area I was due to go north to Seattle on the Amtrak 'Coast Starlight', and my hosts said they hoped I would not sleep too soundly, so that I should be awake in the morning to appreciate the 40-mile long descent of the Cascade Range. They then told me what an almost overwhelming bugbear that incline had been in steam days. Trains weighing about 4000 tons were brought south from Portland by one of the giant cab-in-front articulated locomotives of the 4–8–8–2 type and at Oakridge no fewer than three helper locomotives were added to a train of this size. Practice on this incline was to insert them at various intervals, and the process of cutting the train, with all the attendant technique of dealing with the slack in the couplers, and the remarshalling, was a time-consuming business.

Then they would get under way and make slow progress up the incline with all four locomotives going all out. Such was the effort involved, however, that in no more than twenty miles — *twenty miles* — a stop had to be made for all four locomotives to take water! This again required some tricky and expert work in spotting the locomotives opposite to the water towers, and usually involved dividing the train again, so that two or more locomotives could be watered simultaneously. Again there was the need to draw the various sections of the train up so that the slack was right, when the time came for recoupling. So they would start again and at no more than about 10 m.p.h. thresh their way up to Cascade Summit. Heaven only knows how long it took to lift one of these big trains up the entire forty miles; but spectacular as steam must have been in working up this bank, the advantage with the diesels has been quite phenomenal, quite apart from the saving in locomotive crews.

A visitor from Europe takes a little time to get over his astonishment at the way in which automobiles are carried on the American railroads, with the huge triple-decked trailers loaded with fifteen cars each. These are certainly spectacular, but the transfer from road trucking to railroad brought troubles of its own. The change was not to everyone's liking. Employees of the trucking business, deprived of some work, had their own back on autos travelling by rail by rock-throwing and resort even to firearms, while to plain vandals a glittering array of new autos on a triple-decked trailer car would naturally be a very attractive target! The damage became so serious that General

Motors approached Southern Pacific and other railroads to devise some form of protection. The trouble was not confined to that part of the delivery journey made on the railroad. Fine automobiles like Cadillacs were targets from the moment of leaving the factory, and for these large vehicles the 'Stac-pac' system was devised. Three of them are loaded, one above the other, into 20 ft containers, and four of these containers are carried on a single flat car. For smaller autos the triple-deck trailers are still used, but with the sides and tops completely closed in, carrying fifteen in safety, and having the drive-on, drive-off facility.

For smaller autos, however, the Southern Pacific has introduced the remarkable 'Vert-a-pac' system, which provides for the conveyance of no fewer than thirty autos on a single car. This is a special purpose vehicle of ingenious design. On each side of its 85 ft length there are fifteen doors which are hinged at the bottom, each opening downwards so as to provide a drive-on ramp. Each auto is positioned and secured on its own ramp-door, and then when the door is closed the auto hangs nose down inside securely held, and fully protected. There is great economy of space in this arrangement, which allows twice as many autos to be conveyed on the same length of railroad car as on the older triple-deck open type, and in far greater safety. Another Southern Pacific speciality developed for the automobile industry is the 'Hy-Cube' box-car, which provides 10,000 cubic feet of cushioned load space for bulky auto parts.

The Southern Pacific people talked to me about intermodal traffic. In this present age, in all the advanced countries of the world there can be no monopolies, no 'closed-shops' of one form of transport or another, and Southern Pacific have been to the fore in developing intermodal traffic, using in their respective contexts, rail and road to the best advantage. When writing of Illinois Central Gulf earlier in this book, I referred to the development of piggyback traffic; in this modern process Southern Pacific has a special part to play. In the rapidly expanding volume of world trade the container-ship has revolutionised marine transport, and the way in which its attributes can be co-ordinated with container and piggyback traffic on railroads are being exploited to the full. There was a time when America was seen as the future land-bridge between east and west; now it is in process of realisation, with the Southern Pacific running container trains from Los Angeles to the Gulf ports, in the chain of transportation from the Far East to Great Britain, Scandinavia, and other parts of Europe. The Southern Pacific now has intermodal terminals — rail, road, ship — at Portland, Oakland, Houston, New Orleans, Dallas and St Louis, as well as at Los Angeles. It will be appreciated that although the west to east route from Oakland to the Union Pacific and Chicago is a very important one the greatest artery of traffic on the Southern Pacific is the Portland, Los Angeles, El Paso, San Antonio axis, forking at the last-mentioned to St Louis and New Orleans.

With such a vast and extended mileage operating under C.T.C. and remote control conditions, it is vital to keep the closest scrutiny upon the physical running of the trains, particularly as much of it is in near-desert country. The Southern Pacific accordingly has a very comprehensive arrangement for detecting of hot axle-boxes. On the Pacific lines for example, detectors are installed at no fewer than 266 locations. On the main line between Los Angeles and Tucumcari, in a

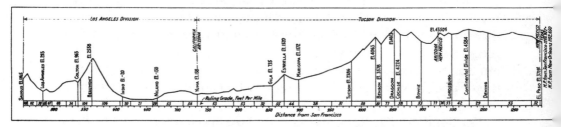

33. Profile of the line between Los Angeles and El Paso

distance of 1147 miles there are 43 installations, at an average distance of 26½ miles. In the neighbourhood of major traffic areas, such as Tucson and El Paso, some of the detectors are uni-directional only, on the few sections of double-track; but the great majority record for both east and westbound traffic. On the coast line, by which I had travelled from Los Angeles to Oakland, as related in Chapter Sixteen, there are twelve detector locations in a distance of 381 miles, an average of 31½ miles. These infra-red heat sensing devices warn trainmen of overheated axle-boxes before they get bad enough to cause a failure of the bearing and possible derailment. With trains of the great length now operated, the major part of the consist is a very long way beyond the personal observation limit of any of the crewmen. On the latest type of hot box detector equipment the warning is linked into the C.T.C. system, and lights are flashed to provide direct warning to the dispatcher as well.

The very few long distance passenger trains working over Southern Pacific tracks are operated by Amtrak, but a busy commuter service is run by S.P. in the San Francisco area. Recently what is known as the Bay Area has attracted much attention from the introduction of the Rapid Transit network; but this is an entirely separate enterprise, not connected in any way with Southern Pacific. The railroad operated commuter service runs from the terminus in San Francisco southwards through the suburbs on the west side of the bay to San Jose, where this line connects with the main north to south route. This is a 47-mile run, and to carry some 10,000 passengers each weekday a fleet of twenty-three locomotives and a hundred double-decker cars is maintained. The service is fast and frequent, and in the rush hours trains run at three-minute headway. But of course Southern Pacific's commuter service operates under the same crippling disadvantage suffered by every similar operation in the world: it is busy only for two hours in the morning and evening peak periods. A very high standard of equipment has to be maintained for safe and fast working during those times, but it is grossly under-utilised during the rest of the day.

I was booked to go north from Oakland on the 'Coast Starlight'. The train was very full, although made up to eighteen cars, and I had some difficulty in finding a seat; but eventually after humping my luggage through several crowded cars I found a very comfortable berth and settled down for the night. After a full programme with my friends of Southern Pacific I was soon asleep, but fortunately I woke soon after first light, when we stopped at Dunsmuir. We were climbing to the high tableland that marks the State boundary between California and Oregon, and happily I was awake to see one of the greatest sights of this route — Mount Shasta. In the unreal half-light that preceded a cloudless midsummer dawn that glorious mountain, deeply snow-clad, had an ethereal beauty. We were climbing steeply among conifers, and then over the summit, and on over level ground at 70 m.p.h. to Khampa Lake. There were distant rearward glimpses of Mount Shasta, and other high mountains to our west. We passed two southbound freights in quick succession, and continued through the conifers at 60 to 70 m.p.h. until coming to Cascade Summit, at around 8 a.m., which I remember more for the breakfast schemozzle in the train rather than for the scenery!

When we were settled in the dining car I saw that we had commenced a steady descent through very beautiful mountain country. This was the gradient to which I referred earlier in connection with steam working with the cab-in-front articulated locomotives. In its constant curvature, tumbled woodlands, and profusion of rhododendrons in bloom it reminded me of some of the Scottish inclines, but on a vaster scale. There were several short tunnels, and avalanche shelters on the approach to some of the tunnels. At times the line swung round and went due south, and we overtook an 88-car northbound freight in one of the loops. By about 9.30 a.m. the valley was opening out, and far below was a vast logging plant; we had to negotiate a spectacular horseshoe bend to get down to its level. This was Oakridge, the one-time steam locomotive helper station for the toilsome ascent to the Cascade Summit. We passed at 9.45 a.m. and then came on to a faster, straighter stretch of line. But it remained a most beautiful country of a broadening valley, with the river widening and masses of early summer flowers in the fields on both banks. With the mountains still of considerable height on both sides this first introduction of mine to the state of Oregon reminded me of certain regions in the Austrian Tyrol.

We were now approaching Eugene, which is a concentration point for the vast timber traffic of the region. Great stacks of it were ranged beside the line, with water playing on it to minimise the risk of fire. So, at 10.50 a.m. we drew into Eugene, nicely on time. The long run through the night, 587 miles from Oakland, had taken 13 hrs 40 min., an average of 43 m.p.h., which in consideration of the hard climbing up past Mount Shasta, and the necessarily slow running down the steep and winding descent from Cascade summit, was very good. We left exactly on time at 11.07 a.m. for the last stage of the journey over Southern Pacific tracks. It is 122 miles to Portland, Oregon, and the time allows only two minutes short of three hours for the run. I have notes that the country looked very English (!), mostly open and level valley land, with a mountain range some eight or ten miles to the east. We had no cause to hurry unduly and rolled pleasantly along at about 60 m.p.h. The actual approach to Portland was very slow, running for some distance at 10 m.p.h. and crossing a large lifting bridge. Eventually we came to rest at 1.48 p.m., 17 minutes early, having averaged 45·5 m.p.h. from Eugene. And at Portland I said farewell to the Southern Pacific, but carrying a host of pleasant memories, sheaves of notes, and many interesting photographs. From now onwards we should be on the tracks of the Burlington Northern.

CHAPTER NINETEEN

Pacific Northwest — The Milwaukee

The building of transcontinental railroads in North America was an exciting business prompted by a variety of incentives. The famous link-up between the Central Pacific and the Union Pacific at Promontory in 1869 was originally strategic, while the heroic drive of the Canadian Pacific through the uncharted wilds of British Columbia was to redeem a pledge to the western provinces on the formation of the Dominion of Canada. But the race to the Pacific North-West — for race it became! — had only one objective, trade. One has only to glance at a map of Washington State, or still more so a large-scale map of Seattle and its environs to appreciate what magnificently protected harbours and anchorages had been provided by nature; and across the Pacific lay the riches of the Orient, the sea routes to Australia and New Zealand, and of course Hawaii. The Northern Pacific reached the west coast first, completing the line into Tacoma in 1877 by the route I shall take the reader eastwards in the next chapter; but then there came into the Pacific North-West that tremendous character, James Jerome Hill.

Hill was one of the syndicate of four that got construction of the Canadian Pacific really moving. It was he who brought in that colossus of railroads, W. C. Van Horne, confidently expecting that the great American entrepreneur would support his contention that the Canadian Pacific main line to the west should be carried through Sault Ste Marie and the south side of Lake Superior, to Duluth and thence north-westwards to Winnipeg. It would then have passed through a large tract of United States territory and connected admirably with his other interests in Wisconsin and Minnesota. But Hill's Canadian colleagues were strongly opposed to this project, and to his fury Van Horne, his own protégé, came down solidly on the side of Donald A.

238

Smith and George Stephen. Hill severed all his connections with the Canadian Pacific and set out to build his own line westward from Minneapolis, and running as near as was expedient to the Canadian border, to be a fierce rival to Van Horne's road. It is amusing to see how Hill's Great Northern sent out a whole series of branches towards the international frontier. The Great Northern reached Seattle in 1893 and at once became a strong rival of the Northern Pacific, for through-transcontinental business, though intermediately, because of the different territories traversed, they were complementary rather than competitive.

Hill, backed by the great financier J. Pierpont Morgan, obtained control of the Northern Pacific; but even this combination failed to achieve what Hill had most dearly in mind, to carry his railroad interests directly into Chicago. In this he was blocked by another of the great nineteenth-century railroad barons, E. H. Harriman of the Union Pacific, behind whom there loomed another giant financier, William Rockefeller. Hill's empire-building tactics were inclined towards two railroads that were already in Chicago, the Chicago Burlington and Quincy, and the Chicago, Milwaukee and St Paul, though any hopes of an approach through the latter were dashed in 1881 when Rockefeller joined the board, bringing with him the 'Standard Oil' interests. But where the Morgan-Hill combine failed with the Milwaukee they succeeded eventually with the Burlington, and this determined the Milwaukee upon the construction of a line through to the Pacific. The control of the Burlington, secured in 1901, was a joint project of the Great Northern and Northern Pacific. After receiving some favourable estimates of the cost, the board of the Milwaukee in November 1905 voted to build the line through to Seattle and Tacoma. The chosen route shows that the railroad map across the states of Montana, northern Idaho, and Washington was becoming rather congested; but the Milwaukee, at the expense of cutting through five major mountain ranges, obtained a route from Chicago to Seattle that was 150 miles shorter than the combined Burlington-Northern Pacific route, and 80 miles shorter than that of the Burlington-Great Northern.

It was expensive to the Milwaukee in another way. By 1906, when the first ground for the extension was broken, the days were long past when new railroads received land grants as an incentive towards opening up virgin country. The Milwaukee had to buy the land it needed. But with more modern machinery than that available in pioneer days the 2300 miles of line from Evarts, near to the border of North Dakota and Montana, and Seattle, was built in no more than three years. Less than two years after the completion of the line the Milwaukee introduced, in May 1911, two highly competitive passenger trains between Chicago and the North-West, the 'Columbian' and the 'Olympian'. There were then three major routes scrambling for the traffic over this particular 'corridor', and despite the tremendous capital outlay incurred by the Milwaukee in building its extension west of Evarts, the management was soon thinking of electrifying the mountain sections. Steam operation was difficult, with winter temperatures down to 40° below zero, and having in mind that water-power for generating electricity was abundant, and that large deposits of copper for electric wires were available at Anaconda, Montana, contracts were placed for electrification in 1912. The first section to be authorised was over no less than 440 miles of line, from Harlowtown, Montana, to Avery, Idaho. This covered the difficult section through the Belt Mountains, the main range of the Rockies, and the Bitterroot Range. The first electric trains ran late in 1915 over the 112 miles between Three Forks and Deer Lodge, in Montana.

It was, however, an unpropitious time to launch such a great enterprise, for although the involvement of the USA in the first world war brought a volume of heavy traffic and prompted the second great electrification project, through the Cascade Range from Othello to Tacoma, the post-war period brought acute financial troubles. Furthermore, the railway scene in the Pacific North-West had been complicated in 1905, when the Great Northern and Northern Pacific jointly had sponsored a direct line to Portland, called the Spokane, Portland and Seattle. Unlike the earlier routes to the west coast, this ran for the most part at river-level grades, beside the Columbia River to Vancouver, Washington, where it made a T-junction. A short line to the south crossed the Oregon State border to reach Portland, while to the north ran the direct line to Tacoma and Seattle. This route, as part of the present Burlington Northern system, forms part of the main route from California. That it was first into Tacoma from the south led to another situation of which I have more to tell later. But the Milwaukee's arrival on the west coast, and its great electrification, marked the beginning of a proud era on American railroads. Though even this was not the first in the North-West, because in 1909 the Great Northern had electrified their line through the Cascade Tunnel.

The Milwaukee was an altogether vaster project. When the two separated sections, Harlowtown to Avery, in 1917, and Othello to Seattle, in 1920, were brought into full operation they represented not only the first long-distance electrification in America, but were, in the aggregate the longest electrified lines in the world, 656 miles in all. The project also represented the first electrification for purely economic reasons. Others had electrified to eliminate smoke in tunnels and terminal stations, to increase line capacity, or to help conventional trains over difficult grades — these conditions applying particularly to the neighbouring Great Northern enterprise. And in all these other cases electrification was an adjunct to the prevailing steam power. The Milwaukee on the other hand abandoned steam altogether on the sections concerned, with the sole intention of saving money and improving service. It certainly offered passengers on the newly-introduced transcontinental expresses a smooth and smoke-free ride through the grandeur of the mountains, a sentiment that is superbly captured by one of Howard Fogg's incomparable paintings, showing the 'Olympian' speeding through the Snoqualmie Pass amid deep winter snows.

After much study of contemporary progress in railroad electrification the world over, the Milwaukee decided upon 3000 volts, direct current, with an overhead line wire. This was well in advance of most thinking at the time. It is now the system standard in Belgium and Italy. The original investment provided for forty-two electric locomotives, each consisting of two semi-permanently coupled cab units and having a nominal horsepower of 4050. When first delivered from the General Electric Company's works in Erie, Pennsylvania, the locomotives were justifiably described as the largest electric locomotives in the world. The most celebrated of all Milwaukee electric locomotives, however, were the five 'bi-polars' of class EP 2, delivered from Alco–General Electric in 1919–20. These were gearless, in that the armature of the motor was also the driving axle.

241

When current was applied and the resulting magnetic force caused the armature to turn, it turned the wheels directly, instead of through gears as on other types of electric locomotives. They were striking in appearance also, having semi-circular coverings to the power units on each side of the central cab. They had the wheel arrangement known technically as the 1−Bo−Do+Do−Bo−1 — rather a mouthful, but representing, from one end to the other, a pair of leading non-powered wheels, two powered axles, four powered axles, four more, two more, and a trailing non-powered axle in rear. They had a capacity of 4120 horsepower, and could run up to 70 m.p.h. The last survivor of these five celebrated locomotives is now in the National Museum of Transport in St Louis.

In February 1973, however, after long studies, the Milwaukee announced its intention to phase out the remaining electric operations. It had been a great period in western railroading, fifty-seven years of it; but in the present state of motive power development, particularly as the two sections of electrified line were separated by the 110-mile non-electrified section between Avery and Othello, it was no longer convenient to operate the ageing equipment. In these days a single diesel, or group of diesels, can be worked through between Chicago and Tacoma without the necessity for engine changing at both Avery and Othello, which was involved while the electrified sections remained. Until the diesels came upon the scene the Milwaukee had worked the transcontinental trains with huge 4−8−4 steam locomotives between Minneapolis and Harlowtown, and between Avery and Othello. They were part of a programme of motive power development on the whole line, that included a class of new 4−6−4s for the easternmost end of the line between Chicago and Minneapolis, the track that was later to become famous from the exploits of the stream-lined 'Hiawatha' express. So far as loads and schedules were concerned, the new 4−6−4s introduced in 1929 could have handled the 'Olympian' and other trains throughout the western sections as well, but climatic conditions impose severe handicaps. During the winter months heavy snow and intense cold are frequently experienced, and high winds prevail at most times of the year. For this reason the 4−8−4 type was preferred, because it was found capable of handling the heaviest passenger trains without recourse to double heading.

242

The Milwaukee 4−8−4s of Class S 1, built by the Baldwin Locomotive Works in 1930, had two cylinders 28 in. diameter by 30 in. stroke; coupled wheels 6 ft 2 in. diameter, and carried a boiler pressure of 230 lbs per sq. in. They had a boiler and firebox of classic proportions, and a tractive force of 62,130 lbs. The new 4−6−4s used south-east of Minneapolis were of generally similar appearance, but of correspondingly smaller dimensions, providing a tractive force of 45,820 lbs. Both the 4−6−4 and the 4−8−4 were coal burners, and the combustion characteristics are emphasised if one compares the boiler and firebox proportions with those of a contemporary British locomotive of roughly the same tractive force, thus:

Loco. class	L.M.S. 'Princess Royal'	Milwaukee 'F 6'
Type	4−6−2	4−6−4
Tractive force lbs	40,300	45,820
Total evaporative heating surface sq. ft	2314	4205
Superheater sq. ft	653	1815
Grate area sq. ft	45	80
Boiler pressure lbs/sq. in.	250	225

With reasonable quality British coal the boiler of the 'Princess Royal' class 4−6−2s could sustain a high output of power for long periods, with hand firing too! The great disparity in the boiler proportions underlines the different conditions of working.

The City of Portland marks the entry to the area known as the Pacific North-West, and on the 'Coast Starlight' we were going forward over the tracks of the one-time Spokane, Portland and Seattle Railroad. Having arrived from the south seventeen minutes early we had a long wait, during which time locomotives were changed. We had, for the last four hours of the long journey, one diesel in the Amtrak colours and one in the green and white of the Burlington. Mention of the latter company reminds me to add that the financial merger of 1970, which formed the present Burlington Northern was, however, no more than eventual full amalgamation of four railroads that had been working under closely co-ordinated control since 1905, namely the Northern Pacific, the Great Northern, their joint protégé the Spokane, Portland and Seattle, and the Burlington itself. We left Portland at 2.20 p.m. with just four hours allowed for the remaining 185 miles to Seattle, and crossing the Colombia River we passed from Oregon into the State of Washington.

The river turns through a full right-angle to the north at Portland, and for nearly fifty miles we were running near to its right bank through a very pleasant country of lakes and waterways. It was a leafy, lush area, with meadows interspersed with woodlands, though east-wards there were glimpses of high mountains. The running was brisk, though our schedule did not demand any real speeding. We had run through several changes of weather since that cloudless dawn beside Mount Shasta, and as we neared Centralia, the lowering skies turned to heavy rain. The 92 miles from Portland to this picturesque station had been run in 110 minutes. The influence of the Great Northern was evident here in the chalet-type station buildings characteristic of that line. We were running here with train order signals, the masts of which were prominent on the station buildings.

Soon after leaving Centralia and, happily, running into clear sunny weather once again, we came alongside the first of the picturesque salt-water inlets that make up the extensive watery complex of Puget Sound, on which the cities of Tacoma and Seattle have grown up. It was a very pretty run, often close to the water's edge, and I enjoyed seeing the numerous little piers, many pleasure boats going and com-ing, and broad views across the water to what is known as the Olympic peninsula. It takes its name from the capital city of Washing-ton State, Olympia, one of the oldest communities in the Pacific North-West. It lies at the southernmost tip of Puget Sound, some miles to the west of our present route and reached by a branch line. Though far surpassed in size by Seattle, Tacoma, and Spokane, Olympia became territorial capital in 1853, long before railroads came to the area. We passed close to the spectacular Tacoma Narrows Highway bridge and then after a long tunnel, in which our direction changed from going due north to south-east, we came into Tacoma itself — 54 miles from Centralia in 65 minutes.

The railway complications of the area will be apparent from the

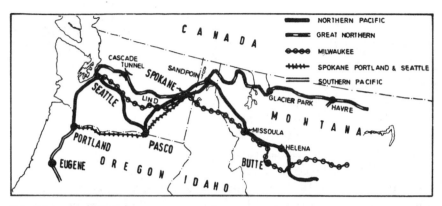

34. Lines into Seattle

map. We left Tacoma alongside the Puyallup River amid much industrial activity. From our own course on the left bank I could now see the track of the Milwaukee across the river, and when we swung round to the north again we were running parallel to it, and from Auburn almost alongside. I was to see much more of this area on the following day when the Milwaukee had a special expedition arranged for me; and now my thoughts were directed towards journey's end, and the keen anticipation of seeing yet another major American city. In Chicago, some three weeks earlier, Jim Scribbins of the Milwaukee had met me and outlined something of the programme they had in mind, and now he had travelled across to be my personal guide and was waiting to meet the train as we drew into the handsome King Street station of Seattle. We spent a busy and pleasant evening finalising arrangements, and then next morning we went to see the port facilities.

All along the dock sides there are well-used railroad tracks leading to loading ramps of a kind I had not seen before. The container traffic is heavy, and with the relatively short jetties the long trains had to be split up into many sections before loading. Beyond the ramps, which have to adjust themselves according to the rise and fall of the tide, is a floating section on to which cars are propelled. This has a number of parallel railroad tracks on which cars to be loaded on to the ships are positioned. This floating section is pushed broadside by tugs as required to bring the tracks into line with the tracks on the ramps.

Among incoming traffic I was interested to see large quantities of timber from British Columbia, and many cars from the British Columbia Railway — the former Pacific Great Eastern — the operations of which I described in the book *Railways of Canada*, in the present series. I saw also in operation the ferry service to Victoria, the capital city of British Columbia, situated at the southern-most tip of Vancouver Island, and only 100 miles away by water.

The highlight of my visit to the Pacific North-West was, however, a run with a freight train southwards from Tacoma. Coming in from the east the Milwaukee had an almost level run over the last three miles from Black River Junction, but it was another matter when the enterprising company decided to 'muscle-in' on the traffic from the Seattle-Tacoma area to the south. The Northern Pacific-sponsored S.P. & S.R.R. was there first, and had secured a water-level route beside Puget Sound, even though it meant the long tunnel under Point Defiance Park where the line is swinging round to come alongside the water again in Commencement Bay. The Milwaukee had to find another way. In the ordinary course of expansion competing American railroads had shown no reluctance to build new lines running cheek by jowl with their rivals, but in this case there was literally no room. So the Milwaukee followed here the tactics it had adopted in building its long transcontinental line westwards from Evarts: it took the shortest way, regardless of gradient. It leaves Tacoma indeed, like going up the side of a house, on a gradient of 1 in 27. It is not very long, as one has to do no more than reach the high ground to the south of the city, but to surmount 1 in 27 with freight trains of 2000 tons or more needs plenty of power, and Jim Scribbins took me to see how it was done.

A freight of fifty-six cars and its caboose was going south from Tacoma to Portland. Its road locomotive power consisted of three 2800 horsepower units, but this would be totally inadequate to get a trailing load of about 3500 tons up the hill. A helper was to be provided, and in the locomotive yard at Tacoma I saw this mighty concentration of power: six units, of the first generation road-freight type of General Motors diesel. But although this 9000 horsepower behemoth was engaged in no wider field of activity than helping southbound freight trains up the grade to Hillsdale, it was extremely well turned out in the orange and black livery of the Milwaukee, and beautifully clean. The lead unit had the handsomely-styled nose cab of this type of diesel, and made a striking sight in the locomotive yard.

We made our way out on a connection with the line from Seattle and soon our train arrived alongside. It was then divided so that there would be thirty-one cars ahead of us, leaving twenty-five and the caboose behind. The insertion of the helper multi-unit locomotive naturally took a little time, with the lead units drawing the front part of the train ahead, to provide space for us to cross over and couple on to the rear portion, and then for the two sections to be recoupled with us in between. Then there were the usual brake tests. In some cases of helper locomotives on heavy gradients that I have seen and described, where the helper is needed for a considerable distance the 'Locotrol' system of radio control of the helper is used, thus obviating the need for any crew on the helper; but this was no more than a short distance operation, and I rode with the engineer and brakeman on the leading unit of the sextuple helper. So we started up the hill. The effort of the helper was applied gradually, and it was four minutes after we started before we were going flat out. It was an extraordinary experience. I can quite understand why some American commentators talk about diesels growling; that is just what it seemed like, grinding, growling up that hill at about 10 m.p.h. The track includes a number of curves, and along the line of box-cars ahead of us, in cuttings, beside the dwellings of upper Tacoma, one could rarely get a sight of the road locomotives at the head end. So, after a quarter of an hour's all-out growling we came to Hillsdale, and power was shut off.

With the precision born of much experience the long train was stopped so that we, on the helper, were just short of the switch for the passing track. Uncouple, front part of the train to draw ahead; helper locomotive draw into the passing track; front part to set back and recouple. My friends of the Milwaukee had other things to show me in the neighbourhood of Tacoma, and an auto was waiting beside the line. There was time for another photograph of the lengthy helper engine as it set off for its base depot again, and then we took the road. One of the distant sights hereabouts was the beautiful Mount Rainier some sixty miles away to the south-east, rising to 14,410 ft, with its snow-clad peak seemingly detached and floating above any foothills, the form of which was lost in the haze of the intervening landscape. I was to pass much closer to this truly splendid mountain on the following day.

We drove back into Seattle on a highway that closely paralleled the two main railroads, one used by the Union Pacific and the Milwaukee, and the other by the Northern Pacific section of the Burlington. We stopped briefly at Kent to watch two lengthy freight trains, a northbound of the Milwaukee and a southbound hauled by union Pacific locomotives. So ended a long and varied day, with yet more aspects of American railroading vividly displayed.

CHAPTER TWENTY

East by the 'Empire Builder'

From Seattle I travelled for the best part of 2½ days across some 2300 miles of America. The 'Empire Builder' is one of the few Amtrak services to retain one of the old titles. It took its name from that stop-at-nothing tycoon James Jerome Hill, for as 'empire builder' he was known as much by his enemies as by his friends. The 'Empire Builder' of old was of course a Great Northern train, but nowadays, under the Amtrak banner, there is ample evidence of cross-breeding. It follows, successively, routes of the Northern Pacific, the Great Northern, and of the Milwaukee in reaching Chicago. By way of variety the second Seattle-Chicago service, the 'North Coast Hiawatha' takes the Great Northern route west of Spokane, and then that of the Northern Pacific to Minneapolis. The route I was to take was the only one entering Seattle from the east that was steam worked all the way — until of course the coming of the diesels. Of the electrification of the Milwaukee Road I have written in the previous chapter, but that of the Great Northern, though not covering so great a mileage, was equally interesting.

The present Great Northern route through the Cascade Range is the third since this part of the line was built in 1892. The first went over the mountains in a series of very sharply-graded switchbacks and then, in 1900, a tunnel 2·6 miles long was opened, eliminating the switchbacks on the summit reaches. But even so, this first Cascade Tunnel was approached by long gradients of 1 in 45, and in the wild mountain country extensive protection of the line by snowsheds was necessary. Because of the difficulties experienced in working, not least from the fumes and smoke in the single-line bore, the tunnel section was electrified in 1907, using the three-phase system which had been favoured for heavy grade working in Italy. This met the immediate situation, but the enterprise of the newcomer in this area, the Milwaukee, and the electrification of so much of its new line, put the Great Northern on its mettle, and in the booming, optimistic, but short-lived era after the end of the first world war, the Great Northern embarked upon a major improvement of their line in Washington State, constructing a new and shortened route through the Cascade Range, 41·1 miles long. It was electrified between Appleyard, near Wenatchee, and Skykomish, a distance of seventy-one miles. The principal feature of this new line was the new Cascade Tunnel, 7·8 miles long, and the longest in the USA.

Cutting through the mountains at a much lower level not only shortened the route by 8·9 miles, but eliminated 18¼ miles of 1 in 45 gradient, 3·7 miles of other tunnels, and no less than 7½ miles of snowsheds. Work on the new tunnel began in January 1926. It is entirely straight and on a uniform gradient from end to end, the inclination being 1 in 64, against eastbound trains. The bore of the tunnel is 18 ft wide and 25 ft high and needless to say the line was electrified from the outset — not only the tunnel section, as previously, but throughout. In this newer project the system of electrification chosen was 11,000 volts alternating current, in some way an acknowledgement of the success of high voltage a.c. traction on the mountainous main lines in Switzerland. The Baldwin-Westinghouse locomotives each consisted of two duplicate units of the 1−D−1 type, which meant that each had four powered axles. The total weight of one of these 'twins' was 330 tons (Imperial). The maximum starting tractive force was 189,000 lbs and the continuous tractive force at 15 m.p.h. was 88,500 lbs. The opening of the new line, with electric traction throughout its forty-one miles, enabled the time of through passenger trains to be reduced by one hour between Spokane and Seattle, while with freight trains there was an acceleration of no less than three hours. Unfortunately the new line, brought into service in January 1929, could hardly have been inaugurated at a more unpropitious time, on the eve of the great depression, when the general decline in traffic failed to offset the high capital investment in the line and the long tunnel.

I chose to travel eastward from Seattle by the 'Empire Builder'

250

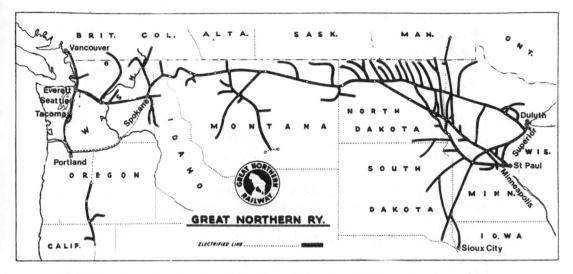

35. The Great Northern, and its lines to the Canadian border

rather than the 'North Coast Hiawatha' because its earlier departure time of 11.55 a.m. enabled the run to Spokane to be made almost entirely in daylight, and also gave a conveniently earlier arrival in Chicago on the third day. Jim Scribbins was travelling with me as far as Spokane, and together we went down to King Street station to 'watch the trains' for an hour or so before our own departure time. The 'Coast Starlight' for Los Angeles was due to leave at 11.05 a.m., and before then there was an Amtrak connecting train from Vancouver, British Columbia, which had left the Canadian National station in the latter city at 6.15 a.m. It is known as the 'Pacific International', but apparently there is not a great deal of connecting traffic because it arrived with only two coaches. The 'Coast Starlight', however, as when I had travelled on it, was a heavy train, though the provision of five locomotives at its head was not necessary for traction purposes. It had an 'E 8' diesel leading, resplendent in the Amtrak colours, two Burlington road freights, and two diesels from the far-off Southern Railway — clearly being worked back after some unbalanced allocation. My own train had twelve cars, including four 'domes', and was hauled by two of the standard Amtrak 'SD 40' type diesels, of 3000 horsepower each.

251

We left on time, and as usual drew very slowly out of the yard. Then we stopped, and during a long wait we learned that an earlier train had collided with a highway truck on one of the level crossings and although the railroad is double-tracked at this point, only one track was in use — the other still being obstructed by debris from the collision. Then we proceeded down the line I had seen on the previous evening as far as the triangle junction at Auburn, where we turned eastward, shortly afterwards calling at East Auburn to take on passengers from the Tacoma area. This was our last stop for nearly 2½ hours. Because of the initial delay in Seattle Yard we did not leave East Auburn until 12.54 p.m., eighteen minutes late, and then, with Jim Scribbins, I went up into one of the domes to enjoy to the full the ride through the magnificent scenery of the Cascade Range. We had to climb 2770 ft in the fifty-three miles between East Auburn and Stampede Tunnel, but climbing does not begin in earnest until one is about fifteen miles on the way, and this initial stretch on which we worked up to 53 m.p.h. gave me a chance to get accustomed to the lineside features of the route. Naturally I was keen to secure a good record of the locomotive working, because for a distance of thirty-eight miles the average rate of ascent is 1 in 67. Although I had a front seat in one of the dome cars I could not see any mileposts, but the mileage is displayed on the posts of all the automatic colour light signals — in each case to the nearest tenth of a mile — and they could easily be spotted.

By the time we were ten miles out of East Auburn and bowling smoothly along at about 50 m.p.h. we had entered a beautiful country of forest lands that reminded me much of the eastern Highlands of Scotland. Mount Rainier, which I had seen distantly on the previous afternoon, was now much closer at hand and on a day of almost cloudless sunshine it looked glorious. The steepening gradient was making its effect on the speed, and some of the curves were already sharp enough to make the wheel flanges squeal. As we made our way up I thought of the days when this line was steam operated, and when the Northern Pacific had some enormous 2−8−8−4 simple articulated locomotives, which with their boosters in action had a tractive force of 153,400 lbs, not all that much short of the starting tractive force of the Great Northern twin-electrics. But there was too much to

252

see and to record without any day-dreaming, and I delighted in the wild flowers by the lineside, amid the pine woods, and great masses of crimson foxgloves on the banks. One curve hereabouts brought us down to 34 m.p.h. but for the most part we were holding around 40 m.p.h. We passed Palmer Junction whence a branch line goes south into the heart of the mountains, and by then, on an increasing winding track we were climbing into the heights of the Cascade Range.

This was the Stampede Pass. Speed was around 40 to 45 m.p.h. and at a passing place about twenty-eight miles from East Auburn we crossed the westbound 'Empire Builder'. It was then Thursday afternoon and it would have left Chicago at 1.40 p.m. on the Tuesday. It was running well on time. As we climbed into higher, wilder regions there were fences to detect the fall of boulders on to the track. This is of course a very necessary precaution on a line with so few places regularly manned, and on which traffic operation is regulated by remote control. The signals hereabouts were of the three-position electric upper quadrant semaphore type, and in conformity with standard American practice those that were automatic had pointed, rather than fish-tailed ends. I noticed that the backs of the automatic signal arms were painted black, with a white chevron. We were climbing well. Between the signals at 77·6 miles (from Ellensburg) and 60·6 we took 25½ minutes — an average speed of exactly 40 m.p.h. As we entered upon the last miles up to the summit, which is in Stampede Tunnel, the scenery became more and more spectacular, and the alignment of the railroad still more so. We crossed a very high trestle, getting a superb view down the valley; then we went into even sharper curves, next a broad horseshoe location with a breathtaking vista, and a last glimpse of Mount Rainier. The speed was now just under 30 m.p.h. and we threaded the first Stampede tunnel, only a short one. Then after a location that had clearly been a facility for replenishing water supplies on steam helper locomotives, we entered the main tunnel. We had climbed 42 miles in 65½ minutes, an average of 38·5 m.p.h.

Coasting very slowly at first down from the tunnel thoughts turned to steam again, and the Northern Pacific, like the Milwaukee and the Great Northern, used the 4—8—4 type for passenger service, but unlike the latter they burned soft lignite coal from Rose Bush. This has a very low calorific value compared to what was used, for example, in Great Britain, amounting to no more than 8700 British thermal units per pound, against about 13,000 B.Th.U. per lb for the best Welsh and Yorkshire grades. 'Rose Bush' had a moisture content of more than 20 per cent. Accordingly the fireboxes of the large Northern Pacific locomotives were of special design. The 'A 2' class 4−8−4s introduced in 1934 had a grate area of no less than 115 sq. ft, for a locomotive that developed a tractive force of 69,800 lbs. Comparing this with an L.M.S. 'Duchess' class 4−6−2, with 50 sq. ft of grate, for 40,000 lbs tractive force, the respective ratios of grate area to tractive force in Imperial tons are 3·7 (N.P.) and 2·8 (L.M.S.) If one compares the above figures with those of a Great Western 'King', a type specially designed to use the very best Welsh coal, the ratio is only 1·9, or little more than half that of the Northern Pacific 'A 2'. The latter were distinguished by a very tall, large-diameter tapering chimney, that might have suggested some arrangement of multiple-jet blastpipe; but this was not so. The drawing shows how this came about, through use of the so-called Cyclone spark arrester. Spark-throwing was to be avoided as far as possible in a country so densely forested as that traversed by the Northern Pacific in the Cascade Ranges.

About six miles downhill from Stampede summit I saw another line drawing alongside us from the north, and realised this was the Milwaukee. We were running in the same canyon, and I saw how the rival line had been constructed with massive stone viaducts. At a point about thirty-eight miles short of Ellensburg it crossed over our line,

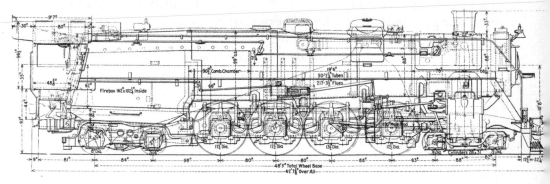

36. The Northern Pacific 4–8–4 showing its unusual front end

but continued to run relatively close at hand in this still narrow valley. By now however the track was becoming much straighter, and the speed rose considerably. Although there were many slowings for curves, we had some good spells at 65 to 70 m.p.h. and I noted that the riding was smooth and most comfortable. On one particular stretch we got up to a full 79 m.p.h., the maximum permitted in territory not equipped with cab signalling, and for a stretch of twenty-three miles we averaged 66 m.p.h. The last miles into Ellensburg involved some further slowings for curves, always with the Milwaukee not far abreast of us, and we finally pulled into Ellensburg 102 miles from East Auburn, in 143 minutes, then only 11 minutes late.

From this station the Northern Pacific line makes a broad sweep to the south, through a country that is bleak and desolate at first. The track is very winding, in a deep valley where the course of the river had necessarily to be followed. Until we passed Wymer this was no place for speeding, and for the most part we were barely making 30 m.p.h. Great outcrops of rock on the hillsides added to the rather forlorn aspect of the country, and it was not until the valley began to open out at Pomona that there was any chance of making some speed. The first 30 miles out of Ellensburg took just under 45 minutes. As we began to speed up, a backward look to the hills through which we had just passed did make them appear most forbidding. But now, down beside the Yakima River we were coming into a fine ranching country, and equally by way of a change, vast areas of fruit growing. We stopped at Yakima, 37 miles from Ellensburg, in 56 minutes, and were away again 5½ minutes later, now only a minute late. The time allowance for the section just traversed is generous on account of the curvature; but although we had made up time the riding was at all times most smooth and comfortable. Yakima is quite a centre for the fruit traffic, and at the motive power depot many diesels in the green and white of Burlington Northern were in evidence.

We got away from Yakima to make some considerably faster running. I took a lot of timings, from the mileages on the signal posts, and this part of the journey consisted of a series of intermediate spurts with slowings through each of the stations we passed. For the most part it was open, fairly level country, with much desert-like scrub, and patches of land beautifully green from irrigation. We had speeds of

75 m.p.h. before slowing at Wapato, 73 m.p.h. before Toppenish, and a fine spell at a full 79 m.p.h. before easing down for Mabton. By now, in this rather parched country the train was throwing up dust from the track, and despite the intermediate slowings we had covered a stretch of 40 miles in a little over 36 minutes. After we passed Prosser, however, the line became very winding once again, and our gay progress could not continue. Moreover we were climbing to a miniature summit as well, and after crossing this at a point twenty miles short of Pasco, we ran at around 60 m.p.h. down towards the valley of the Columbia River, frequently throwing up dust as we went. Many years ago I had read of the almost intolerable dust of travel in American trains in the dry seasons; now, in the air-conditioned seclusion of the dome cars on the 'Empire Builder' I could quite well imagine what it must have been like in former years.

We entered Pasco across a long bridge over the Columbia River, second only to the Mississippi in volume of flow, and joined nearby by its greatest tributary, the Snake River, itself 1038 miles long. At Pasco the railroad is down to no more than 379 ft above sea level. It is a general junction, because not only does the Spokane, Portland and Seattle line come in from its run along the northern bank of the Columbia River, but there are also several branch lines serving termini in the Blue Mountains in the south-east corner of Washington State. It was just after 6 p.m. when we left Pasco on our non-stop run of 146 miles to Spokane and we were taking the track of the Spokane, Portland and Seattle, which parallels that of the Northern Pacific for almost the whole distance. By 7.15 p.m. we were leaving the valley and the rivers and gradually mounting into an extraordinarily barren country, which subsequently changed into a terrain that reminded me of the Nullarbor Plain, in Australia. Up in the front seat of one of the domes again, after dinner, I could see from the restrictive aspects of the signals ahead that we were following another train closely, and before long we approached a loop in which I could see a lengthy freight had been parked out of our way — but not quite.

From correspondence with my American associates in the signalling industry, and from study of their technical literature, I had become familiar of many practices in operating the remote control C.T.C. panels, and particularly of the skill sometimes shown in regulating the signal aspects that two opposing trains on a single-line section passed each other at a loop without either having to stop; the Mallard technique. But here, out in the open grasslands near Lamont was a crossing, or rather an overtaking of an ingeniously contrived kind. The freight on which we had closed up was a lengthy one of 139 cars, drawn by six locomotives, all in the Burlington Northern colours — so I eventually saw. When we came to the loop we had no more than a restricted signal to take the main line; but then, as we drew slowly alongside the freight, I noticed that it had started to set back. Apparently it was too long for the loop; but the dispatcher, some fifty miles away in Spokane, had instructed its engineer to draw up so that its rear end was clear into the loop. Then the moment we had cleared the facing points at the entry, radio communication instructed the engineer to set back, so that the head end would become clear of the main line at the outlet points; and this was done so smartly that we did not have to stop at all. It struck me as a remarkable example of close co-operation by three men at some distance from each other: the engineer and conductor of the freight train, and the dispatcher in Spokane, who would of course be watching the movements by the indication lights on his control panel. We reached Spokane at 9.15 p.m. dead on time, having taken three hours exactly for the 146 miles from Pasco. Jim Scribbins was leaving the train here, and after he had taken his farewell I turned in for the night, in a cosy little roomette.

During the night we changed from Pacific to Mountain time, and I put my watch on one hour before retiring. I hoped to be awake in time to see something of the beautiful scenery around Glacier Park, where we were due to call at 6.43 a.m. The distance from Spokane is 329 miles, and allowing for the change in time the running allowance is eight hours. We had entered the region of the Glacier National Park before I was astir next morning, but I was up in the dome by 6.30 a.m. in time to witness the crossing of the Marias Pass summit, at an altitude of 5213 ft, the lowest crossing of the Continental Divide north of New Mexico. We had been on the former Great Northern line since passing Sandpoint at 10.58 p.m. last evening, and this was evident from the very picturesque stations in the style of Swiss chalets. They blended admirably with the impressive mountain scenery, forested with firs reminding me of British Columbia — the mountains craggy, grey-green, with patches of snow on the higher ranges. By the time we drew into Glacier Park station at 6.50 a.m. the sun was lighting the mountains, and in a most curious way; its low altitude, and the direction from which I was looking showed hardly any shadows — a most strange 'flat' effect.

In the succeeding 1½ hours we descended from the mountains into the wide open region of the prairies. The line was now running only about fifty miles south of the Canadian border. There were grain elevators at Cut Bank, and then at Shelby, reached at 8.27 a.m., we were in the heart of Montana's oil-rich areas. From here a branch line goes north to connect up with the Canadian Pacific, and continue to Lethbridge, Alberta, on the line that goes west through the Crowsnest Pass. Shelby is a characteristic prairie town, and our own line was busy with freights; we met, or overtook five within a space of half an hour. After leaving Shelby, over the flat prairie land we made much faster running. Some time had been lost during the night, and we had left Shelby 16 minutes late; but by covering the 105 miles to our next stop, at Havre, in 91½ minutes we were then practically on time. I was curious to learn the pronunciation of this important divisional point, where we were scheduled to stop for twenty-five minutes; it is Havver, not the least bit French! While the locomotives and the train equipment was being serviced, I walked just outside the station to see the great spectacle of the place, one of the magnificent 4−8−4 steam locomotives, No. 2584, which is preserved on a pedestal.

In retrospect I think it would be difficult to decide which were the finest and most handsome of all American steam passenger locomotives. In making this tour of the USA I have already commented on many 4−8−4s, notably those of the Norfolk and Western, the Union Pacific, the Santa Fe, and of the Southern Pacific — all distinctive in appearance, and with an impeccable record of performance. And here, outside the station at Havre was another. In a wire cage to protect her against vandalism, No. 2584 is not well placed for photography, but in outward appearance the design which was known as the 'Empire Builder' class was one of the most attractive of them all. The fourteen engines were built by the Baldwin Locomotive Works in 1930, at a time when there was general move to tidy up the externals of American locomotives, following the deep impression created by the English *King George V* at the centenary celebrations of the Baltimore and Ohio, in 1927. The 'Empire Builder' 4−8−4s had not only a very 'clean' external appearance but the boiler and cylinder claddings were finished with aluminium paint. This was subsequently changed to a pale green. The striking logo of the Great Northern was carried prominently on the tender. The preserved engine was in beautiful condition when I saw her, with the smokebox and chimney treated with aluminium paint, and the green of the boiler and cylinders quite immaculate.

These 4−8−4s were not only handsome to look at. They were capable of hard work on the road, and in 1937 when my friend Baron Gérard Vuillet, of Paris, travelled on the 'Empire Builder' train from St Paul to Seattle, it was hauled by three of them in succession, from Breckenridge to Minot, thence to Havre, and finally to Whitefish, through runs of 332, 429·7, and 257·2 miles with a load of 1340 tons as far as Havre, and 1260 tons onwards. While all the earlier part of the journey was made over rolling prairie land, which I myself travelled over in the reverse direction from Havre, the third engine concerned on Baron Vuillet's trip had to climb from Cut Bank to the Continental Divide, and this was done without recourse to any helper locomotives. Although the gradient is nowhere steeper than 1 in 100, a stop had to be made at Fort Browning, right on the grade. The restart, with a 1260 ton load and no slipping was quite an achievement. Baron Vuillet describes it thus:

The train was held on the gradient by the air brake with all the slack stretched out. The reversing lever was placed in full forward gear, the throttle 'cracked' and the air released. The train slowly dropped back about a quarter turn of the driving wheels and then, as it was brought to a standstill by the compression of the steam in the cylinders, the throttle was pulled wide open and the train started as a unit with all the draft gear stretched and without jerking.

With the locomotive working 'all-out', in full forward gear and full throttle, the speed rose to 27·5 m.p.h. on the gradient, and was sustained so until another stop was called for at Glacier Park. For the record, the 'Empire Builder' 4−8−4s had two cylinders 29 in. diameter by 29 in. stroke, 6 ft 8 in. diameter coupled wheels, and a boiler pressure of 225 lbs per sq. in. The tractive force was 58,300 lbs and the fuel used was oil.

Even at 10 o'clock in the morning it was blazing hot in Havre, and I was glad to get back into the air-conditioned comfort of the train, ready for some fast running over the prairies. We were booked away from our next stop, which was Malta, in only 72 minutes from Havre; and as the distance is 87 miles, there was clearly to be no dawdling on the way. The track was a little below standard in places on this section, and there were some intermediate slowings; but with several spells at 75 to 79 m.p.h. we reached Malta in 73¼ minutes, a good average speed of 71·3 m.p.h. from start-to-stop. The country was reminiscent of the Canadian Pacific, with rows of grain elevators beside the intermediate stations, and the next stage of sixty-six miles took us to Glasgow — Havre, Malta, Glasgow in rapid succession. The Great Northern mileposts were easy to pick up from a vantage point in the dome, and I clocked more fast running, up to around 80 m.p.h., and the start-to-stop average from Malta over this section was 69·3 m.p.h. We had a speed order shortly after leaving Glasgow, but then from Milepost 272 (from Minot) we had our fastest sustained spell — 41 miles in 30½·minutes at an average of 81 m.p.h. Our engineer was slightly 'bending the rules' here, but the riding up in the dome was most comfortable. The complete 50 miles from Glasgow to Wolf Point took just 42 minutes, an average of 71·3 m.p.h. start-to-stop.

Inappropriately, while we were at lunch, we had some rather rough and uncomfortable riding after leaving Wolf Point, albeit at much reduced speed, This is allowed for in a slower scheduled speed on to Williston. We took 107½·minutes for this stretch of 106 miles, and coming into the zone of Central Time, and putting watches on another hour, we left punctually from Williston at 4.27 p.m. We were now in the State of North Dakota, and as we sped over mile after mile of continuing prairie lands, each station with its row of elevators, I was studying the map of this area and reflecting upon the extraordinary number of branch lines that Jim Hill, the 'empire builder', had thrown out northwards, each ending within a few miles of the Canadian border. Williston lies almost on the same longitude as Regina, and the line we were now traversing is paralleled, in Canada, by that of the C.P.R. through Brandon and Portage la Prairie. Between Stanley, our own next stop, and Grand Forks Junction, a distance of 260 miles, no fewer than thirteen Great Northern lines extend north in this way, showing an iron determination on Jim Hill's part to capture as much of the grain traffic of the area as he could. Curiously enough there are scarcely any lines extending south in a corresponding way from the main line of the C.P.R.

We reached Minot at 6.36 p.m., four minutes early. This is an important divisional point, with a large marshalling yard and extensive locomotive facilities. It was there that haulage of the Great Northern's steam continental trains changed from 4−8−2 to 4−8−4 haulage, and eastbound ourselves, we continued on to a stretch of line where the names were even more intriguing: Rugby, a little town out on the prairies; York, a row of elevators, a few houses and little else, and then Leeds, not much bigger. It was amusing to an Englishman to go from York to Leeds, passing both places in 6½ minutes! It had been another long day of sightseeing and note-taking, and the smooth riding up in the dome was beginning to be slightly soporific; but when I went down to the bar to get a drink, I found the air-conditioning had failed. It was not very comfortable, though good for business across the counter. In the meantime we had covered the 57 miles from Rugby to Devils Lake in just 25 seconds over the hour, and refreshed I went back to the dome to enjoy once more the glorious colours of a sunset, in a cloudless sky, over the prairies. So, at 10.38 p.m., on time, we came into the major junction of Grand Forks. Here the main line turns south, keeping just on the western side of the state border line with Minnesota; but darkness having fallen I gave up note-taking for the day. We had covered 812 miles from Glacier Park in 15¾ hours, including all stops, an excellent overall average of 51·5 m.p.h., and I retired to my roomette for the night.

CHAPTER TWENTY ONE

The route of the 'Hiawathas'

It was inevitable that great rivalry should develop in providing an express passenger train service between two such centres of population and industry as Chicago on the one hand, and the twin cities of Minneapolis and St Paul; and from early days three major railroads, the Burlington, the Milwaukee, and the Chicago and North Western were in the field. The last named, as will be seen from the sketch map, had perhaps the most direct route, but it had an alternative running via Milwaukee, closely beside the Milwaukee's own main line, and over this in the 1930s there developed some of the fastest regular running in the USA, entirely with steam traction. Americans love anything new, and in 1934 for more than a year previously the subject of passenger train speed had occupied the mind of the public probably as never before. Newspapers, magazines and newsreels had featured the new diesel-powered streamlined trains, and predictions were freely made that this new type of power was the only answer to the demand for higher speeds. Then, on 20 July 1934, the Milwaukee made history.

Two years earlier, in England, the Great Western had made a world record by running the 'Cheltenham Flyer' from Swindon to Paddington, 77·3 miles at a start-to-stop average speed of 81·6 m.p.h., with a flying average of 87·8 m.p.h. over the 65·9 miles from Shrivenham to Ealing Broadway. This the Milwaukee set out to beat, with the regular 9 a.m. express out of Chicago, which was normally scheduled to run the 85·6 miles to Milwaukee in 90 minutes, non-stop. The entry to most American city areas is mostly very restricted, and both Chicago and Milwaukee are no exceptions. The locomotive was one of the '6400' series of 4−6−4s introduced in 1930, with a rated tractive force of 45,820 lbs and a total weight, engine and tender, of 297 tons

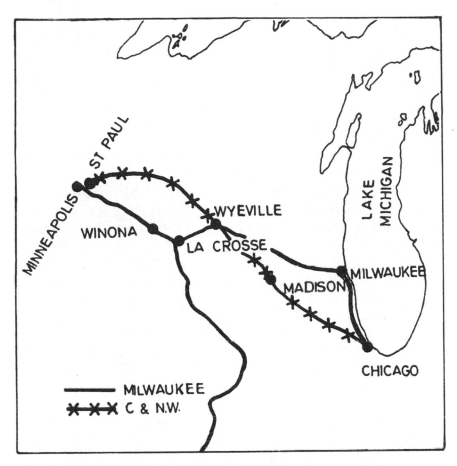

37. Lines between Chicago and the Twin Cities

(Imperial). The weight of the five cars making up the train was 365 tons. The ratio of trailing load to locomotive weight was therefore 1·225, as compared with that of 1·84 in that of the Great Western 'Castle' class 4−6−0 making the 'Cheltenham Flyer' record in June 1932. The Milwaukee train took 9 min 37 sec. to cover the severely restricted 5·6 miles out to Pacific Junction and it was even then not until Edgebrook had been passed, 12·3 miles out, that really fast running began. Then the 65·6 miles to Lake were covered in 43 minutes, an average of 91·5 m.p.h., and definitely surpassing the

English record for this distance. Moreover, in the course of some fluctuations en route the speedometer reached a maximum of 103·5 m.p.h. Overall, because of the slow start and finish the Great Western start-to-stop record still held, for the time from Chicago to Milwaukee was 67 min. 35 sec., equal to 76·07 m.p.h.; but it was a great effort, and in popular parlance it fairly 'started something'.

Within a year the Chicago and North Western had replied, putting on the '400' high-speed train covering the 408·6 miles between Chicago and St Paul in 7 hours, at an overall average of 58·4 m.p.h. including intermediate stops at Milwaukee, Adams and Eau Claire. The start-to-stop time between Chicago and Milwaukee was 80 minutes, 10 minutes faster than the Milwaukee Road was scheduling up to that time. But even before the year 1934 was out the Milwaukee had taken delivery from Alco of two specially designed and streamlined 'Atlantic' engines; and in May 1935 the 'Hiawatha' express was introduced, cutting the time between Chicago and St Paul to 6½ hours. The heat was now on in earnest, and the time between Chicago and Milwaukee was reduced to a regular 75 minutes. In competition with the Milwaukee and the North Western, the Burlington put on the diesel-powered streamliner, the 'Twin-Cities Zephyr'. By the summer of 1936 the fastest start-to-stop runs regularly scheduled on the three rival lines were:

Railroad	Run	Distance miles	Time min.	Speed m.p.h.
Milwaukee	New Lisbon–Portage	43·1	35	73·9
C. & N.W.	Eau Claire–Wyeville	86·2	76	68·1
Burlington	East Dubuque– Prairie du Chien	54·6	44	74·5

Both the Milwaukee and the North Western remained steadfast with steam during the exciting period of the later 1930s, and by the time Europe had become involved in the second world war the fastest runs in the 'race' to the Twin Cities 'had become:

264

Railroad	Run	Distance miles	Time min.	Speed m.p.h.
Milwaukee	Sparta – Portage	78·3	62	75·8
C. & N.W.	Chicago – Racine	61·9	49	75·8
Burlington	East Dubuque – Prairie du Chien	54·6	42	78

The two first mentioned were, bracketed first, the fastest regular steam worked runs in the USA, but in non-stop running between Chicago and Milwaukee the rivals had not cut their time below 75 minutes, an average of 68 m.p.h. The Chicago and North Western were then running the '400' with the streamlined 4–6–4s of Class 'E 4', while the Milwaukee had superseded the 'Atlantics' of 1934 by the 'F 7' streamlined 4–6–4s. These latter were primarily introduced in 1938, for working heavy sleeping-car trains, but they also took turns on the 'Hiawatha'. The original trains put on in 1935 consisted only of six cars, with a weight of 313 tons, but such was the mastery displayed by the special streamlined 'Atlantic' engines that the standard formation, in response to increased patronage, was increased to nine cars, making a load of about 420 tons. No difficulty was experienced in making the run between Chicago and Milwaukee in the scheduled 75 minutes, even when delays on account of track work of up to ten minutes were experienced en route. Maximum speeds up to 105 m.p.h. were regularly attained.

After the introduction of the 4–6–4s the load of the 'Hiawatha' was increased to twelve cars, and with very little effort these remarkable engines attained speeds of 120 m.p.h. on level track. The Milwaukee engineers felt that the regular schedules were not fast enough to bring out the best performance of the locomotives, and a sensational cut in the Chicago-Milwaukee time from 75 to 60 minutes was proposed. But despite the keen competition for traffic between Chicago and the Twin Cities there was a gentleman's agreement between the three, on minimum overall times, and because the other two were not in a position to follow the Milwaukee had to abandon their ideas of such a startling acceleration. Runs made by the 4–6–4s in 1942 and 1943 showed that the 60-minute run could easily have been accomplished.

Records are on hand of one southbound run in 65 minutes with a 14-car train, and another with no fewer than sixteen on, in 63 minutes. On the first run a distance of 48 miles was run at an average speed of 105·5 m.p.h. Those 4–6–4s were most strikingly-styled locomotives, in orange and silver, and one can imagine what a breathtaking sight one of them would be storming along the track at over 100 m.p.h.

When I turned in that night at Grand Forks, it was in anticipation of another great day's travelling, because from Minneapolis onwards we should be on the route of the 'Hiawathas', for the rest of the journey into Chicago. I was awake before 6 a.m. on a sunny morning, in time to see our arrival in Minneapolis. The station was beside the Mississippi, but whatever it may have been like upstairs the train shed was one of the semi-underground, cavernous affairs, devoid of anything except tracks and dark platforms. Some shunting was in progress, for what purpose I could not ascertain, and I was glad when our waiting time of thirty minutes was up, and we drew out into the sunshine at 6.55 a.m. And now our route lay beside the right bank of the Mississippi, and at this early hour it was a sheer delight. How different the great river was from the vast, highly commercialised waterway I had seen earlier in my American travels, in New Orleans, near Cairo, and from the air over St Louis. It was strange to realise it *was* the same river, now 1100 miles, as the crow flies, from New Orleans. It was now like the Thames or the Marne at their best, but much wider. There were beautiful riverside homes, bungalow townships, and at times the river as wide as a lake. Meantime we were bowling gently along at about 60 m.p.h.

Even in the most hectic days of the steam-hauled 'Hiawathas' this was not a fast stretch. The midday south-bound train leaving St Paul at 1 p.m. was allowed 100 minutes to cover the first 103 miles to Winona, with no booked pass-to-pass average speed of more than 67·8 m.p.h. On my trip 60 m.p.h. was quite fast enough, because the track was rough in places. The moderate speed, however, gave a better opportunity to enjoy the scenery, and note the picturesque wooden-built lakeside dwellings, and the many waterlily pools in full flower. Our line was double-tracked until we came to River Junction, when one line of the Milwaukee continued down the right bank while we turned east, crossing four arms of the waterway on single-tracked bridges to enter La Crosse. The 140 miles from Minneapolis had taken 3 hrs 35 min., an average speed of 39 m.p.h. that reflected the nature of the track on this section. The line then has a run of nearly 200 miles eastwards before reaching Milwaukee. It was once the scene of some of the fastest steam running in the USA, with many booked point-to-point average speeds at more than 80 m.p.h. Just now, however, it is not in very good shape. The country itself was beautiful, but I found the incessant jolting very tiring. There was a seemingly derelict track of the Chicago and North Western not far abreast of us. It looked in a terrible state; but for a time, judging by the riding of the cars, ours was not a great deal better! We took the scheduled 3¼ hours to cover the 131 miles from La Crosse to Columbus — average 36 ·5 m.p.h. — and for once I was glad that we did not have to travel faster! In 1939 the southbound morning 'Hiawatha' covered the 78·3 miles from Portage in 63 minutes, and the 28 ·2 miles on to Columbus in 24 minutes, in each case start-to-stop, at *average* speeds of 74·8 and 70·5 m.p.h.

After lunch, and leaving Columbus at 1.53 p.m., on time, I did some detailed recording and noted that we covered a stretch of 17 miles in 18¾ minutes. The fastest mile here was taken at 62 m.p.h., but we were well on time, and completed the 65 miles from Columbus into Milwaukee in 96 minutes with some very slow running over the last few miles. Now, on the threshold of what was once the world's greatest steam railroad speedway, I felt rather like the young English enthusiast who had listened enthralled to a lecture about the old times, and remarked afterwards that he had been born too late. So far as steam operation is concerned I had, of course, come to the Milwaukee much too late; and in an era when the newer forms of railroad motive power are far surpassing the greatest achievements of steam, it was sad to find such a decline in the speed of transit over so famous a route. Inclusive of a brief stop to set down passengers the 'Empire Builder', with 6000 horsepower at the head end, was allowed 95 minutes for the run into Chicago, with speed limited to a maximum of 70 m.p.h. I will not dwell upon the reasons for this present situation. The Milwaukee has an uphill fight on its hands. Instead, may I reflect for a moment upon the anatomy of what may be set down as the world's fastest steam locomotives.

I know that by the last remark I shall be bringing English, and particularly L.N.E.R. enthusiasts down upon me like the proverbial ton of bricks, in that the record of the Gresley 'A 4' streamliner *Mallard* at 126 m.p.h. has not been surpassed. But this latter was achieved at the expense of thrashing the engine almost to the point of disintegration downhill, whereas the Milwaukee 4−6−4s attained speeds up to 120 m.p.h. — on level track. In maintaining the 75-minute timing of the morning 'Hiawatha', one of them ran the 58·5 miles from Oakwood to Morton Grove in 35 min. 42 sec., an average of 98·5 m.p.h., with a trailing load of 465 tons. The basic dimensions of these engines, contributing to a tractive force of 50,300 lbs were, cylinders 23½ in. diameter by 30 in. stroke; coupled wheels 7 ft diameter, and a boiler pressure of 300 lbs per sq. in. But the piston valves were very large in relation to the cylinder volume, and with very generous port openings provided for that free flow of steam which is more efficacious than any external streamlining in promoting a fast-running locomotive. They were coal burners, having a grate area of 96·5 sq. ft to suit Indiana coal, with a heat value of 11,840 British thermal units per pound — far better stuff than the lignite burned in the giant Northern Pacific locomotives referred to in the previous chapter. A maximum speed of 125 m.p.h. is claimed for one of the Milwaukee 4−6−4s, the design of which may be further studied from the accompanying drawing.

Between Milwaukee and Chicago the rival lines lie very close to each other for all the way. The North Western follows the shores of

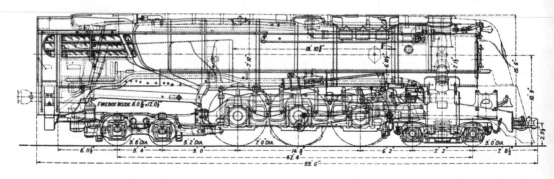

38. The streamlined 'Hiawatha' 4−6−4

Lake Michigan, passing through Racine, Kenosha and Waukegan, and the Milwaukee only a short distance inshore — both over practically level track. But although making comparable times the North Western never seemed to attract the publicity enjoyed by the Milwaukee, even though its streamlined 4–6–4s were selected for the A.A.R. 100 m.p.h. trials in 1938, as referred to in Chapter Eleven of this book.

The 'E 4' class, which were built by Alco in 1938, although streamlined and designed as much for high speed as their Milwaukee counterparts, were not directly intended for the '400' service, but rather for heavy sleeping car expresses run between Chicago and Omaha, and there handed over to the Union Pacific. Dimensionally they were more powerful than the Milwaukee 4–6–4s, having cylinders 25½ in. diameter by 29 in. stroke, but like their rivals having 7 ft diameter coupled wheels, and carrying a boiler pressure of 300 lbs per sq. in. Though not so startling as the 'Hiawathas' in their colour scheme the streamlined style was most impressive, and the livery of dark green with gold bands gave an immense dignity to them. So far as I can trace they were not used on the Twin Cities '400'. That service was in any case changed over to diesel traction in 1939.

Reverting to the Milwaukee, on the 'Empire Builder' we started very slowly out of Milwaukee, including one slack to 2 m.p.h. and for 20 minutes or so we were making no speed worth mentioning, even by present standards over the route. In overtaking a freight train near Sturtevant we were running briefly at 70 m.p.h., this part of the line being signalled for running in both directions. The freight was on the right-hand track at the time we overtook it. Shortly afterwards we were slowed to cross from the left-hand to the right-hand track, the latter of course being the normal arrangement on double-track sections in the USA.

Then at last we got going, and the 33·6 miles from Somers to Deerfield were covered in 28½ minutes, at an average of 70·5 m.p.h., and we pulled into Glenview, 67·6 miles from Milwaukee, in 73¾ minutes. The average speed of 55 m.p.h. thus involved was quite good in the circumstances, though of course the availability of 6000 horsepower from our two diesel locomotives enabled very rapid acceleration to be made from the various speed restrictions. From

Glenview, speed can be around 70 m.p.h. as far as Tower A5, but after that it was very slow running into Chicago. Once again I could not help being amazed at the complexity of the railroad network as we ran in. The line continues dead straight from Morton Grove inwards, crossing the North Western at Mayfair and then swinging round until, from Western Avenue, the direction is due east and heading straight for the spectacular skyline of the city centre. In a maelstrom of converging tracks we rode gently in and then made a sharp right-angle turn to enter the Union station, 95¾ minutes from Milwaukee, and a minute late after our long run of 2287 miles from Seattle.

On the following day, a Sunday, Jim Scribbins had arranged another interesting trip for me, to Milwaukee and back on one of the turbo trains, riding in the driving cab on the outward journey. With Jim I also had the pleasure of the company of Al Cini, manager, train operations. The train, booked to leave at 8.30 a.m., consisted of five cars as follows from the leading end: power, club parlor; coach-dining car; coach; coach; coach-power. By this time in my tour I was getting used to the everyday talk of American railroadmen, to the extent that I was beginning to use some of them such as getting the 'highball', for what we should call in England the 'right away'; but in starting from Chicago Union station that morning I was interested to hear a cheery 'Let's go' passed from one engineman to the other. As is often the case in Great Britain these days, with non-steam forms of motive power, the 'fireman' — a term still used — Bernie Rohrpasser, actually operated the train, with the engineer, Eric Siffert, working as second man. It was certainly a pleasant little party in the cab. We pulled out of the Union station with the bell tolling, according to the rules applying within yard limits; round the left-hand curve, to head due west for a time, and not exceeding 50 m.p.h. before reaching Western Avenue. Just beyond that station we slowed to 20 m.p.h. We had been running alongside the main line of the Chicago and North Western, and at Tower A2 we had to cross it on the level to get to the north side and then swing round on to our true course to the north. By Tower A5 however we were at last making express speed and running at 60 m.p.h. but because of the many initial restrictions the 5·4 miles to passing that interlocking had taken 10½·minutes.

By that time we were going well, and from the driving cab I could appreciate the splendid alignment of the Milwaukee road, that had enabled such exciting schedules to be set up when the 'Hiawatha' trains were put on. There were one or two brief restrictions to 60 m.p.h. but for the most part we were now running at a steady 70 m.p.h. One of the slight restrictions, to 60 m.p.h., was at a grade crossing with the North Western just before Mayfair station. This was the direct line from Chicago to St Paul, via Madison. The alternative route via Milwaukee, over which the '400' ran, branches away to the north also at Mayfair but before the level crossing with our route. After that we settled down to a steady 70 m.p.h. and the riding was very smooth and comfortable. I noticed that we were still tolling the bell at the many highway crossings. We were still within the city limits of Chicago, and use of the horn is not permitted, by city ordinance. We did not reach the city limit until nearing Morton Grove, some 13½ miles out. We passed the latter station, 14·3 miles from Chicago Union, in 18½ minutes, and shortly afterwards drew into Glenview, our first stop, in 21½ minutes. Schedule time allows 23 minutes to the restart, and we were away exactly on time.

I was interested now to see the accelerative capacity of this train on a straight level track with no restrictions other than the overall limit of 70 m.p.h. We attained this line maximum in about 1½ miles from rest, and then ran steadily at 69 to 70 m.p.h. until nearing Rondout, beyond which there is a lengthy stretch limited to 60 m.p.h. But between Glenview and Rondout, on a magnificently straight and level stretch I could well imagine how the steam hauled 'Hiawathas' used to tear along at 100 m.p.h. Just beyond Rondout we met turbo train No. 322, with four cars on; the combined speed was not more than 120 m.p.h., and in photographing her approach I was able also to record a good impression of this potentially fast stretch of line. I thought briefly of an experience not many months previously when I was riding in the driver's cab of one of the H.S.Ts on the Western Region, at home, and I tried to record similarly the passage of two such trains at full speed. The combined speed was just 250 m.p.h., and the photograph was not very successful! While still on the 60 m.p.h. stretch of the Milwaukee we met an eastbound freight, hauled by three GP−38−2 class diesels. It also must have been travelling at little less than 60 m.p.h. and apart from the straightness of the track, the most interesting feature of the photograph I secured is the impression of the enormous box-cars towering up high above the locomotives. Despite the hampering effect of the 60 m.p.h. speed restriction we completed the 44·4 miles from Glenview to the stop at Sturtevant in a few seconds under 43 minutes, though the schedule here demands a run in 38½ minutes to be able to restart from Sturtevant in 39 minutes. A start-to-stop average of 69 m.p.h. with an overall speed limit of 70 m.p.h. seems something of a counsel of perfection; with the temporary imposition of '60' for more than half the distance, it was of course impossible.

On the last stage into Milwaukee the schedule allowance of 30 minutes for 23·2 miles allows ample margin for recovery, because for most of this distance we were able to run at the full 70 m.p.h. We passed Milepost 79 (from Chicago) and 17·2 miles from the start at Sturtevant in 15¾ minutes, 16 of which miles had been run at an average of exactly 70 m.p.h.; but we then had to slow down to 40 m.p.h. approaching the oddly named Kinnic-Kinnic bridge, and the final approach, from Washington Street Junction was, as usual, slow. The 23·2 miles from Sturtevant had, however, taken no more than 25¼ minutes start-to-stop, and we arrived exactly on time. The total running time from Chicago was 89½ minutes. The station at Milwaukee is another of those dark, rather clinical train sheds, characteristic of recent constructions in the USA. They do not encourage that pastime that Canon Roger Lloyd once described as 'station sauntering', purely for the pleasure of being among trains.

In Milwaukee that day with Jim Scribbins and his wife, it was a pleasure to meet David P. Morgan, the distinguished editor of *Trains Magazine*, and Mrs Morgan, to talk trains, to lunch with them and then enjoy a drive along the elegant lake front of the city. Jim and his wife and I returned to Chicago by the 2.50 p.m. turbo train, but on this run the train was held at the Kinnic-Kinnic bridge, which at first could not be closed properly. The westbound 'Empire Builder' and two freights were also held on the far side. So we were nearly half an hour late leaving Sturtevant; but by running the 44·4 miles to Glenview in 41¼ minutes, and the last 17·4 miles into Chicago in 19¼ minutes, we were only 22¾ minutes late on arrival in Chicago.

CHAPTER TWENTY TWO

Pennsylvania — grandeur and decline

To the countless enthusiasts who study railroads and especially to those whose interests lay beyond their own backyards, the Pennsylvania stood out as one of the greatest of them all: a colossus, in the land of colossi. In America the Pennsylvania had a status closely akin to that of the London and North Western in Great Britain— the 'Premier Line' — though not all its contemporaries, and least of all its arch-rival the New York Central, would concede that supremacy. In that, there was a close parallel to the attitude of the Midland Railway in England. Connoisseurs of operating and engineering practice looked with admiration, and perhaps a little envy, to the magnificent permanent way of the Pennsylvania; to its reputation in locomotive designing, because although a great many of its engines were built by the Baldwin Locomotive Works, the official hand-outs often bore the legend 'built to Company's prints'. Then there was the great works at Altoona with its pioneer stationary locomotive testing plant, and in Chapter Three of this book I have told how the railroad was taken beneath the Hudson River and into New York City.

This is no place to try and trace exactly what went wrong from the slump years of the 1930s. To say that competitive modes of travel, some of which were indirectly supported by government finance, cut severely into railroad traffic was true enough. But it was not the whole story. One day someone must write a definitive history of what developed into one of the most catastrophic business collapses of all time. To British observers, to whom the effects of deferred maintenance expenditure was becoming only too obvious, the first real surprise was the merger of the Pennsylvania and the New York Central to form Penn Central, in February 1968, an amalgamation in which the New York, New Haven and Hartford was included less than a year later. But like that of the London and North Western and the Midland in Great Britain, merged by Act of Parliament to form the main financial buttress of the new London Midland and Scottish system, the amalgamation was far from a happy one. And Penn Central had no Guy Granet to realise very soon that something was going wrong, and to bring in a Josiah Stamp, who was equally skilled in personnel management as in his already towering reputation as an economist. Penn Central endured twenty months of bitter infighting between the two major factions, and in June 1970 it went bankrupt. Never mind about the N.Y.C., but the Pennsylvania bankrupt — it was unthinkable! Within two years the Lehigh Valley, the Reading, the Lehigh and Hudson, and the Erie Lackawanna had gone the same way.

But I must go back to the great days of the Pennsylvania, before the first world war, when its prosperity seemed as assured as that of the London and North Western. As an engineer myself I have always been attracted to its locomotive history, which in many ways was one of the most remarkable in the USA. The Pennsylvania at first was in the very forefront of the development of really large locomotives for express passenger traffic, and in seven years Altoona works had progressed from the 'K 2' Pacific of 1907, non–superheated, and having a rated tractive force of 33,400 lbs, to the almost legendary 'K 4' with a 33 per cent increase in tractive force for an increase in total weight of only 15 per cent. What is extraordinary however is that the 'K 4' remained the standard passenger locomotive of the railroad until 1942. Twenty–eight years was a very long time for anything to remain unchanged on an American railroad, particularly in view of what was happening elsewhere in the country in the years between 1914 and 1942. The 'K 4' was a mighty engine, and it is interesting to compare its basic proportions with those of other famous classes of non-articulated types that have already been mentioned in this book.

The factor that, of course, stands prominently out in this comparison is the boiler pressure. While 205 lbs per sq. in. was normal enough in 1914, it had become completely outmoded in the 1930s; and it is a matter of no more than simple proportion that if a high pressure version of the 'K 4' had been built, with other dimensions unchanged the tractive force would have gone up to 64,500 lbs! As it was, however, the 'K 4' was a beautifully balanced design for its size and power, and there could be no doubt that the much lower boiler pressure made it a far cheaper engine to maintain. Seeing that the design of the 'K 4' in all its essentials dated back to 1914 it was astonishingly successful in its continued dependability in a class of service virtually unheard of when it was first introduced. In 1937 for example, on the 'Broadway Limited', Baron Vuillet clocked an average speed of 77 m.p.h. for ninety miles, with a 630-ton train, while on the 'Manhattan Limited', another engine of the class, hauled 880 tons and attained a maximum speed of 85 m.p.h. on level track. On the lines west of Pittsburgh, however, the nominal limit for one of those engines in the fastest running era before the second world war was 870 tons, and many of the heaviest trains had to be double-headed, with a pair of 'K 4s'. The Pennsylvania certainly had plenty of them, 425 in all.

Inevitably one falls to wondering why, in view of the outstanding success of this design, in its own power range, the Pennsylvania did not develop it into a larger and more powerful version. That the 'K 4' had to be flogged to maintain schedule times with its maximum rated loads is no more than incidental, because all American locomotives were driven in the same way, without any apparent falling off in thermal efficiency. On the run with the 'Broadway Limited' referred to earlier, the coal consumption may have been 135 lbs per mile — more than double what one would expect to see on a strenuously driven British express locomotive — but it was not excessive in relation to the work done. It is generally believed, however, that the high policy of the Pennsylvania in holding back from the development of express passenger steam power, was in anticipation of a westward extension of its electrified system. Certainly from the traction point of view electricity would have paid off on the mountain section between Altoona and Pittsburgh, where heavy trains sometimes required the services of *three* 'K 4' engines in climbing westbound to Gallitzin summit. There the line rises 966 ft in 10·8 miles, an average gradient of 1 in 59, and for this distance it was the practice to pile on the locomotive power rather than to reduce train loads. The maximum tonnage for an unassisted 'K 4' was 390 tons (six cars). The climbing speed was 35 to 40 m.p.h., which was remarkably good, seeing that if allowance was made for the severe curvature of the line, including the famous Horseshoe Curve, the equivalent gradient in places is about 1 in 50. My own experience on the Horseshoe Curve is told in Chapter Twenty-four.

Although their rated tractive force was not a great deal less than that of the Santa Fe '3460' class, and of the Milwaukee 'Hiawathas', the 'K 4s' suffered from the relative age of the design. I do not mean that there had been any deterioration of the material over the years, because until 1930 the standards of maintenance were very high. It is that a great deal had been learned about the design of cylinders, ports, passages and valve gear since 1914, and the later engines were inherently much freer runners. In 1929 it is true that the Pennsylvania did introduce two experimental 'Pacifics', known as Class 'K 5'. Outwardly they looked very much the same as a 'K 4', but with a higher boiler pressure of 250 lbs per sq. in. and a longer piston stroke of 30 in., the engine was about six tons heavier, because of the thicker plates needed to carry the higher boiler pressure. But that increase in pressure brought the tractive force up to no less than 58,000 lbs and made by far the most powerful 'Pacifics' ever built anywhere, far indeed above the 4—6—4s of their neighbours and rivals. One of these two experimental engines with the standard Pennsylvania arrangement of piston valves and valve gear was built at Altoona; the second, which had Caprotti poppet valve gear, was built by Baldwins.

Strangely enough, however, when the growing need for more powerful passenger locomotives was becoming evident enough by the frequency of double-heading, no further engines of the 'K 5' class were built. The management were hoping to extend the electrification westward from Harrisburg, over the difficult, heavily-trafficked and mountainous section to Pittsburgh. Operationally the advantages would have been incalculable, but by 1930 the great depression had set in, and it was no time for the massive capital investment that would have been required for electrification. In the course of ordinary boiler renewals on such a large stud of passenger locomotives as the 'K 4s' there must have been a great temptation to supply them with 250 lb boilers as applied to the 'K 5'. This, without any increase in the piston stroke would have increased the tractive force from 44,000 to

53,700 lbs and allowed the maximum load for one engine on the fastest trains west of Pittsburgh to be increased from 870 to at least 1000 tons, and thereby saved much double-heading. But the majority of the 425 'K 4s' were relatively old engines by American standards, and in all probability the frames would not have been able to stand the stresses involved in the transmission of the 20 per cent increase in tractive force. So the 'K 4' remained the standard passenger locomotive of the Pennsylvania for another thirteen years after the appearance of the two 'K 5s'.

This is not to say there was no development. In 1918 a freight equivalent of the 'K 4' had been introduced: a 2−8−2 having boilers that were interchangeable, and from this was evolved the 4−8−2, which could be described as a fast freight version of the 'K 4', with 6 ft diameter coupled wheels, and a boiler pressure of 250 lbs per sq. in. They were also intended to assist in working passenger trains over the Gallitzin summit, in the Allegheny Mountains. This was a very successful design, first introduced in 1926, and followed in 1930 with 'M 1 a' class having enormously larger tenders. These fine engines had a tractive force of 64,550 lbs, but although they had relatively large coupled wheels they were not utilised to any extent on the faster sections of the line for working passenger trains, and reducing the amount of double-heading needed. A prominent external feature of these engines was the forward extension of the firebox in a very large combustion chamber, 8 ft 2 in. long providing 164 sq. ft of heating surface additional to the 206 sq. ft of the firebox proper. The 'K 4' class had a firebox heating surface of 205 sq. ft.

One of the standard Pennsylvania locomotive classes that has always interested me very much is the 2−10−0 heavy freighter, of which I saw a fine example preserved in the grounds of the Westinghouse Air Brake works, at Wilmerding, near Pittsburgh, and appropriately overlooking the scene of its former labours on the Pennsylvania main line. After the building of a prototype in 1916, at Altoona, the standard version, Class 'I 1 s', was built in bulk from 1922 onwards. They were extremely powerful engines, having cylinders 30½·in. diameter by 32 in. stroke, and a boiler pressure of 250 lbs per sq. in. With coupled wheels 5 ft 2 in. diameter the rated tractive force was no less than 90,024 lbs. Even so this was less than might be worked out from the basic dimensions just quoted, but the valve gear was arranged so that when working in full forward gear steam supply to the cylinders was cut off at 50 per cent of the piston stroke, instead of the more usual 80 to 90 per cent. The underlying idea of this design was to reduce steam consumption in all-out working conditions, and tests on the Altoona stationary plant showed that this aim had been very successfully achieved. The rated tractive force is calculated on a basis of 70 per cent of the boiler pressure being available for supply to the cylinders, instead of the usual 85 per cent normally used in tractive force. At the same time a special feature was introduced to give an additional boost when starting. Small auxiliary starting ports were cut in the valve liners, and opened into pockets formed in the cylinder ports. While those small ports allowed sufficient steam to pass into the cylinders to provide a boost when starting, once the locomotive was running the steam passing through them was so small and so throttled as to have no appreciable effect.

The 'I 1 s' class, of which there were eventually 475, proved remarkably efficient locomotives in traffic. As with all other Pennsylvania types they were very thoroughly tested on the stationary plant in Altoona works, and with one of them working practically 'all-out', with the cut-off point of steam in the cylinders at 47 per cent of the piston stroke, the horsepower in the cylinders was 3863 at a speed of 30 m.p.h. More important, however, was the relatively low basic coal consumption. In this, however, consideration must be given to the very high quality of coal used, a high-volatile bituminous grade from the Crows Nest mine, having a calorific value of no less than 13,658 British thermal units per pound. This is equal to the very finest Welsh steam coal used in Great Britain. In the highest development of British steam locomotives, with economy in working preached and practised assiduously, a consumption of 3 lbs of coal for each horsepower exerted on the drawbar at the back of the tender, per hour, became the acknowledged hallmark of a good locomotive in express passenger service. An 'I 1 s', on the Altoona test plant, slogging away at a typical 'all-out' freight speed of 22½ m.p.h. showed a consumption consistently below 3 lbs per drawbar horsepower hour until the power output rose above 2500 horsepower; then, as is characteristic of the conventional steam locomotive when approaching maximum

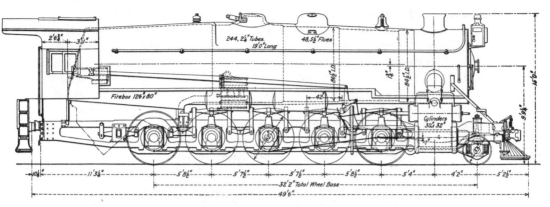

39. The Pennsylvania 2–10–0 freight locomotive

output conditions, the consumption rose steeply to 4 lbs per D.H.P. hour.

Certainly in the 'K 4', the 'M 1 a' and the 'I 1 s' the Pennsylvania had a stud of excellent standard locomotives, and in the 1930s although there were no visible signs of development the general trend of world locomotive practice was being watched very carefully at Altoona. They certainly had within their grasp an express passenger locomotive in the 'K 5', which was nominally equal, or better than the 4–6–4s on other lines, but equally the design staff were looking towards a high-speed passenger engine with eight driving axles. Towards the end of the 1930s, when recovery from the depression was making possible a programme of capital investment, the 4–8–4 was being developed to great success on many of the American railroads, as earlier chapters of this book have described. In a paper read before the New York Railroad Club in 1945, Ralph P. Johnson, then Chief Engineer of the Baldwin Locomotive Works, explained why the Pennsylvania had not followed this particular trend. He said:

Coincident with the use of the 4–8–4 for fast heavy service, came a breakdown of the old habit of changing locomotives with the varying characteristics of the terrain. The 4–8–4, with its big boiler and high wheels is at its best possible over fairly level country but its weight also enables it to do an effective job in mountainous regions. This resulted in longer and longer locomotive runs until now it is common to run

279

this type of locomotive as much as 1800 miles at a time. This type of operation makes monthly averages of 20,000 miles fairly common. Naturally, the more intensive use of power showed the necessity for high class maintenance and justified the use of such devices as roller bearings not only on axles but on main and connecting rods as well. Locomotive designers began to give intensive thought to means of increasing availability and lowering maintenance time and costs.

One of the means for accomplishing this which suggested itself was the lowering of the piston thrust on crank pins by using four smaller cylinders in place of the two cylinders of conventional design. Many of the modern 4−8−4 type locomotives with boiler pressures around 275 pounds per square inch have piston thrusts of 160,000 pounds and one fleet with 300 pounds per square inch boiler pressure has 185,000 pounds. Such thrusts require large crank pin bearings, but the lengths of crank pins are restricted by clearances and the diameters by available space in the wheel center. With four cylinders the piston thrust can be cut in half and even with 300 pounds per square inch boiler pressures can be brought down to 90,000 pounds. This smaller load makes possible smaller bearings at the back end of the main rod and eliminates heavy moving parts.

Four-cylinder locomotives have been common for years, but with articulated frames. Such engines, while powerful, were not suited to high speeds, since the front unit is not sufficiently stable, as spring centering devices are not effective against slight lateral displacements. In addition, the hinged connection between front and rear units has always been a high maintenance item. A four-cylinder arrangement with a rigid frame and rear cylinders between the two groups of driving wheels had been proposed by The Baldwin Locomotive Works several times, notably in March 1932 to the Baltimore & Ohio Railroad, and in December 1935 to the Florida East Coast Railroad; and in January 1936 to the New Haven Railroad. This design had been rejected in all cases on account of the long rigid wheelbase.

Johnson went on to tell how the Pennsylvania, following the setting up of an advisory committee in 1937, on which the three leading manufacturers, Baldwin, Alco, and Lima were represented, designed and built at Altoona the colossal non-articulated 4-cylinder locomotive 'S 1' having the 6−4−4−6 wheel arrangement. The display of this extraordinary locomotive at the New York World's Fair in 1939 was, I am afraid, regarded by many as a piece of showmanship rather than of serious locomotive engineering, and a more practical application of the 4-cylinder non-articulated principle came in 1940 with the placing with the Baldwin Locomotive Works of an order for two 4−4−4−4 high-speed passenger locomotives, designated Class 'T 1'. The basic requirement was the haulage of a load of 880 tons at 100 m.p.h. on level track. In actual service these engines, of which there were eventually fifty-two, were able to sustain speeds of 100 m.p.h. with considerably more than 1000 tons trailing load. They could exert 6000 drawbar horsepower at 80 m.p.h.

Regarding their striking external appearance Johnson remarked:

Many critics of the steam locomotive deplore the fact that it has changed so little in outward appearance over the years. This criticism reflects ignorance of both engineering and economic facts, as no type of boiler commercially practicable has been developed which, subjected to the same space limitations, can generate more steam or generate it faster than the internally-fired fire-tube boiler. This just suits railroad work, where the power demand changes rapidly and widely. By using the exhaust steam to furnish draft for the furnace, the locomotive has an automatic adjustment of the draft to the power requirements that is as simple as breathing. And in addition, the steam locomotive is rugged and has low maintenance. All of these characteristics have contributed to the so-called 'lack of progress' in steam locomotive design, but in reality, economics has dictated this. Many types of experimental locomotives have been built through the years with higher thermal efficiencies than the conventional types, but none of them have survived because the higher efficiency has been gained at the expense of simplicity, original cost and maintenance.
However, the steam locomotive has always looked functional, rather than aesthetic, and while this is beautiful to a railroad man it was recognized that the traveling public might prefer the locomotive 'dressed up'. Therefore, Mr. Raymond Loewy, one of the foremost industrial designers of this day, was retained to 'streamline' these new four-cylinder locomotives. This styling was not carried to an extreme as it left accessible all moving parts for inspection.

So far as test results were concerned, the 'T 1' was a great success; but even before the first of the class had been delivered from Baldwins the Pennsylvania had nailed their colours to the mast of rigid frame 4-cylinder locomotives by building at Altoona works the first of

281

the fast freight class 'Q', with the $4-4-6-4$ wheel arrangement. This was their answer to the ten-coupled freight locomotives in service elsewhere in the USA. It was to provide a fast freight locomotive with a capacity much in advance of that of the 'M 1 a'; it had, indeed, a tractive power of 100,816 lbs, or 56 per cent greater than the 'M 1 a'. It was proportionately larger in every way, and when one of these locomotives was put on to the test plant at Altoona in 1945 it produced the highest output of power ever recorded on that plant. The plant itself had had to be rebuilt to accommodate the 'T 1' $4-4-4-4$ passenger engine when the first of these was put through 'full dress' trials in 1944, and a drawbar horsepower of 6000 was registered at 80 m.p.h. The 'Q 2' attained 7016 drawbar horsepower at 49 m.p.h.

In 1945 competition from diesel traction was becoming a serious consideration, and although the test results from the 'T 1' showed that it could out-perform a 5400 horsepower diesel at all speeds above 26 m.p.h., performance on the road was not everything, and in June 1945, R. P. Johnson, then Chief Engineer of the Baldwin Locomotive Works, wrote privately to E. C. Poultney:

On American roads, the Diesel locomotive sells — not so much on account of its superior thermal efficiency, but because of its superior availability, and it is our hope that the Turbine locomotive will improve the availability of the steam locomotive.

In September 1944 the Baldwin Locomotive Works had delivered to the Pennsylvania an enormous geared turbine locomotive with the $6-8-6$ wheel arrangement. It could be described as a greatly enlarged American version of Sir William Stanier's Turbomotive on the L.M.S. in Great Britain. The locomotive did well in service, though showing no fuel economy over the 'T 1' class. It was built for power, and increased availability rather than economy. In 1945 it was working daily over the 580 miles between Crestline and Chicago with loads of 900 to 1200 tons at overall average speeds up to 64 m.p.h.

Although the Pennsylvania had, since 1939, made some remarkable strides forward in the maximum capacity of its steam locomotives, with the 'T 1' $4-4-4-4$ high-speed passenger, and the 'Q 2' $4-4-6-4$ fast freight, the adoption of the rigid frame 4-cylinder arrangement, though strongly supported by the Baldwin Locomotive

American Express Locomotives

Railroad	Pennsylvania	Santa Fe	Milwaukee	N.W.	Union Pacific	Santa Fe
Type	4-6-2	4-6-4	4-6-4	4-8-4	4-8-4	4-8-4
Class	K 4	'3460'	Hiawatha	'J'	'FEF1'	'3771'
Cylinders dia. in.	27	23½	23½	27	24½	28
stroke in.	28	29½	30	32	32	32
Coupled wheel dia. ft. in	6-8	7-0	7-0	5-10	6-5	6-8
Total evaporative heating surface sq. ft	4058	4770	4166	5271	4597	5513
Superheater sq. ft	962	2080	1695	2177	1473	2366
Grate area sq. ft	70	98·5	96·5	107·7	100·2	108
Boiler pressure lbs/sq. in.	205	300	300	275	300	300
Total weight engine tons	138·5	184	163	220	211·4	227·5
tender tons	95·5	177	167·5	168·5	181	201·5
Tractive force lbs	44,000	49,300	50,300	80,000	53,400	66,000

Note: weights are in Imperial tons

283

Works, was by no means generally acclaimed, and in the final days of steam traction in the USA the Pennsylvania was, in fact, the only railroad to adopt it. In 1945, E. S. Cox, whose experience in British steam locomotive design and in analysis of all the varying traits of performance have hardly been equalled, was sent on a fact-finding tour of the USA, and he spent a considerable time on the Pennsylvania. He concluded that the 4–4–4–4 type was definitely inferior in adhesion to the 4–8–4s on other railroads and that their performance suffered from excessive slipping. It was a brave last fling, but as elsewhere in the USA steam was soon to go down before the diesels.

CHAPTER TWENTY THREE

Steam on the New York Central

I expect some readers will be surprised that in the collection of data for this book my field-work has not included any personal travel over the lines of the former New York Central System — the route of the 'Empire State Express', the 'Commodore Vanderbilt,' and above all the 'Twentieth Century Limited.' I must admit, however, that in my voluminous reading about American railroads, now extending over more than forty years, and in my professional studies of their engineering and operation, the New York Central, as a route, never gained the attraction for me that some of the others induced. I suppose it was because it is a water level route, with no dramatic mountain ranges to cross, no great estuaries to wind beside, no great tunnels. All the same, there developed a very keen appreciation of its locomotive practice. It is perhaps significant of its place in the American railroad scene of forty years ago that the locomotive prowess of the New York Central was more completely documented in the British technical press than that of any other administration, partly through the interest and authorship of the late E. C. Poultney. But in another respect it was the very levelness of the main line, in relation to the high average speeds demanded by the traffic department, that made vital a very high standard of engine performance.

At first sight this may seem strange to some, in that a hilly, mountainous road would appear to be more demanding. But in the New York Central there was a close analogy to the case of the Great Western, in England. On a level route there is no let-up. The effort has to be sustained continuously, and when that effort involves the haulage of a train of about 1000 tons at 80 m.p.h. it is no mean 'effort'. Some years ago a learned paper was presented to the Institution of

Mechanical Engineers, in London, analysing test performances of a variety of locomotives, in which it was recommended strongly:

> . . . that locomotive tests be not confined, as is so often done, to very heavily graded routes, but that tests be made on level or easily graded routes with maximum train loads and at high average speeds. Far greater differences are likely to be found between different types of locomotives under these conditions, and it is perhaps not without significance that the one British railway company which has standardised the long-lap valve . . . [one of the keystones of efficient performance] . . . is the railway whose main line is level and whose trains are scheduled at the highest average speeds.

That paper was presented in 1927, and the railway referred to was the Great Western. Similar operating circumstances on a much larger scale applied equally to the New York Central.

Before passing on to a most wholehearted commendation of N.Y.C. locomotive practice between the two world wars, and to the introduction of the sadly short-lived 'Niagara' class 4−8−4s, I trust I shall be forgiven for quietly 'debunking' an oft-repeated myth of American railroad speeding. In 1893 there was a great international exhibition in Chicago, and in that year some very fast running was being made by the 'Empire State Express', run by the New York Central and its western associates. The 'star' locomotive on the job was one of the largest 'American' 4−4−0s ever built, the '999', and there was surprise, and not a little consternation among British locomotive men when it was reported that on 9 May 1893 she had reached a maximum speed of 102·8 m.p.h., and more so when two days later the sensational maximum of 112·5 m.p.h. was claimed. In the very first volume of *The Railway Magazine*, however, the pioneer train-timer Charles Rous-Marten wrote:

> It happened that two friends of mine, both being engineering writers and train-timers of much experience, travelled by the same train which was alleged to have achieved this marvellous feat. Their timing, taken quite independently of one another, brought out the rate of travel as a mile in forty-four seconds, or 81·8 m.p.h. But after the British record had been made in the 'race' of 1895, the Americans, as in patriotic duty bound, at once set to work to beat it, and used No. 999

for that purpose. A 'tie' was the virtual result. But in the official report is is expressly stated that the maximum speed attained by No. 999 during that supreme effort at record-braking was 'about eighty-one miles an hour'. I may well leave these indisputable facts to speak for themselves.

It is nevertheless astonishing how often that mythical '112·5' is quoted, even today, on behalf of No. 999!

The steam locomotive prowess of the New York Central needs no such artificial embellishment to set its record, for all time, at the very highest level. By the year 1905 the 'Atlantic' type had been developed to a high degree of efficiency, but in 1906 the first 'Pacifics' were introduced. Both types were then non-superheated, and the 'Atlantic' in particular had an exceptionally large boiler and fire grate. In fact, on paper, the 'Pacific' did not appear to represent a very big advance, despite its increased length and weight, thus:

NEW YORK CENTRAL Express Locomotives

Type	Atlantic	Pacific
Cylinders dia. in.	21½	21
stroke in.	26	28
Coupled wheel dia. ft in.	6−7	6−1
Total heating surface sq. ft	3321	3457
Grate area sq. ft	50·3	50·2
Boiler pressure lbs/sq. in.	180	200
Weight of engine only tons	86·2	92·4
Tractive force lbs	23,300	28,800

But in 1907 the shape of things to come was more clearly revealed in a batch of superheater-equipped 'Pacifics' built by Alco for the Lake Shore and Michigan Southern section of the line. These had a total evaporative heating suface of 3784 sq. ft and a further 705 sq. ft in the superheater. The grate area was 56·5 sq. ft and the tractive force 30,900 lbs. From that notable stage the development was steady and strong up till the introduction of the 'K 5' class in 1925-6. These engines were distinguished by their having huge tenders carrying 15,000 gallons of water, and running on two 6-wheeled bogies. This permitted the progressive elimination of service stops and the making of longer through runs with one locomotive. But in these engines the maximum physical size for the 'Pacific' type had been virtually reached, and a survey taken in 1926 of probable future requirements for express passenger locomotives led to the conclusion that an entirely new design and type must be developed. Among many desiderata laid down perhaps the most important of all was to achieve a high degree of reliability for uninterrupted service under conditions of dense traffic, requiring simple but adequate machinery combined with the use of well-proved auxiliary equipment. The New York Central favoured Alco as a manufacturer, and the latter company and the Superheater Company were taken fully into consultation. The result was the introduction in 1927 of the first locomotive to be built in the USA of the 4—6—4 type, and in view of the N.Y.C. affiliation it was named 'Hudson', although the type already in use in Europe was known as the 'Baltic'.

Type names apart, however, the N.Y.C. 'Hudsons' were an outstanding success. To meet the demand for exceptional steaming capacity at sustained high speeds, with heavy loads, ample heating surface was essential, with an extra large superheater and a grate area sufficient to ensure an economical rate of firing in maximum conditions of steam generation. To carry the added weight thus imposed on the rear of the locomotive, without excessive loads on trailing or coupled axles, the 4-wheeled trailing truck was used, thus securing the advantage of providing for large firebox capacity with comparatively light individual axle loads and consequently low rail stresses. For some time the New York Central had standardised the use of boosters on its large 'Pacific' engines to provide for rapid acceleration from station stops, and the trailing truck had one pair of wheels 4 ft 3 in. diameter, as on the 'Pacifics', on to which the booster engine drove, and the second pair of wheels were of 3 ft 0 in. diameter. The tractive force of the main engine was 42,360 lbs, with the booster supplying an additional 10,900 lbs when cut in. The general layout of this historic and epoch-marking American locomotive can be studied from the accompanying drawing. The extent of its success can be appreciated from the N.Y.C. taking delivery of no fewer than 205 of them from Alco between 1927 and 1931.

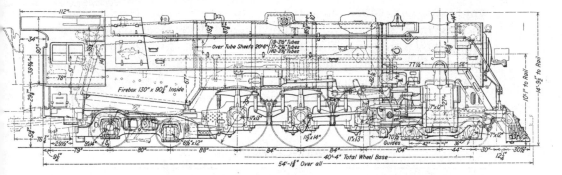

40. The first New York Central 'Hudson' type express lcoomotive

Performance and capacity tests of the new locomotives in comparison with those of the larger 'Pacifics' were carried out over the Mohawk Division of the line, between Albany and Syracuse, a distance of 140 miles. Apart from a very severe uphill start out of Albany, for three miles on a gradient of 1 in 61, up which rear-end helper assistance is always provided with heavy trains, the line is an easy one on gentle undulating gradients. Tests were made with the dynamometer car, and empty standard steel coaches, varying in number from ten to twenty, which together with the car provided train weights of 780 to 1465 tons. The comparison between the 'Pacific' and the 'Hudson' can best be summarised in that the drawbar horsepowers were 2530 at 45 m.p.h. by the former, and 3240 at 58 m.p.h. by the 'Hudson'. Moreover, although the coal consumption was naturally heavy in securing feats of high-speed performance with very heavy trains, the basic values, which corresponded closely with those obtained on contemporary tests on the Great Western Railway in England, showed an improvement of 14·6 per cent by the 'Hudson' over the 'Pacific'.

The 'J 1' class 'Hudsons' saw the New York Central through the great depression, but in that time consideration was being given to the future development of the 4−6−4 type, in anticipation of greater power demanded by the constantly increasing weight of trains, and the need to accelerate the schedules. The basic requirements for a modified design of 'Hudson' emerged, that should provide an output of about 20 per cent greater at much higher speed, but with an

289

approximately equal rated tractive force, and the least possible increase in overall weight. The fundamental change was to use a much higher boiler pressure, and smaller cylinders, and to streamline and enlarge all the internal steam passages to provide the freest possible flow of steam. The outcome was the 'J 3' class, introduced in 1937, the relative dimensions in comparison with those of the original 'J 1' 'Hudsons' is shown below:

NEW YORK CENTRAL 'Hudsons'

	'J 1'	'J 3 a'
Class		
Year introduced	1927	1937
Cylinders dia. in	25	22½
stroke in.	28	29
Coupled wheel dia. ft in.	6−7	6−7
Total evaporative heating surface sq. ft	4484	4187
Superheater sq. ft	1951	1745
Grate area sq. ft	81·5	82
Boiler pressure lbs/sq. in.	225	275
Tractive force:		
main engine lbs	42,360	43,440
booster lbs	10,900	12,100

The 'J 3 a' proved a very profitable investment for the New York Central. They amply fulfilled the designers' aim to get greater power at higher speed, and they proved capable of maintaining scheduled time over the Mohawk Division with loads of up to twenty-three coaches, 1609 tons. This severity of working involved a coal consumption of 139 lbs per mile, or a ton of coal every sixteen miles!! But such a voracious appetite must be related to the work done, and if comparison is made with one of the classic English test series of all time, those with the Great Western 4−6−0 *Caldicot Castle* in 1924, the coal consumption per indicated horsepower hour — that developed in the cylinders — was 2·10 lbs for the 'Castle', and 2·19 lbs for the 'J 3 a' in maximum load conditions. When the latter was hauling a medium weight train of only 1253 tons — only 1253! — the coal consumption was 2·03 lbs per I.H.P. hour. The New York Central had certainly got a very efficient locomotive. The contrast between the original Hudson 'J 1' class and the later engines is brought out by the conditions in which maximum power output was attained: 3900 I.H.P. for the 'J 1' at 67 m.p.h., but the 4725 I.H.P. of the 'J 3 a' was at 75 m.p.h. In view of such test results the records taken by travellers on the crack trains of the New York Central, of speeds of 95 m.p.h. with loads of more than 1000 tons are understandable enough. There were fifty of the 'J 3 a' class, of which some were streamlined, and allocated to prestige trains like the 'Twentieth Century Limited'. The extent to which the New York Central adopted the 4−6−4 type for its heaviest passenger duties is shown by the total of 275 in service by the year 1940, while in the whole of the rest of the United States there were only 162 more! Eventually the total on other lines advanced to 225.

Even with 275 'Hudsons' available, there were times when the N.Y.C. had not enough of them for all the first class passenger traffic, and recourse had to be made to the older 'K 3' Pacifics. But these were not really up to the modern problems of haulage, neither was the expedient of using the 4−8−2 'Mohawk' type freight engines, because these latter were limited to a maximum speed of 60 m.p.h. So in 1940 a new series of general service 4−8−2s was introduced, the 'L 3' class, that could be used in both fast freight and passenger service. With the experience in design and testing of the 'J 3 a' 'Hudsons', and careful attention to the balancing, it had been found possible to produce a locomotive having the 5 ft 9 in. coupled wheels considered ideal for fast freight, but which would run freely and smoothly up to 80 m.p.h. or more in passenger service. A total of fifty of these fine engines was supplied by Alco, twenty-five of which were equipped for passenger working. It was another very successful design, and led up to the final N.Y.C. steam locomotive class, the 'Niagara' of 1945.

These large engines were designed and built in direct response to the diesel challenge that was developing in its intensity by the end of the second world war. The New York Central already had some diesel-electric 5400 horsepower freight locomotives. In a paper presented to the American Society of Mechanical Engineers in January 1942, entitled 'Modern Steam Passenger Locomotives — Research and Design',

P. W. Kiefer, chief engineer, motive power and rolling stock of the New York, after describing the inception and progress of the 'J 1' and 'J 3 a' 'Hudsons', and of the new 'L 3 a' 4−8−2s, had this to say on 'Present thoughts'.

Future development of the steam locomotive in some radically new form, such as the steam turbine condensing or combustion type, as recently proposed, should show a substantial increase in thermal efficiency, but until the stage has been reached where such units of proved dependability in daily operation can be produced of moderate size, weight and cost, it is the author's belief that basic lines of development should be continued by taking advantage of the possibilities for further betterment of the conventional reciprocating design without radical changes in the type of boiler or resorting to the mechanical complication of multiple expansion of steam. It should be possible now to produce a highly serviceable two-cylinder single expansion locomotive of the 4−8−4 type at a weight per indicated horsepower closely approaching that represented by the 4−6−4 class 'J 3 a' described in this paper, capable of delivering 6000 cylinder horsepower when required. Such a design should include the largest practicable superheater, with ample firebox volume and grate area, carefully proportioned steam passages from boiler to exhaust and a working steam pressure probably up to 300 p.s.i.

So, in 1942, was foreshadowed the 'Niagara' or 'S 1' class. In view of the easy gradients of the New York Central it was perhaps not surprising that it was one of the last of the great American railroads to adopt the 4−8−4 type. The Santa Fe and the Rio Grande had introduced it as long previously as 1929, and the Rock Island, the St Louis South Western, the Milwaukee, the Burlington and the Great Northern followed within a year. But the 'Niagaras' of the N.Y.C. were built with the prime object of competing with the diesels, and with the massive bank of experience built up in operation of those 275 'Hudsons', in very heavy and intense service, the design of the 'Niagaras' was packed with every conceivable feature that would minimise day-to-day attention, and shorten servicing time, as well as producing a locomotive capable of the hardest sustained power output on the road. In November 1944 the New York Central announced the forthcoming completion of what was called an 'experimental 4−8−4 type

292

steam locomotive' in the following terms:

Although the importance of new kinds of motive power other than modern conventional steam, such as improved Diesel and straight electrics, and steam and gas turbine locomotives, is fully realized and developments along these lines are being progressed, it is regarded as most important constantly to improve the reciprocating steam locomotive in order to stimulate and expedite progress in the entire field of the motive power design art. To this end, a new design of two cylinder single expansion steam locomotive of the 4−8−4 wheel arrangement, capable of delivering not less than 6000 indicated horse-power in the higher speed ranges when required, has been developed. Construction was authorized in April of this year and delivery is expected during the spring of 1945, to be followed immediately by comprehensive boiler and locomotive capacity and performance tests. For further increase in productive capacity and efficiency, a new design fire tube boiler is to be used from which the steam dome has been omitted. This change from present practice permitted increase in barrel diameter, thereby making possible, within permissible weight and clearance limitations, the use of improved tube and flue layouts with correspondingly larger gas areas and better superheater proportions, additional firebox and combustion chamber volume, more nearly level grates and larger ashpan capacity necessary for long locomotive runs, as compared with the best present boilers as represented by those of the class J 3 Hudson type and classes L 3 and L 4 Mohawk type engines. Other important features consist of roller bearings on all locomotive and tender journals and in side and main rods and valve motion to increase availability and serviceability through freedom from heating difficulties and reduced wear of machinery parts. Steam passages from boiler to exhaust have been improved for reduced pressure drop and correspondingly greater power and better engine efficiency. High tensile carbon silicon steel is used in the shell courses for weight reduction, with firebox construction in carbon steel and working pressure of 290 lbs per square inch. The design is arranged for both 79 in. and 75 in. diameter driving wheels. An extra set of wheels of the latter diameter will come with the locomotive so that performance and capacity tests may be made with both sizes, with interpolation of results for the 77 in. diameter wheel. Reliable data thus will be made available on which selections may be based for future steam motive power of similar character for main line freight, passenger, or combination service.

Dimensionally the 'Niagara', as fitted with 6 ft 3 in. coupled wheels and having a tractive force of 62,330 lbs was one of the least powerful of all American 4−8−4s, but it proved very efficient in service on the road, as would be expected from the design team that had produced the 'J 3 a' 'Hudson', and the 'L 4' 'Mohawk'. After the initial acceptance trials no time was lost in forming a general assessment of their overall performance against the latest diesel-electric locomotives from General Motors. The 'Niagaras' cost £59,750 each, at the exchange rates then prevailing, while a 4000 horsepower General Motors diesel cost £125,000. This was not strictly a fair comparison because the 'Niagara', as expected, could produce 6000 indicated horsepower. The frequently quoted price ratio of that period of 2½ to 1, diesel to steam, for equivalent power output was about right at that time. Then came one of the fairest and most representative comparisons of steam and diesel performance that has ever been carried out, setting units of the most up-to-date designs against each other.

On the New York-Chicago run one locomotive worked through over the 930 miles between Harmon and Chicago, with changes of crew at the various divisional points. Harmon was the limit of the electrified area on the N.Y.C. from New York. Six 'Niagaras' were set against six diesels of approximately equivalent tractive power, on this service, which involved hauling trains of 1000 tons or more at sustained speeds of 80 to 85 m.p.h. on level track, and the twelve locomotives were kept under strict observation for a whole year. The average results for the six 'Niagaras' worked out as follows:

Total hours per annum	8760
Time allocated to shops and routine inspection	672
Hours available for traffic dept.	8088
Not available due to servicing	1435
Available for running	6653
Hours available but not used	573
Hours used	6080
Per cent availability	75·9
Per cent utilisation	69·4

During the year of observation the average mileage reached the high total of 314,694, equivalent to 862 miles a day. The average for the whole stud of 'Niagara' engines was averaging about 260,000 miles a day, against a diesel average of 330,000. The Diesels were showing a definite advantage in this respect though nothing large enough to offset the big disparity in first cost.

For how long the 'Niagaras' would have kept the complete dieseli-sation of the N.Y.C. motive power stud at bay is problematical, but unhappily an unexpected difficulty arose. Reference was made in the advance publicity issued that to reduce weight the boiler shells were made of high tensile carbon-silicon steel. After a disappointingly short time these developed cracks. It would, of course, have been possible to replace these boilers by new ones with shells of the conventional carbon steel, though a very expensive expedient on practically new engines; but this very serious defect 'sold the pass' to the diesels. Although the 'Niagaras' had so relatively short a life, that year of working, turn and turn about with diesels on the Harmon-Chicago run, showed what a high percentage availability could be secured with a well designed, and efficiently serviced steam locomotive. That it was the 'swan-song' of steam on the New York Central was sad.

CHAPTER TWENTY FOUR

Conrail — massive freight operations

The 'Broadway Limited' landed me in Pittsburgh at 6.30 in the morning. The overnight journey from Chicago had not been one of the most restful, but a cheery greeting from Joe Harvey, who had come over from Philadelphia to be my guide for the next few days quickly dispelled any 'hangover' I might have had from the night's run. Almost immediately we were to go out to Conway Yard, breakfasting on the way, though before we left there was time for a look at the unusual forecourt of the Pennsylvania passenger station. Even the most perfervid railway enthusiast is not very much inclined to study station architecture, subsequent to arrival well before the normal civilised hour for breakfast, but this one could not fail to arrest one's attention. I cannot better the description of it in Carroll L. V. Meeks' book *The Railway Station*:

The constricted site did not permit the architect, Daniel Burnham, to indulge in the bombastic show he liked. The office building was hardly different from the semi-skyscrapers he designed for banks and department stores. There was one feature, however, where he could let his imagination run riot: the carriage concourse in front of the head house. It was built a little later than the two more essential parts. The design was revised from an earlier scheme, which had timid arches, to the more daring scheme of a single dome resting on wide four-centered arches. It is a fantastic conception reminiscent of a Beaux-Arts *Esquisse-Esquisse*, an imaginery exercise in which 'buildability' is unimportant; in spirit it is like Binet's audacious main entrance to the Paris Exposition of 1900. Here again we see an impressive glass cage subordinated to the fore building. Only the carriage concourse tells us that this is a station and not just another office building.

I was so taken with it at a very first glance so early in the morning that I went back, after a long day out on the line, for another look at it. The pity of it is that there are now so few passenger trains, and this spectacular rotunda passes virtually unnoticed.

We were soon heading out to Conway Yard, twenty-two miles west of Pittsburgh on the main line to Chicago. Claimed as the world's busiest electronic freight marshalling yard, it serves as a gigantic clearing house for much of Conrail's enormous east-west traffic between the Middle West, the Great Lakes and the Eastern Seaboard. Instead of going through several classified yards en route, thousands of cars are moved unclassified to Conway and sorted centrally, then relayed in solid block loads direct to their ultimate destinations. This follows the same principle on which the great yards I had

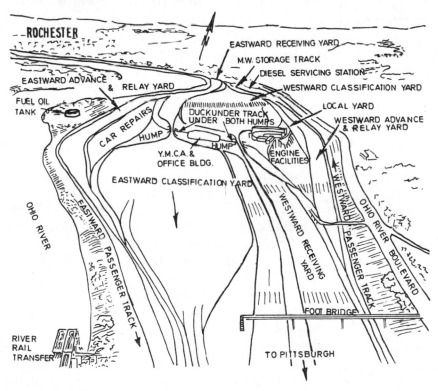

41. Conrail—a pictorial sketch of Conway Yard

seen out in the west are operated, at Barstow on the Santa Fe, and at West Colton on the Southern Pacific. The Pennsylvania Railroad had always been to the fore in developing freight train handling facilities, and here in the heart of Pennsylvania territory I saw an installation into which has been built every known advance in automation and technology that can speed the movement of freight cars. The diagram map shows its strategic location.

It is one thing, however, to study a diagram of traffic flows, stick in a pin, and say 'there we will have our great classification yard'. It is not so easy in a terrain like that surrounding Pittsburgh. The main line of the former Pennsylvania to Chicago and St Louis runs on the right bank of the Ohio River, on a relatively narrow strip of land between the river bank itself and a range of high hills, and when one is thinking of a yard complex that is going to need nearly *one hundred* tracks abreast, it would not have been easy to accommodate it. A marshalling yard is not the kind of activity that one can put underground, by tunnelling into that range of hills; but at Conway nature provided the answer. Between the townships of Baden and Freedom, a distance of about 3½ miles on the main line, the river makes a wide sweep to the south, briefly increasing the distance between the original main line location and the river bank from 70 to just over 2000 ft, and on that area of flat land the yard was built, after a brilliantly ingenious piece of railroad planning.

The pictorial diagram gives an excellent impression of how the various facilities were arranged and during their planning the engineers of Conrail must sometimes have thought enviously of their counterparts on the Santa Fe, when laying out Barstow Yard, in the wide open spaces of the Californian desert lands, even though the latter had immense troubles of their own that were non-existent at Conway. In that limited area there had to be contrived two classification yards with fifty-three and fifty-four tracks leading from the respective humps, and each providing space for about 3500 cars — cars, moreover, of the huge size now common in the USA. Both the eastbound and the westbound yards had nine reception tracks and nine relay tracks, which with the auxiliary yards, shop yards, engine facilities and connecting lines made up a total of nearly 170 miles of track in this relatively small area. The whole complex was designed to

298

cope with a maximum of 9000 cars classified per day, though at the time of my own visit the actual number had not exceeded about 7000. Even so that represents a pretty massive throughput, as the expression goes. There are twenty-seven daily scheduled departures in each direction, and often several extras. In the ordinary way the average number of cars per train is ninety-seven, though at the time I was there a typical day's working on the main line between Pittsburgh and Harrisburg was twenty-six freights eastbound, and thirty-one westbound, which with an average of ninety-seven to a train would mean a daily movement of 5500 cars on this one line alone.

Taken all round, I was very impressed with Conway, because of the skill that has been shown not only in the application of highly sophisticated control equipment but in the physical layout that has enabled such a mammoth traffic handling capacity to be installed in such a relatively confined space. It provides a remarkable example of the evolution in marshalling yard design and operation when compared to another Pennsylvania yard in the Pittsburgh area, at Pitcairn, about fourteen miles east, on the main line to Philadelphia. Like the Markham yards of the Illinois Central, to which I referred in Chapter Eight, this was one of the earlier installations of power operated retarders that we, in England, studied very closely in the early 1930s when the first mechanised yards were being planned. I went to see it some years earlier than my present round trip when I was visiting works in Swissvale and Wilmerding, east of Pittsburgh. Its equipment, the last word when it was installed in 1929, was by then very much outdated. Unhappily too, it was at the time when Penn-Central had entered bankruptucy, and much of the track was in poor condition. Pitcairn as originally installed was equipped for eastbound traffic: a point of concentration of traffic from the major industries of the area, and along the left bank of the Monongahela River. As first installed it had 34 classification tracks fed through 25 retarder control.

On the next day arrangements had been made for me to ride one of the heavy freights right through to Harrisburg, 258 miles. Joe Harvey warned me that it would be something of a marathon trip, and as it turned out we were on the road for very nearly twelve hours. It was one of the most interesting I have ever made on a locomotive, in its extraordinary variety of scene, operating conditions, and sheer hard work required from the locomotives. In the first place we were routed up the Conemaugh Line, which bypasses the Pittsburgh passenger terminal area, and at first runs near to the right bank of the Allegheny River. It is purely a freight line, and just over thirty years ago made world history in the development of power signalling and automatic train control. Until the end of the first world war the American railroads in general did not have a good safety record. With the growth of traffic and acceleration of train schedules operation with train orders only was not easy and collisions were all too frequent. The Interstate Commerce Commission laid down certain broad requirements for improved signalling and automatic train control, out of which four distinct systems were evolved:

1. Intermittently controlled cab signals.
2. Same as '1', but with automatic brake application added.
3. Continuously controlled cab signals.
4. Same as '3' but with automatic brake application added.

The Pennsylvania decided upon type '3', and by the outbreak of the second world war most of its main line trackage was equipped. By that time such confidence in the continuously controlled cab signals had been established that on the freight-only Conemaugh Line the epoch-marking step was taken of dispensing entirely with the lineside signals, and relying only on the cab signals. Thirty years ago this was considered a most revolutionary step, but since then lineside signals have not been provided on several important lines, including of course the Japanese high-speed Shinkansen passenger network.

The diagram on page 302 shows the Conemaugh Line, in relation to the main line, and the Monongahela branch, and before setting out on our trip with the eastbound freight and leaving the Pittsburgh area I must mention the celebrated Panhandle tunnel, single-tracked, leading to the bridge across the Monongahela River to the Pittsburgh-St Louis main line. It is not so much the tunnel itself as what happened at its western portal one day in 1868 that made world railroad history. On that day the Steubenville 'accommodation' on the Panhandle Railroad made its first trip after being fitted throughout with the earliest form of George Westinghouse's air brake. It left the Pittsburgh Union Station, and set off through the Panhandle tunnel;

but when emerging at the west end, at a smart pace, a cart drawn by two horses was just entering upon a highway crossing ahead. The engine whistled; the horses and their driver panicked, and it seemed certain they would be run down. But the locomotive engineer made a full application of the air brake and stopped clear of the terrified animals. The incident became front page news throughout America, and gave a tremendous boost to the Westinghouse brake!

Joe Harvey and I joined the freight at Etna Yard just after 11 o'clock. It was made up to a total of eighty-seven cars, sixty-five loaded and twenty-two empty, making up 4867 tons. The lead unit, on which we rode, was a 2500 horsepower 'GP 35', still in the colours of the Reading Company, with a 3600 horsepower 'SDP 45' in the Conrail livery behind us. We made the usual very gentle start, but in less than four miles we had topped 40 m.p.h. until we had to slow to take the loop track at Harmar. Then after getting away again, on easy gradients beside the river we were not making as good progress as our engineer anticipated, and the trouble was found in a hand brake sticking. A stop of seven minutes sufficed to locate this, and rectify it. Some slow running followed until the rear brakeman had boarded the caboose, now in beautiful country in the valley of the Allegheny River, and after negotiating Harris loop we crossed the river on a large girder bridge, just before it is joined by the Kiskiminteas. We headed up the deeper and narrower glen of this river now, passing the junction at 'AJ' Tower. Our progress this far had not been rapid, because the 24½-miles from our start at Etna had taken 78½-minutes. But we were not getting clear signals in the cab, a replica in miniature of the standard position light aspects used on the Pennsylvania. The next seventeen miles, uphill and in magnificent river scenery, took twenty-seven minutes.

At Truxall we passed beneath an overhead coaling plant, beneath which steam locomotives were coaled while standing on the main line. Beyond this we had a speed order, to reduce to 15 m.p.h. crossing a 3-span girder bridge over the river. We were now mounting into the higher ranges of the Allegheny Mountains, amid gloriously wooded heights, and our diesels were fighting back against the gradient after that awkwardly sited speed restriction. We gradually got back to just over 30 m.p.h. and the ten miles between mileposts 23

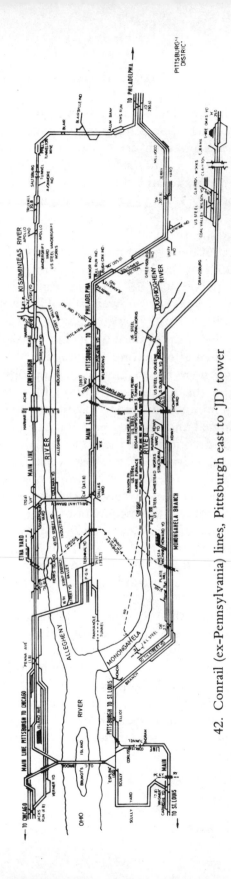

42. Conrail (ex-Pennsylvania) lines, Pittsburgh east to 'JD' tower

and 13 took a few seconds under twenty minutes. This series of mileposts originates near to junction 'JD', where the Conemaugh Line joins the main line, high up in the mountains. There were more checks, including one to cross from the eastbound to the westbound track and eventually we passed milepost 0 in 3 hours and 5 minutes from Etna, 72½ miles. As will be seen from the sketch map there are extensive facilities at 'JD', which is actually nearly four miles east of milepost 0 on the Conemaugh Line. We were crawling forward under restricting signals to stop short of the junctions. We were waiting for a heavy 3-engined westbound freight before we could cross over on to the third track of the main line. 'JD' Tower is 290·6 miles from Philadelphia, and thenceforward we were running on the main line series of mileposts.

One noticed now a big change in the nature of the road. While the Conemaugh is an important through route it is definitely a subsidiary, and looked it. From 'JD' Tower we were on the main line of the one-time premier railroad of the USA, a magnificent multi-tracked road into the mountains, well aligned, finely ballasted and very impressive between the great crags on both sides. With clear signals, now, lineside as well as cab, we gathered speed to a sustained 40 m.p.h. and then the unexpected happened. There was a sudden hiss of the air brake and we came to a precipitate halt. The front brakeman, riding in the front cab, seized a spare brake hose and jumped down. First thoughts were that a hose had burst, and he ran backwards down the train looking for trouble; but then on the walkie-talkie radio from the rear came the explanation — a more serious fracture. A coupling knuckle towards the rear end had broken, and the train had parted. Spares are carried, and the conductor and the rear brakeman set about the job. It was no light task, but these two heroes worked with a will, and seeing that they had nothing but brawn and muscle power to heave the heavy parts about they did remarkably well to give us the 'high ball' once again in just forty minutes from our first stop. In that time they had to walk some considerable distance forward to find what was wrong, then fit a new knuckle, replace the brake hose, which of course had been torn in half, and then signal to our engineer to set back and recouple. Then back in the caboose the brakes had to be tested before we could start away. It so happened that the mishap took

303

place on a straight stretch of line, so that at first neither the conductor nor we at the front end could see what had happened. After all, our great train was about 1¼ miles long.

While we were standing, two heavy westbound freight trains passed, and on restarting our diesels had to fight against the rising gradient. But the inherent characteristic of the diesel locomotive showed up well here, and when we passed Johnstown and the great plant of the Bethlehem Steel works, deep in the mountains, we were doing a steady 30 m.p.h. We were now nearing the foot of the steep final ascent to Gallitzin tunnel and at 'AO' interlocking we stopped for two pusher locomotives to couple up in rear. This operation, which of course was completed by making the brake test, occupied 11½ minutes, and then we started away. The line was now quadruple tracked, and the allocation as to direction was, from left to right: westbound; either; eastbound; eastbound. At this particular time the line happened to be much busier in the westbound, and since we had started from the broken knuckle incident, we had passed four westbound freights in the space of half an hour. The ascent was very curving at first, a continuous succession of S-bends, and our four locomotives accelerated the load to 40 m.p.h. But the terrain was typical of what I had seen of the Alleghenies earlier in my tour, in Chessie country. I have a note that it looked like Rattery, in South Devon, rather than like some great summit.

Beyond South Fork the gradient briefly eases out to dead level, and there the Pennsylvania took the opportunity of laying in water troughs — an American counterpart of Tebay. With all four locomotives going at full power we attained a full 60 m.p.h. at this point. It was a thrilling sight looking back at our huge train, winding its way among the hills; but we were now on the final ascent, and speed was soon down to 30 m.p.h. past Cresson. So we came to Gallitzin. From the time we took our pusher locomotives we had taken exactly 45 minutes, and the twenty-two miles between mileposts 270 and 248 (the summit) occupied 39¼ minutes; 33·5 m.p.h. in very heavy grade work. Then came the most dramatic part of the run, the very steep descent to Altoona, and the perambulation of the Horseshoe Curve, to which I had especially looked forward. One can think of many spectacular railroad locations, like the Montagu Pass in South Africa; the

Western Ghats; the hill railways of Northern India, and our own Horseshoe Bend on the West Highland line in Scotland; but none of them, I found, were remotely like this astonishing Pennsylvania location.

First of all, the line is quadruple-tracked. Then the mountain sides are thickly wooded right to their summits, as I saw from the air when flying to Huntington with my Chessie friends. We kept the two 'pushers' on for the descent, and came down steadily at 25 to 30 m.p.h. with the dynamic brake in action. At the actual 'horseshoe' the line is high on the hillsides, and although the afforestation is as dense as everywhere else in this region, the slope is such that the line can be seen clearly across the neck of the curve. When we were on the far side I took a photograph, not of the rear of our train but of three triple-deck auto-carrying trailers that were about two-thirds of the way back, and they were exactly broadside to us, and travelling in the opposite direction! My friends in the cab had warned me to be ready with my camera for another 'sight' at the horseshoe location — none other than a preserved 'K 4' 'Pacific', a real exhibition piece by the lineside. The resulting snap is clear enough to show the engine's number, 1361, but the light was on the wrong side, and the picture is of little more than sentimental value. But it was a pleasing gesture to install this representative of so famous a class beside the scene of its former labours.

So we ran cautiously down the last five miles of the descent and at 5.50 p.m. we stopped at Altoona. The 133 miles from Etna yard, with all the intermediate delays, had taken 6¼ hours, a not very spectacular average of 21 m.p.h.; but our actual running time was roughly an hour less, and there had been difficulties enough in such a terrain. At Altoona we changed crews and in the meantime I was interested in the place itself. Sometimes called the 'Crewe' of America. I could not imagine two places less alike, at any rate from what I saw of it during the hour we were standing. Of course, the whole character of the railway activity has changed since the superseding of steam, but the yard where we stood was like that of an upland divisional point, rather than the centre of such a tremendous locomotive engineering design, constructional and testing activity. It was 63 minutes after our arrival that the new engineer moved us gently out of Rose Yard, but not until

7.10 p.m. that we eventually got the 'highball', and took the main line at Antis Tower, 232½ miles from Philadelphia. We began very slowly until we heard on the radio that the rear end was out of the yard and on to the main line. Then began a splendidly undelayed run down the valley of the Juniata River. The track is fairly winding at first, and is a section that has the reputation of being very foggy at nights. In the first twenty miles from Antis Tower we did not much exceed 40 m.p.h., but then we really began to move.

From the 212th milepost, near Spruce, our engineer began to pile it on, and we ran forty miles on end at an average of 51 m.p.h. The fastest mile I clocked here was at 55·5 m.p.h., so that the speed was very steady with our 1¼-mile-long train. We slowed to about 30 m.p.h. past Lewistown passenger station, and we had hardly recovered when we were slackened to 30 m.p.h. at Mifflin to cross over on to the relief line because of engineering work on the main track. Up to this point the permanent way throughout from 'JD' Tower, where we came on to the main line, had been excellent, but this relief line was not too good, and for the eighteen miles we were on it the speed was barely 30 m.p.h. We crossed back on to the main at Port and immediately speeded up to over 50 m.p.h. By this time it was dark, but as usual on American railroads when riding in the cab I could pick out the mileposts easily, lit up by the engine's headlight. This however was the last of our fast running. At Duncannon Junction, where we came alongside the Susquehana River, we were slowed down and eventually brought to a stand at Banks Tower, the end of the Allegheny Division of the line. The 117 miles from our start at Rose Yard, Altoona, had taken one minute over three hours, an average of only a shade under 40 m.p.h. The running average between mileposts 230 and 115 was 42·2 m.p.h. We were held up some time at Banks, waiting for the westbound 'Broadway Limited' to pass before we could cross over and take the line leading into Nadola Yard, Harrisburg. Joe Harvey had got things well organised, and when we finally checked in at the yard there was a car waiting to take us into Harrisburg City for the night.

It had been a fascinating trip, every minute of its twelve hours duration. It seemed there had been something of everything! The details I took fill thirty pages of one of my notebooks, and when it was over and we climbed down from the locomotive in Nadola Yard at 11.25 p.m. I felt so little tired that Harvey and I sat up until the small hours enjoying more than one refresher, and just yarning about railroads. Next morning we caught one of the smart electric passenger trains for Philadelphia and again I was favoured with a ride in the cab. But although it was fun clocking the speeds up to 75 m.p.h. between stops it was freight again that took my attention. We passed five westbound 'Piggyback' freight trains within a space of forty minutes, and overtook a heavy eastbound freight in the same period. So eventually we came into Philadelphia, and my 13,000 miles circuit of the USA was ended. I called into the Conrail headquarters to thank Howard Gilbert for the arrangements he had made for me, and then I relaxed.

Alone for the first time in several weeks, with half a day to spare before a final engagement before I flew home, I retraced my route on the map of America, and realised more keenly than ever before how much there was that I had not seen. When in Chicago I would have liked to go back to the Pacific North-West by the North Coast 'Hiawatha', and then to have returned across the Sierra Nevada Range, and then by the Union Pacific route. I would like to have made the long run through the arc of the Golden Empire from Los Angeles to New Orleans, and seen more than the inside of the airports at Detroit and St Louis. But while I can never be satiated with seeing new places and viewing fresh countryside, I realised that so far as railroads are concerned in the USA today additional journeys would have been very little more than variations upon the major theme that I had already absorbed. The change from steam to diesel traction has brought about a general standardisation in motive power throughout the country, however bright and distinctive some of the different liveries may be. So on reflection I felt content, and with a heart full to overflowing with gratitude for what the A.A.R., the individual railway companies, and Amtrak had arranged for me in this short time. As one of my Westinghouse friends at King of Prussia put it: 'After all, you've seen more of the country in six weeks than many Americans have seen in a lifetime.'

Bibliography

Air Brake Tests, Westinghouse Air Brake Co. Wilmerding, Pa. 1904.

American Heritage, Dec. 1970 issue.

American Locomotives, 1830-1880, John H. White Jr. Johns Hopkins Press, Baltimore, 1968.

Atchison, Topeka & Santa Fe, History of, Keith L. Bryant, Macmillan, New York, 1975.

Baltimore & Ohio, History of, William Cotton, Macmillan, New York, 1975.

California, Mary Austin, A. & C. Black Ltd, London, 1914.

Greenbrier Heritage, William Olcott, Arndt, Preston, Chaplin, Lamb & Keen Inc.

Gulf, Mobile and Ohio, James H. Lemly, Richard D. Irwin, Inc. Homewood Ill. 1953.

Illinois Central Railroad, History of, John F. Stover, Macmillan, New York, 1975.

Locomotive Engine, Running and Management, Angus Sinclair, John Wiley & Sons, New York, 1885.

Louisville and Nashville, History of, Maury Klein, Macmillan, New York, 1975.

Main Line of Mid-America, Carlton J. Corliss, Creative Age Press, New York, 1950.

Northern Pacific, History of, Robert L. Paterson, Macmillan, New York, 1975.

Railroaders, The, Keith Wheeler, Time-Life Books, New York, 1973.

Railroads at War, S. Kip Farrington Jr., Coward McCann Inc., New York, 1944.

Railway Reminiscences of Three Continents, Gérard Vuillet, Thomas Nelson, and Sons, Ltd. London, 1968.

Railway Signalling, E. E. King, McGraw-Hill Book Co. Inc., New York, 1921.

Railway Station, The, Carroll L. V. Meeks, The Architectural Press, London, 1957.

Rails West, George B. Abdill, Bonanza Books, New York, 1958

Steam Locomotive, The, R. P. Johnson, Simmons–Boardman Publishing Corporation, New York, 1942.

Steam Locomotive in America, Alfred W. Bruce, W. W. Norton & Co. Inc., New York, 1952.

Westinghouse, A life of George, Henry G. Prout, Charles Scribner's Sons, New York, 1922.

Periodicals:

Baldwin Locomotives, Baldwin Loco. Works.

Institution of Railway Signal Engineers Journal, from 1910, London.

Railway Age, (USA)

Railway Gazette, London.

Railway Mechanical Engineer, (USA).

Railway Magazine, London.

Trains, Milwaukee, Wis., USA.

Index

311